Native American Religions

An Introduction

Native American Religions

An Introduction

Denise Lardner Carmody and
John Tully Carmody

PAULIST PRESS
New York, N.Y./Mahwah, N.J.

Library of Congress Cataloging-in-Publication Data

Carmody, Denise Lardner, 1935–
    Native American religions : an introduction / Denise Lardner
Carmody and John Tully Carmody.
        p.   cm.
    Includes bibliographical references and index.
    ISBN 0-8091-3404-7 (paper)
    1. Indians—Religion and mythology.   2. Indians of North America-
-Religion and mythology.   I. Carmody, John, 1939– .   II. Title.
    E59.R38C37   1993
299′.79—dc20   93-15547
                                                                            CIP

Published by Paulist Press
997 Macarthur Boulevard
Mahwah, New Jersey 07430

Printed and bound in the
United States of America

CONTENTS

For Kevin O'Connell

LIST OF ILLUSTRATIONS

PREFACE

This book is an introductory text intended for undergraduates. Non-specialists in the field of native American religions should also find it useful. Several features may be worth noting. First, we survey the entire Americas—North, Meso, and South. We spend the most time on northern traditions, because those seem most likely to interest our probable readers, but we do not slight Mesoamerican or South American traditions. Second, we treat the materials with a consistent format, to facilitate comparisons among the different geographical groups. Thus for each area we discuss the historical and geographical background, views of the natural world, social thought, convictions about the self, views of ultimate reality, and spirituality.

Third, our Introduction deals with both the plan of attack we have developed and the attitude we have assumed toward our materials. Suffice it to say here that we come to the native American groups we study with a strong will to appreciate their achievements and no will to deprecate them. Fourth, our Conclusion surveys the Americas as a whole, offering summary thoughts about how native peoples tended to regard the animal world, tribal life, taboos, the surrounding spirits, death, the afterlife, and several other topics.

Our thanks to Kevin Lynch and Larry Boadt of Paulist Press for sponsoring this project, and to Don Brophy of Paulist Press for several helpful suggestions.

Chapter 1

INTRODUCTION

The Plan

Our plan in this book is to survey the major blocs of native American religion. This has meant dealing with Eskimos (Inuit) of the far north and natives of Tierra del Fuego living at the southernmost tip of South America. It has meant moving across what is now the United States, and much of Canada, to treat tribes of the eastern woodlands, the central plains, the southwest, and the west coast. We provide a bulky chapter on Mesoamerican traditions, paying tribute to the impressive cultures developed in what is now Mexico. We consider how native South Americans of the Andes, the tropical forests dominated by the Amazon, and the Gran Chaco tended to organize their lives, create myths and rituals, think about the gods and spirits, and orient their children.

Our assumption is that nowadays these native American peoples are likely to receive a sympathetic hearing. As little as two generations ago, that would not have been the case. Apart from a few anthropologists and ethnographers, most scholars would have considered native religious ways "primitive." Only with the advent of the more sophisticated understandings of myths, rituals, symbols, and social organizations that social scientists have developed since World War II has it become clear that native Americans, like native Africans and Australians, have had a genius equal to that of native Europeans or Asians. Nowadays the majority of serious scholars are attentive to this genius, coming to the native peoples they study with an inclination to appreciate rather than dismiss.

The 500th anniversary of the arrival of Christopher Columbus in the new world has only reinforced this change of attitude. In reviewing the effects of European influence in the Americas, virtually all

3

dispassionate observers have found much to blame in Europeans' treatments of natives. The cultures that European dominance altered or tried to replace were usually damaged seriously, if not destroyed outright. While some rabid Christians might argue that destruction was proper and good, because such cultures were the works of Satan, they are not the majority of commentators or the most representative. Inasmuch as theologians have developed a consensus that God works through native cultures, inspiring them with grace, the cultural imperialism that Europeans often visited on natives now strikes most Christian theologians as ill-advised, if not seriously sinful. Saying this does not imply that Christians should abrogate their conviction that explicit faith in Jesus the Christ is the greatest of cultural gifts. It does imply Christians' being considerably more humble about the offices of Christ's church than has been the norm throughout most of Christian history.

How does one best introduce the native religious cultures of the various American peoples? No doubt there are as many different answers to this question as professors dealing with it. In our opinion, however, one does best by blending empirical information with interpretative analysis. Students need empirical information: facts about the geography and history of a given area, examples of myths and rituals that given native peoples developed, clarifications of conceptual convictions such peoples possessed about the structures of nature, social life, the self, and ultimate reality. Until students know a fair amount about how native peoples tended to live, what their cultures stressed and assumed, "native peoples" will seem like Martians. Simply by noting where they lived, what they ate, how they interacted with the plants and animals of their habitat, how they thought about the life cycle, and the like, one makes native peoples less exotic, more like one's own tribe.

Survival, Meaning and Religion

Second, however, students also need "interpretative analysis. All peoples are preoccupied with making a living and constructing meaning. Whether "making a living" entails hunting buffalo or stalking clients on Wall Street, it draws the same bottom line. Human beings have to obtain food, shelter, clothing. They have to find ways to cure their sick, bring healthy children into the world, educate their young people so that they become competent, mature members of the tribe. All groups are involved in passing on their traditions, the practices

It is important to understand and respect the dignity that individuals feel when they are given the freedom to feel positive about their cultural roots.

and beliefs that make them who they are. "Making a living" means mastering the material resources, the practical underpinnings, necessary to sustain family life, build villages, transport goods, and so forth.

Nonetheless, life is more than food. Human beings are not made human by bread alone. They require meaning. The human spirit is hungry for more than food, shelter, sex, excitement, pleasure. In their depths people long for beauty, justice, holiness. They feel a profound need to integrate their lives with the larger cycles of nature, the greater powers that they intuit are responsible for the world's original coming into being and present operation. What we call "higher culture" deals with these issues. It is meditative, contemplative, artistic, scientific—disciplined, yet free of workaday narrowness. It calls people to vacate their ordinary assumptions and wander imaginatively in new realms, where new ways of thinking about nature or designing social arrangements or understanding human destiny can flourish.

In most native American cultures leadership in such matters of higher culture has fallen to tribal elders and shamans. The elderly have been assumed to have gained the experience necessary for wisdom. The entire tribe has needed such wisdom in order to live well— to prosper in spirit, as well as body. Shamans have been ecstatics, people who knew how to move out of ordinary consciousness and encounter the spiritual forces really running the world. From such travel shamans typically have gained the ability to cure the sick, guide the dead to their place of rest, discern the sources of hard times, and help those troubled in spirit find their way back to peace.

There is no native American group that has not traditionally been religious. Certainly, many groups long had no special word for religion. Certainly, the ordinary rule among native Americans has been that culture has been holistic, making no rigid separation between secular affairs and sacred. Nonetheless, traditionally sickness, education, hunting, gathering, procreating, celebrating harvests,·mourning the dead, and all other significant aspects of culture have entailed interactions with the gods or spirits whom the people credited with the major say in their prosperity or suffering. One could not come of age without the help of such spirits, and one could not pass out of this mortal phase of existence without facing their primacy. All significant infusions of power, from the rage that warriors needed to fight well to the fertility that visited women each month, involved one in an economy of sacred forces. Inasmuch as such involvements are much of what we mean by "religion," we can say that traditional native Americans were virtually to a person religious.

Now, once again we have to ward off possible misunderstandings.

The beauty and vastness of the land were major influences in Native American culture.

To say that traditional native American cultures were religious is not to say that no members of the tribe were skeptical about traditional ways, wondered at the silences or apparent caprices of the gods, saw through the myths and rituals to their sources in human invention and psychological need. Native Americans were not schooled to criticism, skepticism, the way that Europeans have been since the 18th century Enlightenment. They did not bring to their culture the "hermeneutic of suspicion" that has developed in the wake of Marx and Freud. But they could be wise about the ambiguity of human motivation, the impurity of human desires, the man-made, woman-shaped character of many traditional stories and ceremonies. For instance, as soon as Hopi Indians passed out of childhood, they realized that the kachina dancers were human beings, not gods pure and simple. However, that did not vitiate the kachina dances. Most native Americans have realized instinctively, intuitively, that the sacred needs human, material vehicles, if it is to make an impact in human affairs. As well, they have realized that when one donned the kachina mask one's consciousness changed. A certain loss of ordinary identity occurred, so that in a significant if still symbolic way one became the spirit one represented.

Native American Consciousness

For traditional, pre-modern peoples the world over, the line between the self and "outside" realities has not been as sharp or rigid as it became for Europeans after the Enlightenment. Reality has remained more mysterious and symbiotic. It has made psychological sense that the shaman would become a bird, so as to fly away to the heavens and deal with the celestial forces, or become a jaguar, to contend with the forces of beauty and death that roam the jungle. What such a "becoming" entailed could never be rendered with mechanical precision. Yet that has not made it unreal or fully suspect. It has happened, and its happening has honored a primal truth of traditional native American life: human beings have a great deal in common with the animals of their habitat. The bonds between hunters and hunted have been supple, complex, rich, a two-way street. The same for the bonds between agriculturalists and the maize, beans, or squash they raised, between gatherers and the roots, berries, or nuts on which they subsisted. The spawn of the salmon in the spring traditionally was more than a flat, natural happening. Brothers and sisters were on the move. Their beauty and purpose had profound implications for the psyches as well as the supper tables of those who fished for them.

We take it as relatively obvious, then, that the peoples we study in this book have been religious. If, etymologically, "religion" means being retied to one's primary sources, reconnected with the gods who made the world and one's species, then virtually all important aspects of traditional native American culture have been religious. Everywhere native peoples have tried to gain harmony with the gods, the spiritual powers in charge. Always this harmony has been the great treasure of native cultures, the great yield that a trusting acceptance of traditional ways has provided, generation after generation.

Although we consider such staples of traditional native American cultures as peoples' relations with the natural world, their sense of tribal identity and ideal organization, their understanding of the composition and destiny of the individual self, their conception of ultimate, divine reality, and the spiritualities they have fashioned to guide people to health and wisdom, distinctions among these different concerns are somewhat artificial. The holistic character of traditional American cultures shows through clearly in the inability of natives to distinguish thoroughly between nature and divinity, or between the self and the group. Native consciousness has not fashioned air-tight distinctions among such categories. Native rituals and myths have tended to deal with all of them at once, all of them together.

So, what we employ as serviceable tools for organizing our data, lest they prove completely unmanageable, are only useful fictions. We need always to remember that our distinctions break down when it comes to the actual functioning of traditional native American consciousness, conscience, culture. Admittedly, native thinkers have fashioned their own categorical schemes, as though to remind us that categorizing reality, working taxonomically, is endemic to the human intellect. But their "sciences" have been less rigorous than our European ones, so they have suffered less temptation to hypostatize their categories—give them the status of independent entities, forget that they are merely useful fictions.

Last, we should note that the diversity of practices and beliefs that emerges as we describe the traditional cultures of native American peoples on two large continents should be a salutary reminder that no overview, least of all an introductory one, can pontificate about how things seemed, how reality configured itself, to the typical member of a given native tribe. Tribes evolved considerably through the centuries, indeed the millennia, that they interacted with changing environments and ecosystems. Individual natives may not have prized their uniqueness as passionately as modern western cultures have taught many Europeans to do, but they were not simply interchangeable ants sharing a common hill, interchangeable drones or workers serving a common queen bee.

Consequently, it is hard to overestimate the variety and diversity of the religious experiences that natives of North, Meso, and South America have enjoyed through the centuries. The more that our categories become lenses suggesting this variety and diversity, rather than intellectual containers leveling natives' experiences to tidy, manageable portions or recurrent patterns, the better they will introduce the actual historical reality of religious life in the Americas.

The Attitudes

If our plan of attack is to group native Americans according to traditional geographical areas and investigate their customary ideas about the natural world, the organization of their tribe, the meaning and destiny of the individual, the disposition of the ultimate forces running the world, and the spirituality one espoused, if one wanted to become wise, our attitude is a blend of respect and intrigue. On the one hand, we are dealing with traditions that enabled human beings to survive in the Americas for thousands, perhaps tens of thousands, of years. Minimally, then, they deserve our respect, for through them people have kept their tribes going. On the other hand, many of those traditions are so foreign to a contemporary western mentality that they seem exotic, more than passing-strange. "Intrigue" may be a properly neutral word through which to convey this second characteristic of traditional native American cultures.

We can only be intrigued by something if its foreignness is not so marked that we feel we could never understand it. We have to find grounds for hoping that, with fuller acquaintance, native ceremonies or myths or convictions about death could become coherent for us. The deeper ground of intrigue is the possibility of discovering that humanity, what we share with any other members of our species *homo sapiens,* is richer, more surprising, than we tended to assume. Strangers become truly interesting, even our benefactors, when they show us other ways that we could mature as women and men, other roads in the yellow wood that we might have taken as paths to rich meaning.

In the case of the meaning of human existence, the most persuasive data are individuals who give every evidence of having become fully mature. Full maturity as a human being, an animal capable of reflection and profound communication with others through knowledge and love, entails a robust realism. The fully mature or wise woman or man knows the measure of the world, the self, the human community in which she or he lives. Without sentimentality, mature people love this measure, find nature and other people so full of beauty and wonder that they could never imagine becoming bored.

A prime problem that maturity has to negotiate is death. Human beings die, like all other animals. Our span is limited. We don't even know how long it will be, when we shall end. We don't even know whether our ending will be peaceful or painful. So, related to death, are the problems of pain and injustice. We live in a world that causes most people considerable suffering. Equally, we live in a world that does not give all people a fair shake, a square deal. Wisdom entails accepting these foundational facts without acquiescing to them. It may pass through phases where one rails against the universe or the gods, but when it has settled so as to become a stable disposition, wisdom lives beyond railing, raging, shaking one's fist.

For the fact is that we never get clear answers to our questions about why we have to die, why we have to suffer, why the world is not just. Relatedly, we never get clear, empirically incontrovertible answers to our questions about where we came from, where we go at death, what is the best thing we can do at present. The myths and traditions that our cultures offer us hint at answers to these questions, but they cannot give us certitude. Inseparable from being mature as a human being is having to live by faith, having to toss one's bread upon the waters and trust that it will come back not soggy but enriched. Shamans and sages learn to live by faith, with mystery, so that it becomes as congenial as the air they breathe, the sea in which the fishes swim.

Ordinary people who have become mature nearly always have passed through much suffering, both physical and spiritual. Traditional native Americans, like traditional religious people in other parts of the world, have known that wisdom and holiness lie on the far side of spontaneous, sensual human judgments and choices. One cannot become wise without realizing that the spirit tends to wax fat as the body fasts, becomes ascetic, moves away from ease, luxury, carnal pleasure. Equally, one cannot become wise or holy without realizing that riches, honors, the esteem of one's fellow human beings are no substitute for searing confrontations with ultimate realities like death and unexpected surges of joy. There is a huge difference between dreams of vainglorious success and tough, testing confrontations with one's own nothingness. Ashes to ashes and dust to dust. How is it that a body marked for the grave can house a spirit yearning for immortality? How is it that beyond even the pride and stoic toughness that carry many shamans and sages away from mediocrity, toward spiritual distinction, something humbler and more loving dwells?

The Spiritual Life

These are the paradoxes, the intrigues, of the spiritual life, as one finds the heroes of traditional native American cultures, African cultures, Asian cultures, and European cultures to have discovered them. These are the deeper reasons for studying people who originally strike us as bizarre but soon turn out to have much the same agenda as we do. We want to make it through the day without cracking up, and so do they. We want not only bread but also roses, art, intercourse with something so compelling that we might sell all we had and follow it wholeheartedly, and so do they. Once we see that all continents have housed people with these aspirations, religions with these goals, we begin to consider any store of traditional cultural lore a potential treasure trove for ourselves. Eskimo shamans, or ordinary Eskimo survivors, no longer seem like members of another species.

Substitute the cultural wilderness induced by modern secularism and technology for the wilderness of ice and snow that traditional Eskimos have had to conquer and you find kith, kin, soulmates. The same with plains Indians dancing to the sun, piercing their breasts with thongs of leather for the sake of the hoop of their nation, the social circle they want to keep from breaking. Their mode of asceticism may not suit a contemporary European psyche, but what they were trying to achieve through the sun dance is completely relevant to the spiritual projects many Europeans have pursued. At the least, we can appreciate the signal humanity they have displayed.

"Appreciation," then, need not be merely a bland slogan. If it names an intrigue powered by a genuine desire to learn more about the greatest of human tasks, which is to become mature in face of bedrock realities like death, it can connote a peculiar, telltale excitement. Inasmuch as the human spirit has been fashioned to pursue meaning, significance that might orient it in a mysterious world so as to live with peace and joy, the human spirit takes flame when it comes across reports of people who fashioned lives of manifest peace, joy, dignity, conviction that they had a significant place under heaven. People who have felt that they fitted into schemes much bigger than themselves or human inventions, that their lives ran in harmony with

Their mode of asceticism may not suit a contemporary European psyche, but what they were trying to achieve ... is ... relevant to the spiritual projects many Europeans have pursued.

truly cosmic processes or divine, providential dispensations of space and time, stand out from the rest of us, especially us modern Europeans, as singularly blessed.

Where we may doubt deeply that there is any master plan, any overarching providence to give every time a purpose under heaven, they have felt that their prayers raised the sun each day, sent it racing across the sky with joy, and put it to bed peaceful, full of a sense of accomplishment. Or, they have felt that their work in the earth helped Mother Earth be fruitful, bring forth healthy children, bless the world with an amazing bounty. Or, they have felt that their hunting brought them into fascinating relations with the game they stalked, such that the game eventually might give their lives willingly, under the assurance that human beings appreciated their sacrifice and would commend them to the Master of the Animals responsible for their replenishment. In traditional, pre-white America, animals and human hunters were locked in a strange, wonderful economy of life and death. They had not chosen this economy. It had been imposed on them. But they could hallow their time if they observed its rules well, and by observing its rules well they could become both dispassionate about the need to kill and compassionate toward all mortal creatures.

On and on the potential appreciations of the riches of traditional religious cultures go. The more one learns about native American, African, Australian, Middle Eastern, Asian, European, or other cultural ways, the more one realizes that no people has been without a great passion to understand its situation. As soon as they had assured themselves physical survival, every people we encounter by studying the historical record has striven to enrich its life with beauty, religious meaning, a profound sense of the cosmic scheme into which it ought to fit. It is our privilege as writers of this book to suggest some of the chapters of human striving lived out in the Americas. It is your opportunity as readers to discover how different many of those chapters have been from your own, yet also how similar.

Chapter 2

TRADITIONS OF THE
EASTERN WOODLANDS

Background

The northern portion of the area that we treat in this chapter falls roughly within 90 degrees to 70 degrees west longitude and 35 degrees to 47 degrees north latitude. Three main geographical areas are included: the upper Great Lakes and Ohio River valley, the lower Great Lakes, and the eastern coastal regions. Several different types of lifestyle have occurred: nomadic hunting, semi-permanent settlements in villages, and permanent agricultural settlements. Three major language groups stand out: Iroquoian, Algonquian, and Siouan. Most of the tribes that spoke Iroquoian languages were organized along the female line. The tribes who spoke Algonquian and lived along the east coast were organized either along the female line or both the female and male lines. The Algonquian tribes that lived near the upper Great Lakes or the Ohio River tended to be organized either along the male line or both lines. The same held for the Siouan tribes: organization along the male line or both lines. The diversity of languages, lifestyle, and social organization suggests that the tribes of the northeast woodlands represented several different historical lines.

Demographic speculation suggests that at the time of their first contact with whites, native American groups varied considerably in the density of their populations. The most densely populated area was probably along the east coast, in what is now the region of Virginia and North Carolina. The area around the lower Great Lakes was probably next in density of population, while the more northerly regions (upper Great Lakes and what is now coastal New England) were the most sparsely populated. Even the "densely" populated areas had relatively few people: perhaps 300 per hundred square kilometers in Virginia-North Carolina, 25–60 in the lower Great Lakes area, and fewer than 25 in both the upper Great Lakes area and New England.

The implication, of course, is that native Americans of these areas could roam quite freely. Even agricultural tribes felt little cramping. The further implication is that nature would have bulked large and human achievements quite small. Inasmuch as the woods were full of birds and animals, the people would have felt that they had many neighboring creatures. Interacting with them would probably have been less dramatic than the interactions that Native Americans of the far north experienced. In the bareness of northern landscapes, meeting the walrus or polar bear, the caribou or arctic wolf, tended to be a critical event.

Since the advent of whites in significant numbers in the seventeenth century, the traditional patterns of native life in the northeast woodlands have shifted markedly. Many of the tribes were forced to move from the habitats they enjoyed at the time of initial contact. Often we cannot be sure how long they had lived in those habitats, but it seems clear that the disruptions caused by white immigration had severe consequences for the cultural lives of the native Americans. Not only did they have to develop new economies (in the sense of new interactions with their ecological niches, for the sake of survival), they also had to compensate for the emotional losses that migration entailed. The land had never been simply an indifferent site. All tribes had related to their traditional land as to something maternal—a living abode.

The traditional habitat had holy sites: places of special beauty, places where the holy powers were thought to reside in unusual force. Burial sites had long tokened contact with ancestors, and so tribal continuity through many generations. Totemic (emblematic) relations with the animals of a given area had entered into the peoples' sense of themselves. To the extent that traditional native American cultures now seem horribly mangled, perhaps beyond repair, this movement from long-standing sites takes on a tragic aspect. The native American tribes were forced to sacrifice much of their traditional identity. What sort of theodicy (justification of God's ways) such a sacrifice would require has to stand atop the agenda of a theology responsive to native American experience, both in the northeast woodlands and across the entire continent.

When we break down the three main language groups of this geographical area, some familiar tribal names emerge. Among those speaking Algonquian stand the Ojibwa, Ottawa, Potawatomi, Menomini, Sauk, Fox, Kicapoo, Miami, Illinois, Shawnees, Narragansett, Mohican, Delaware, Nanticoke, and Powhatan. Among those speaking Iroquoian we find the Huron, Erie, Neutral, Petun, Seneca, Oneida, Onondaga, Cayuga, Mohawk, and Tuscarora. The tribes in this area speaking Siouan were the Winnebago and Tutelo. Obviously, language is the great carrier of culture. Inasmuch as they belonged to the same language group, a given cluster of tribes tended to think of themselves as relatives. Conversely, they tended to think of tribes that spoke another language as strangers. Being relatives or strangers did not immediately settle the question of friendly or hostile relations, but it did shade that question. Indeed, when the French and English began to contest control of areas of the northern woodlands, they tended to recruit native American allies from different, traditionally somewhat estranged tribal families.

The Southeast Woodlands

The southern portion of the area under discussion in this chapter is roughly that of what white Americans mean by "the south." It extends from about 95 degrees west longitude to the Atlantic coast, and from about 37 degrees north latitude to the Gulf of Mexico. Estimates of the population of native Americans inhabiting this region prior to contact with whites vary considerably. Perhaps a million is a reasonable figure. Obviously, to have only a million people in so large an area means that the population was seldom dense. Such a relatively light population meant that natural surroundings made a great impact on the people's culture and psychology.

The mild weather created conditions suitable for farming, and from late in the pre-historic period (the period prior to contact with whites), native Americans had extensive agricultural projects along the larger rivers. The alluvial soil deposited there was rich, and so farming was relatively easy. Tribes located themselves by rivers, and a relatively complex social organization arose. The rivers afforded easy transportation and facilitated communication among different groups.

Still, the tribes of the southeast were quite diverse. At least five families of languages obtained, making for significant cultural differences. Muskogean was the largest family, but three of the languages found in the northeast woodlands were also present: Iroquoian, Algonquian, and Siouan. The fifth linguistic group was Caddoan.

While the land, and perhaps Muskogean traditions, created a fairly uniform social structure throughout the southeast, the tribes were frequently at war. People lived in villages, or even towns, along the river shores, comprising relatively large social units. They were organized under chiefs, whose power passed from father to son. These families of chiefs constituted a social elite, somewhat separated from the rest of the people, who functioned as commoners. The chiefs drew their importance from their leadership in war. War was sufficiently common and significant to create a militaristic culture. Young men trained for war, and distinguishing oneself in battle was the best way to win prestige.

When Europeans immigrated in large numbers, they discovered the richness of the southern lands and developed ambitious agricultural dreams. This put them at odds with the native Americans, who were no match for their military weaponry. Tribes got drawn into the competition among the British, French, and Spanish for southern territory, tending to side with the European group that was strongest in their traditional area or promised them the richest rewards for cooperation. In fact, the plantation owners of the early nineteenth century disregarded native American claims, trampling underfoot most native rights. The plantation owners were expanding the use of black slaves. Eventually this led to the forced relocation of most native Americans, who had to trek westward to what is now Oklahoma. Only a few groups—Cherokees, Choctaws, Catawbas, Seminoles—had people who avoided capture and managed to stay in the southeast. Some of them intermarried with blacks.

However, the native population had already been decimated by white diseases. By 1755, native Americans in the southeast were perhaps down to 50,000–70,000. This drastic reduction of their numbers, along with the other incursions of white culture, understandably disrupted traditional ways of life. The system of chiefs and commoners went into abeyance and a simpler social structure emerged. Apparently, religious beliefs and rituals also simplified. Since most of our information about native American beliefs comes from nineteenth century observers, it is difficult to picture what pre-contact patterns had been. Some earlier sources, going back as far as the sixteenth century, offer clues, but until the nineteenth century much is conjectural.

Because of their forced displacement, native Americans of the southeast woodlands are poignant reminders of the sufferings that white immigration caused. The new nations that emerged on the North American continent depended on much native pain. The physical sufferings were terrible enough, and native Americans still manifest them: disease, poverty, marginalization. But the worst suffering has been cultural. To become a people without healthy roots, with diseased memories, has meant widespread depression, alienation, and self-hatred. Many native Americans became Christians, of various sorts, but virtually all struggled to retain some hold on their pre-Christian traditions. The efforts at revival during the twentieth century testify to the strong attraction those pre-Christian traditions have exercised.

Nature

For most of the peoples of the eastern woodlands, the land was a source of power. As the seasons changed, or the sun passed through the sky to periodize the day, or the earth brought forth new plants and animals, the vitality of existence touched the people. This power was awesome and holy. It was numinous: a presence of the divine, the sacred, the truly real by reference to which everything else found its orientation. One could not explain this power by reference to anything else. It was the ground and context, the explicator rather than the explicand. And it passed beyond human control. Human beings could find no words in which to capture it, no rites by which to subdue it. Rather, it was that to which human beings had to bow if they were to find right order.

We shall consider some of the names for this power when we treat of how peoples of the eastern woodlands thought about ultimate reality. Here it may be more pertinent to reflect on some of the myths through which tribes explained their origins, or the origins of the land itself, from sacred power. For example, the Menomini of Wisconsin said that the first human beings arose from bears. Two bears, a male and female, arose from the earth at the mouth of the Menominee River. They became the first man and woman. The symbolism is plain yet profound. First, animal life comes directly from the earth. Second, the local waters were the center of the drama of creation—waters as life-giving as the earth. Third, there is an intrinsic tie between animal life, represented dramatically by the bear, and human life. The animal that human beings hunt in greatest fear and trembling is their ancestor. Fourth, sexual differentiation, common to both bears and human beings, is aboriginal. From the time that there were animal species, there has been male and female. Male and female runs throughout creation. It makes sense, therefore, to organize much of one's social and cultural life in terms of sexual differentiation. It makes sense to think that all of nature (all of reality) proceeds by the dialectic of sameness and difference that we find in the relations between human males and females. For both fertility and creative, though sometimes painful, tension, one has to have female and male.

Many native Americans became Christians, of various sorts, but virtually all struggled to retain some hold on their pre-Christian traditions.

The land was a source of power for most of the peoples of the eastern woodland.

Another Menomini myth says that the first human beings came from thunderbirds that descended near Fond du Lac, at a point where a prominent ledge extends into Lake Winnebago. The implication of this story is several-fold. First, perhaps creation took place at several different sites. Second, any outstanding, famous place in the landscape suggested itself as a site that might have been, perhaps must have been, significant to the tribe's origins. Third, by linking the thunderbird with the arising of human life, the Menomini both established an intrinsic tie between human beings and birds and balanced the dependence of human beings on the earth (spotlighted in the first myth) with a dependence on the sky. The thunderbird, a "personification" of the power of the storm, represented the fecundity of rains. For many peoples, the waters of the sky are what fertilizes mother earth, like a fatherly semen. Actually, many woodland tribes tended to speak of the earth as "grandmother" and of the sky as "grandfather," to suggest the venerable character of these natural progenitors. They were old, wise, strong as only the fullest members of the human tribe could symbolize. They stood beyond the wars of maturation that human parents might still be fighting, as fully realized parental forces—powers strong enough to be benevolent and trustworthy in all circumstances.

For the Ojibwa, certain sacred spaces of human manufacture stood for the power that ran through nature and might break out at any exceptional site. In a "medicine rite" (a ceremony designed to tap the power of the cosmos), the Ojibwa would construct a lodge of arched trees. They would place a rock on the earthen floor and erect a pole in the center. The symbolism was meant to recapitulate the structure of the cosmos: earth beneath, sky above, directions (north, south, east, west) arching around the people's life. The pole stood for the people's hope that they were truly connected with the heavens above. Each of the arches of the cardinal directions could also symbolize a water spirit or snake associated with the vital power mediated by that direction (warm wind, gentle rain, cold wind, snow and ice, etc.). Up the tree or cosmic pillar ran the different spirits of the heavens— layers of power. (For shamans, the tree also represented a way to ascend to the powers holding the tribe's fate.)

For the Iroquoian and coastal Algonquian tribes, who tended to live in "longhouses," the ordinary tribal dwelling was a miniature of the cosmos. Thus the Delaware "big house" associated the floor with the earth, the ceiling with heaven, one side with the rising of the sun, the opposite side with the sun's setting. A "good white path" through the house stood for the journey that human beings make from birth to death. In ceremonial dances, the Delaware would exit from a door in the western wall and circle back to the east, as an expression of their hopes for rebirth. A post in the center of the big house stood for the axis of the world. It had twelve levels, to represent the different layers of the cosmos. At the top was the abode of the Great Manitou, the foremost power. The post was like the staff of the Great Manitou, who dispensed the power of creation down it. All around the lower levels of the big house carvings represented spirits who carried this power. The general result was a picture of Delaware life in which the people were always surrounded by numinous, creative power.[1]

Southeastern Themes

Like many peoples in the new world, native Americans of the southeast woodlands pictured the world as having three layers. Above was the sky, an inverted bowl made of stone. Below were the waters— the deeps of the sea. In the middle, as the realm that gave human beings their habitat, was the earth, a circular island floating on the waters. The sky would rise at daybreak and dusk, to allow the sun and the moon to pass beneath it.

This tripartite human realm was bounded by a superior world and an inferior world. Above the sky was a realm populated by the sun, the moon, and the archetypes of all the creatures on earth. Below the waters was an infernal world of monsters and spirits, a source of novelty (a mixed blessing). The uppermost world was the source of order and peace. It was where the human spirit went, when it thought about perfection and fulfillment. The nethermost world was a place of chaos, but also of fertility. Native American thought seems to have intuited that both order and chaos are necessary for the world to be as it is.

In one creation account, in the beginning there were only the uppermost zone and the nethermost zone. The middle zone (in three layers) inhabited by human beings arose when soft mud from the nethermost world, below the waters, rose up to form the island that is now the midmost point of the human world. This island depended from four cords (the cardinal directions) and was precarious. These cords were vulnerable, and failures of human beings (fractures of moral codes) weakened them further. It was possible that one day the cords would break and so the island earth would sink beneath the waters, to be no more. That was the apocalyptic end that some native Americans of the southeastern woodlands foresaw, when they worried about a decline in morals.

Whereas the forest tribes of the north tended to focus on the heavens, the tribes of the south were more interested in the underworld. The Cherokee, closely related to the Iroquois, kept northern traditions alive in the south. Hartley Burr Alexander has rendered their myth of creation as follows: " 'The earth,' they say, 'is a great island floating in a sea, and suspended at each of the four cardinal points by a cord hanging down from the sky vault, which is of solid rock. When the world grows old and worn out, the people will die and the cords will break and let the earth sink down into the ocean, and all will be water again.' Originally the animals were crowded into the sky world; everything was flood below. The Water-Beetle was sent on an exploration, and after darting about on the surface of the waters and finding no rest, it dived to the depths, where it brought up a bit of mud, from which the Earth developed by accretion."[2]

The water-beetle is what students of comparative mythology call an "earth diver." Various peoples have myths according to which an animal—turtle, duck—dives to the bottom of the primeval waters and brings up the bit of sand or mud from which the earth is built up. Apparently most traditional peoples were very impressed by the primacy of water over the surface of the world. Somehow they sensed that the oceans are much more extensive than the lands. The waters seemed more basic and certain, the land areas more precarious. Perhaps this stems from an intuition that the conscious, formed parts of the human psyche are only a small portion of the whole. They rest above all sorts of subconscious and unconscious influences, forces, and memories encoded in our genes through millennia of evolution. Whatever the proper psychoanalysis, it is interesting that so many traditional myths depict creation as a descent into the primeval waters to bring up a bit of solid, defined reality.

Virtually never is the earth-diver a human being. Almost always it is a humble, familiar animal, at home in the water. The assumption of the myth is that human beings are the debtors of such simple, familiar animals. We share a single world with them, and they are closer to its basic structure than we. The traditional myths reflect an intuition that human beings are the odd species out in creation. By our reflective consciousness, we stand apart from the simpler, more instinctual species. They have wisdoms that we lack, just as we have powers that escape them. Even though the myths frequently celebrate such wisdoms, and even though they tend to personify the turtles or water beetles that figure in the creation accounts, an ambivalence remains. The world belongs to the simple animals more than to human beings. They had more to say about its original formation than we, and they move through it more naturally, with fewer hesitations.

Alexander goes on to narrate other parts of the Cherokee story of creation. Once the earth dried, animals came down from the heavens to populate it. They found this difficult and uncongenial, because the earth was dark, so they got the sun to move above it each day, from east to west, to provide light. (One can imagine more reflective Cherokee thinking that night-time is a reminder of how things were before this importing of the sun, and that night-time remains a time of creation—sexual generation among human beings, and the rest that the entire earth needs if it is to be fruitful.)

When the sun arrived to move over the earth, things became too hot. The crayfish suffered from this heat. His shell turned red and his flesh spoiled. That is why Cherokees do not eat crayfish. (Here we have a story to explain ancient customs—what scholars sometimes call an "etiological" myth [a myth about causes or origins]. In addition to explaining the grand order of the cosmos, most peoples have also wanted to explain some of their distinctive customs, or some of the distinctive features of their environment.)

The "conjurers" (probably shamans, certainly people of special power) kept raising the orbit of the sun, to reduce the heat that it shone down upon the earth. They had to do this seven times before they got the distances and temperatures just right. To this day, conjurers speak of the top of heaven as the seventh height. The sun now travels the orbit of the seventh height each day, passing beneath the earth in the evening.

The Group

Death is an event that forces a group to express its deepest convictions about its existence. Among the Fox, the tradition was to have a death announced by a crier. Members of the clan to which the dead person belonged would gather and mourn through the night. The leader of the clan would speak to the deceased, telling him or her not to envy those still alive. Rather, the deceased ought to press on, to the land of the ancestors in the west. After death there was a journey, and the first obligation of the deceased was to see it through. If reunion with the ancestors was the carrot, the stick was the need for those still living to get distance between themselves and the dead person.

This "distance" was both physical and spiritual. By burying the corpse, the clan put the deceased out of sight. By picturing the activity of the deceased as a movement away from the village, the clan suggested that new obligations demanded a firm break. Psychologically, it seems clear that the clan was projecting onto the dead person its own need to make a clean break. However dear the deceased had been, and however healthy it might be to treasure fond memories, life had to continue. It would serve no useful function for members of the clan to regret the death of any member too long or too passionately.

The Fox had the custom of marking the grave with a post bearing the emblem of the person's clan. For six months people could mourn, visiting the marker. To substitute for the dead person at clan events, the clan would adopt a stand-in. The ceremony effecting this adoption made it clear that the stand-in was a kind of continuance of the dead person's presence and role. During memorial feasts, the stand-in would "be" the deceased person. Thus the leave-taking, though firm, was balanced with an effort to maintain the integrity of the clan. The departure of the dead person ought not to leave such a hole in the clan that the clan would be disabled. Not all tribes of the upper Great Lakes area buried their dead as the Fox did. Other tribes preferred cremation or exposing the body.

Tribes of the lower Great Lakes and coastal regions also varied in their funeral practices, but burial was probably the preferred tradition. The Algonquian peoples of Virginia tended to wrap the bodies of ordinary people in animal skins and place them on scaffolds (so that the flesh would decay). Then they would bury the bones. Interestingly, however, they would mummify the bodies of rulers, after a fashion, removing the flesh, sewing the skin back onto the skeleton, and filling the carcass with sand. Priests would attend the bodies of these former rulers.

Even this barest indication of some of the funeral practices of the peoples of the area we are studying shows that death made a tribe or clan express how it thought about its place in the world. No doubt we could come to the same conclusion by studying any other event significant enough to require an elaborate ritual: marriage, atonement for a crime, installation of a chief. Typically, such a ritual would draw on myths about the origins of the first human beings, or even about the origins of the cosmos itself. Singers might recite myths related to the particular phenomenon in question (death, marriage), but the wider context tended to be the structure of the cosmos, which was established at its birth.

The word "clan" appeared at several points in our description of Fox customs. On the whole, our use of terms such as "tribe" and "clan" will not be technical. On the whole, we shall simply mean a discernible, significant unit or group. But here it may be well to indicate that "clan" can serve to specify a social cohort whose members cannot intermarry. Members of a clan might live in various locales, within the general area of the tribe in question. They had duties to provide one another hospitality. By maintaining rules against intermarriage, they forced themselves to have regular contacts with members of other clans, who might furnish them marital partners.

Apparently several instincts were at work in this arrangement. One was a sense that a healthy people requires exogamy—marriage outside the narrow group—for "fresh blood." Another was that nature is a subtle harmony of different forces that both work through various animals and are represented by those animals. So, usually, clans were totemic. They did not establish a strict, one to one, correlation with the supposed characteristics of the animal with whom they identified (who became their emblem—not just their symbol, but the "marker" standing for them in the "game" of harmonizing with nature's laws for fertility and prosperity). But they did use their totemic identity as the clan of the bear or the eagle to shape their understanding of the role they were to play in the overall interaction of the different clans.

Among the Hurons, and some other groups, a double burial was the practice. Periodically (every ten to twelve years) they would exhume the bodies buried during the preceding interval, clear away any remaining flesh, and then rebury the skeletons. By mixing the bones of these skeletons, they would re-establish bonds among the various segments of the group. The unity among the dead stood for the unity that the living ought to accomplish. This "Feast of the Dead" is clearly rich in social significance. It reminds us that the dead remained members of most tribes.

Native Americans, like Asians and Africans, thought that dreams could be important sources of revelation. A typical scenario would be for an ancestor, usually recent and known personally (father, mother, grandfather, grandmother, aunt, uncle), to appear in a dream with a warning, or a message of consolation, or a directive about how to act. It is easy to say that this was simply a mechanism by which a person might take good advice from the subconscious, but on native American terms the matter is more complicated. For the person appearing might be someone whom the dreamer did not know. Only on consultation with an elder or a shaman would it emerge that the person seemed to be a famous chief of several generations back, or a relative who died before the dreamer was born.

In the native American world, the boundaries between past, present, and future were more permeable than they tend to be in modern cultures. Similarly, the boundaries between human beings and animals, birds, and fishes were more permeable. The dead could speak in dreams or visions, and so could denizens of the far future. Birds could cry forth a message from heaven, and bears could promise to be helpers. As we saw with the Inuit, the world was alive with spiritual powers—souls, divinities, localizations of *manitou*. Inasmuch as a people lives by pre-scientific senses of reason, by pre-critical controls on meaning, it is susceptible to suggestion. Granted, the line between what might be and what probably is did not disappear. People did not become wholly credulous. But the more intense an experience, the more likely native Americans were to accredit it.

Taboos

Some of the taboos by which native Americans of the southeast woodlands established social cohesiveness may strike us as strange to the point of being bizarre. For example, children could not touch moles, because moles were thought to have a bizarre life, living under the ground, that might afflict children and make them unnatural. Here we have a rather primitive logic, perhaps thought especially applicable to children, who are unsophisticated. The logic is that touching something puts one in contact with its nature and power. Such a contact might make the ways of moles rub off on children. Even when native Americans would have blushed to have the matter put so starkly, they might have defended this custom by saying that moles, and all other fellow creatures, were not indifferent beings. Each had a field of force surrounding its being. Each brought some of this force or power to bear on everything else with which it came into contact. So no contacts were indifferent. Always one was being weakened or strengthened by encounters with other beings. Children, being vulnerable, had to be defended against dangerous influences. In some twisted way, the subterranean life of moles might appeal to them, or might come to symbolize human equivalents: not living in the light of conscience; burrowing into the dark recesses of their psyches, where violence and deviance might fester.

Another widespread custom was to prohibit combining birds and four-footed animals in the cooking pot. Once again the logic of this custom may escape us, unless we are willing to accredit the native American tendency to mix physical and spiritual influences. Birds were one kind of "people." Four-footed animals were another. And human beings were a third. Though they shared the same world, and could be helpers, it was important to stay aware of their differences in kind. To mix birds and four-footed animals could challenge the way that the creative spirits had laid out the world. Or it could import confusion about the relations among the different creatures. Clearly, moving well in the world, gaining harmony and avoiding turmoil, depended on clarity about such relations. By keeping their pots separate (like Jews keeping a kosher kitchen, with two sets of dishes), native Americans could remind themselves of the need to be precise, disciplined, and traditional in their thinking about their environment.

Still another widespread custom was to separate males and females on given occasions. For some peoples of small-scale societies, this custom would extend to domestic animals. Among native Americans, the accent fell on separating men and women. Once again, the logic becomes an analysis of the importance of difference in kind. Men and women are different kinds of human beings. They are complementary, but different. They carry different powers. Women carry the power to create and bear forth life—an awesome power, celebrated at the menarche and reaffirmed by the separation enjoined during menstruation and childbirth. Men carry the power to kill—animals, enemies. Theirs is the power of death, and after killing they too have to separate themselves from the group at large, until the power that they have roused abates back to normalcy. It could be disastrous for the creative power of women and the destructive power of men to collide. It could make nature, which depends on polar balances, run amok.

The Self

The traditions of the Iroquois tribes have been rich in social organizations designed to affirm life, intensify life, and counter the forces that threaten life. The basic function of most such organizations was to help people gain power, usually by invoking spiritual helpers. If the communal ceremonies of the entire social group aimed at offering thanks for such bounties as the harvest, the ceremonies of smaller, select groups offered the chance to focus on more particular needs. As we consider various Iroquoian associations, we may imagine what impact they were likely to have on the lives of individual members.

Donald St. John has composed a list of eight Iroquoian "medicine societies."[3] (Here "medicine" does not mean a help for curing bodily illness so much as a means of intensifying the significance of life, by stimulating an experience of power.) In earlier times, it seems, individuals gained more of their power through private shamanistic practices. To some extent, therefore, the proliferation of medicine societies in Iroquoian life after the eighteenth century represents a loss of confidence in the ability of the average person to find power on his or her own.

The largest society, known as "Shake the Pumpkin," contained most of the members of other, smaller societies. It sponsored rituals to thank animal helpers who were thought to have pledged their aid in fighting disease and bringing good luck. Some of the practices of this society were very old: juggling hot coals, wearing blinders. The likelihood is that they reflect shamanic practices designed either to prove the possession of power or to help in the acquisition of power.

The "Company of Mystic Animals" gathered together members of such more specialized groups as the Buffalo, Bear, Otter, and Eagle societies. Members would imitate their totemic or tutelary (advice-giving) animals. The roots of this group apparently lie in long-standing shamanic experiences of communication between human beings and animals.

The "Little Water Society" originally served in time of war to facilitate healing wounds. The members would make medicines by mixing parts of animals, plants, and birds. Such medicines had a great reputation for efficacy, and members would meet at night several times a year to renew their potions.

The "Little People Society" also met at night. Its goal was to maintain good relations with the little people—fairies or elfin folk who might be either helpful or mischievous. Many European peoples also believed in fairies, so the practices of this group would seem to have roots in a psychology that imagined luck, whether good or bad, to be the result of personal actions by spiritual forces. The typical person of a small-scale, oral society has been a "personalist" or an "animist," in the sense that he or she did not think of nature or fate as casual. Nature was not a system of impersonal forces. Everything that happened came from an act of will. The agents of history, the makers of fate, were imagined to be like human agents. Not only were they capable of intelligent action, they could be capricious, spiteful, or generous. They were susceptible to flattery and bribes. So one had to be on the lookout and do one's best to appease them.

The "False Face Society" revolved around the manufacture and wearing of masks. The masks carried special powers, so even carving them was a weighty business. Some scholars believe that the Iroquois borrowed the practice of wearing masks from the Hurons. This society would meet in both the spring and the fall, to cleanse the community of disease. By stirring up people's power ("medicine"), it would strengthen its members. Rituals included blowing ashes and handling hot coals. Seventeenth century observers reported members' imitating hunchbacks. The psychology of mask-wearing is very rich. Freeing themselves from their ordinary personalities, members could explore new parts of themselves. Masks allow people to drop inhibitions. They loosen the wearer's sense of what has to be, opening a wider horizon of what might be, in unusual circumstances. Inasmuch as traditional peoples' ways of healing sickness regularly drew on psychic sources, using masks could facilitate healing. Practitioners could draw on extraordinary aspects of the mechanisms involved in both the production of disease and overturning it.

The "Husk Faces" were another group that wore masks. Their purpose was to stimulate success in agriculture. Their masks represented spirits of the fields, important for fertility. This was another group that blew ashes and handled hot coals. (Perhaps the dependence of the Iroquois on a standing fire to see them through the harsh winter made fire an object of awe. Ashes can symbolize death. Inasmuch as one can revive a fire from coals covered with ashes, ashes can also symbolize rebirth. One who can handle hot coals has conquered fear of death and drawn on unusual bodily powers—perhaps the very ones needed to combat sickness or infertility.) At midwinter members of the Husk Faces would burst into the longhouse and announce that they were setting out on a journey to the other side of the world, where they would till the crops. The notion was that the crops had gone away for the winter but would return in the summer, as long as someone cared for them in their exile.

The "Towii'sas Society" was a women's group dedicated to honoring corn, beans, and squash. Women tended these crops. This group sponsored a Green Corn ceremony, to honor the beginnings of the new crop. It also sponsored curing ceremonies.

The last Iroquoian medicine society that St. John describes, the "Ohgiwe Society," would conduct ceremonies for people who had seen ghosts. It would also sponsor ceremonies to honor the dead, whom the Iroquois both reverenced and feared. Such ceremonies (ceremonial feasts) would bring family members together, and they were thought to insulate the entire tribe from attacks by the dead.

These various societies aided individuals in their efforts to enjoy healthy, power-filled lives. Individuals also had access to the power of animal-helpers through personal visions: "During puberty rites or shamanic training a guardian spirit would reveal itself to the individual through the dream-vision. The spirit could take the form of a human being, or animal, or a bird such as a raven or crow. An intimate and powerful relationship was established between the person and the guardian spirit. A person who had such a friendship had greater inner power and confidence than one who did not. The guardian spirit revealed its desires in dreams. To ignore this ally or to fail to understand its desire could result in illness. Such an illness signified a dangerous disruption of the relationship between spirit-forces and humans."[4]

Sexual Roles

Sexual roles obviously impinge on both the group and the individual. For the individual, how a given culture construes what it means to be female or male is enormously important. Human beings grow up trying to fit into patterns reflected to them by their elders. Their elders are their role models, and perhaps nothing is more important to a young person than fulfilling the model of what it means to be a good male or female—a brave man, a beautiful woman (as many cultures have stereotyped things).

The marriage ceremony that prevailed for most tribes of the southeast woodlands gives us clues to how men and women were schooled to think about themselves. First, the kinsmen of the groom presented gifts to the kinsmen of the bride. This suggests that most tribes thought that a wife was a valuable possession. Certainly she might be much more than just a "possession," but she was also that: a productive addition, an increase in a man's "wealth" (whether broadly or narrowly conceived). By giving gifts in exchange for the bride, the groom's kin reset the economic balance between the two family lines. They acknowledged that they were profiting and that her family was losing. To be sure, this could become a crass view of things, but it did not have to be. At its best, it could be a way of honoring the many-sided new value that was coming into the groom's life.

Second, the marriage ceremony itself included acts that symbolized what each of the partners would do in the marriage. The groom had to kill a deer or bear. The bride had to cook a dish of corn. Men were the hunters, expected to provide fresh meat at regular intervals. Women were the farmers, at least concerning corn, the all-important crop. The myths of hunting were staples of male lore, and significant sources of male identity. The myths of the coming of corn had feminine motifs, tying the corn to women's fertility. Women were bound to find in them significant sources of female identity. The marriage was bringing together two complementary identities. The two ways of being human, male and female, had to merge, coordinate, not only in the physical act of intercourse but also psychologically, to create a household. Parenting would depend on this coordination. Happiness in the individual household, and by extension in the whole tribe, would also depend on it. So the symbolic acts of killing a bear and cooking a dish of corn were rich indeed. In effect they were saying that each partner pledged to carry out the tasks expected of him or her—that each would strive to be a good, mature, generous, productive instance of his or her sex.

Women were mothers, as well as wives, and another important dimension of their identity was their bearing and raising children. They would usually give birth apart from men, in the midst and with the help of other women. Frequently the same house to which they withdrew during menstrual periods would be the place for giving birth. That naturally became a center for women's bonding, passing on feminine lore, and strengthening their sense of identity. Some tribes had distinctive societies for women, focused on the cures or thanksgivings that women especially needed. Ideally, women matured to think of their sex as carrying great dignity. Not only were women indispensable for the future of the tribe (procreation), they also had irreplaceable economic roles (for example, cultivating the corn). As is true of people of small-scale societies generally, native American women were not second-class citizens. On occasion they might be subject to abuse by men, but few cultures looked down on female nature or inculcated a sense of inferiority among women.

In addition to their roles as hunters, males were encouraged to be strong warriors. The tribes of the southeast woodlands were militaristic, violent enough to make training for warfare important. As noted, prowess in fighting was one of the best ways for males to gain distinction, and the typical tribal structure made the chiefs who led the people in battle the upper, ruling class.

A military culture tends to school males to obedience and endurance. Fighting well requires both individual courage and a willingness to sacrifice oneself for the overall needs of the group. Certainly native American warriors did not develop their tactics or ethos as extensively as European warriors did. Their societies were much smaller, and so were their wars. But native American warfare added another wrinkle to the bravery that the life of hunting already required. It forced men to confront death from another angle. Women had to confront death as a possible outcome of childbirth. Men had to confront it as a possible outcome of warfare. And whereas women had the consolation that childbirth was oriented to producing life, men had to face the grim reality that warfare directly intended death.

One way of dealing with death, when it is a regular possibility, is to resolve to live intensely, in the present, "seizing the day." Another way is to develop a stoic detachment: what will be will be. Native

Americans tended to blend these two ways. Part of the typical male's respectable profile was a stoic emotional control. Men might show tenderness in private, to their wives and children. In public they had to remember that they were hunters and warriors, called to face down death on a regular basis. The more that they could do to derive satisfaction from each day of life, the easier it was to contemplate losing life in a worthy cause. It would be terrible to die without ever having lived intensely. If one demanded that nature show its beauty, that other people be loyal friends, that one's woman give herself passionately, that one's children grow up strong and healthy, one could say that, whatever the length of one's life, it had been good.

A myth about the origin of corn shows us several features of the socialization to which both sexes were subjected in the southeast woodlands. An orphaned boy is schooled by an old woman, whom he calls "Grandmother," so that he learns to hunt: "Now he went hunting everywhere, but his Grandmother told him he must never pass a distant blue mountain on the horizon. He hunted many things but never discovered from which creature his Grandmother made the *sofky* maize gruel and the blue dumplings of maize and beans. He knew nothing of plants. He decided one day to peep in through the door when she was preparing food. He saw her remove her dress and straddle a corn sieve. As she scratched one of her thighs, a stream of maize poured down. As she scratched the other thigh, a stream of beans descended. When he came in and would not eat, the Grandmother guessed that he had discovered her secret. She told him that now that he had solved the mystery he must leave her and go beyond the blue mountain. To protect him, she made a magical headdress of intertwined rattlesnakes and blue jaybirds which rattled and sang when he put it on. Now Grandmother told him that all was ready for his journey. He must marry the first girl that he met, and then return. As he left he was told to shut the door, with Grandmother inside, and set fire to the house so that nothing would remain but ashes. He did so and the fire consumed everything just as Grandmother had decreed."[5]

The symbolism of this myth is so rich that we defer a full reflection on it to the next section, where we can indicate its implications for the southeast woodlanders' sense of ultimate reality. Here, in keeping with our stress on the role of sexual identity in the native American sense of the self, we need only underscore the obvious correlation of femininity with agricultural fertility, and the interaction between an aged female and an adolescent male. Only when he solves the problem of fertility does the orphan boy come of age, become ready to marry, and receive permission to venture beyond the blue mountains, the prior boundary of his world. And, at his leave-taking, he must slay the one who has provided his food and education up to that point. These facts are pregnant with suggestions about the relations between males and females, youths and elders, in native American culture. Certainly the relations between boys and grandmothers was only one of the key relations in that culture, but by isolating it, the myth-makers gave both boys and grandmothers much to think about.

Ultimate Reality

When we reflect on what this myth suggests about the structures of ultimate reality, we sense a deep dimorphism in native American culture of the southeast woodlands. There are the forms that the boy fulfills: male, young, hunting, concerned with animals. There are the forms that the grandmother fulfills: female, old, agricultural, concerned with plants. The grandmother is a figure of wisdom, which reposes in old age (and perhaps more in females than in males). The boy is a figure of adventurous youth, which must finally escape from the confines at first necessary for its safety and then slay the controls of the prior generation.

A Freudian note enters when the boy observes the grandmother's fertility and then will not eat. Not only is there an interesting link between human fertility and food, there is also the bracketing of adults' sexuality that young people require until they are comfortable with their own sexuality. Before she sacrifices herself, so that the boy can move on to the tasks of full manhood, the grandmother arranges for his protection. The magical headdress is a final gift of her love. The instruction to marry the first girl that the boy meets implies that he must quickly get to work at creating the next generation, because the grandmother's generation is passing from the scene. Soon nothing will remain of her era, which was also the boy's youth, but ashes. Soon she will be burned up by the need for life to go on.

In reality, of course, these motifs are but a few of the very many that crisscross any tribe's life. One could imagine the interactions between older males and younger females, older females and younger females, older males and younger males, etching them so that they ran parallel to this relation between a younger male and older female. Each of these portrayals has something abstract about it, like the "primitive" art that was a trigger for modern abstract art. The effort is to get at the essence of a relationship, not to render the details that domesticate it. Something wild, almost amoral hangs over the story, as the final scene suggests. The forces being depicted are primordial: sex, generation, food, killing. The dualism that runs through the myth says that nature itself is tense with oppositions: life and death, male and female, young and old, constraint and freedom.

The sacrifice of the grandmother consummates her self-giving in devoting her life to the welfare of the young boy. The older generation sacrifices for the younger in many ways, but here the amazing sacrifices of women are foremost. Life comes from women's bodies. The grandmother is a symbol of all the fertility and provision that human beings need. She is both Eve, the archetypal mother, and Mother Nature, source of corn and beans. The boy is nonplussed by this profusion. He can only long to get away, to a freedom not dominated by thoughts of how much he owes. Eventually he may realize what the ashes of his grandmother mean. But she has to take the initiative, provide for her own death. As a figure of wisdom, she says that the most mature humanity is that which reads the signs of the times and is generous enough to let go, become mulch for the next generation.

This is a relatively benign interpretation of the dualisms that appear in the myths of native Americans of the southeast woodlands. A darker dimension appears in their preoccupation with witchcraft. Witchcraft assumes that human beings can direct evil forces to afflict their enemies. In some cases, stories of witchcraft utilized native beliefs about the *uktena,* a composite creature—snakelike, yet possessing wings, horns, and teeth. The *uktena* had a blazing crest on its forehead and functioned in both lore about misfortune and divination to determine witchcraft. If a person saw an *uktena,* bad luck was sure to come. If a person smelled its breath, death was likely. If one could obtain the crest of an *uktena,* one might divine the source of illness or misfortune. Then one could combat the incursions of witches—thoroughly evil human beings who wanted to steal the time of sick people, to extend their own lives.

Theology

Just as the Iroquoian peoples were relatively developed politically, so they were relatively developed theologically. (Perhaps agriculture had given them more leisure in which to think about both politics and theology.) One recent summary of Iroquoian theology describes it as follows: "The concept of supreme power among the Iroquois was expressed in the idea that all existence was a struggle between a duality of light and darkness, of good and misfortune. The concept of evil, as we know it, is not characteristic of primitive religion in any part of the world [a bold claim]. What was called bad was unlucky in material affairs. Great respect was paid to the sun and to the moon and the stars; in particular, the Morning Star was very important. The passage of the seasons and the growth of crops made the people aware of the importance of the calendar. . . . Religion among the Indian tribes of the eastern woodlands is reported to include the concept of an All-Father of the type of [the German god] Odin or Zeus, but it is more probable that this concept had derived from contact with European Christians, which began with the visit of Vinlanders from Greenland about the year 1002. The concept, found [also] among the Northwest Coast Indians, of a sky house, where an angry old chief lived, was no doubt an explanation of meteorological phenomena. The Indians of the great forests had a wider concept of nature, and their thinkers postulated a supreme being, all-embracing, but without form and having little contact with men. The concept was more like an abstract notion such as Time, thought of as the bearer of fore-ordained events. For most people this Great Manitou, or spirit, was an ever present emotive force that took second place to the world of nature spirits who were concerned with daily events."[6]

The so-called "dualism" of native Americans of the northeast woodlands is less a clear theory about the interactions of good and evil than a reponse to the obvious fact that human experience shows some times and places to bring good fortune and others to bring bad. The powers responsible for human fortune must be similarly double or complicated. Since there are no records detailing contacts between whites and native Americans early in the eleventh century, it is purely speculative to suggest that European notions shaped the native American sense of ultimate reality. The relation between a Great Manitou and the spirits involved with more local, particular affairs is reminiscent of the relation between a "High God" and more immediate divinities. Among many African tribes, for example, the ultimate divinity is thought to be remote. Once he was close to the world, but now he stands far off. People may still appeal to him, especially in times of great need, but they do more of their religious business with lesser forces, who seem more concrete, involved, and vital.

Perhaps part of the psychology behind this theology derives from impressions that younger people have of older people. Inasmuch as old age is supposed to be the time when wisdom comes into flower, and the supreme divinity would be nothing if not wise (and long-lived), people might picture the supreme being as detached from everyday affairs, concerned with overarching, even speculative matters. The suggestion of time as an analogue is interesting, for time is nearly unique in seeming to be quite abstract while actually being ingredient in every moment and aspect of human existence.

For the Hurons, the world came from the body of a god and so had a direct tie to ultimate reality. The goddess Ataentsic was thrown by her husband, the chief deity of heaven, through a hole in the sky. She had this hole caused by tearing up the tree of heaven (the world tree). She ended up in the lower regions that make up the human world, where she gave birth to divine twins. Later, she was killed by her evil son. Her good son formed the sun from her face, and the moon and stars from her breasts. From her body came corn, beans, and pumpkins.

One way of interpreting this myth is to see it as a graphic way not only of assimilating the origin of the earth to a sacrificial birth but also of making the point that everything partakes of the same mystery of being. There is nothing that exists apart from the whole of existence. To suggest the whole of existence, many peoples refer to the divinity who stands at the beginning of the process through which the world came into being. That is the closest they can come to the notion of the font or source of what is. Agricultural peoples, impressed by the need for the seed to fall into the ground and apparently die, are often especially interested in the sacrificial aspects of the relations between ultimate reality and the concrete, diverse, proximate world that they know. To picture this world as the result of a primordial sacrifice of a divine body can seem to make it a great gift and explain why it remains full of the power of the farthest, most ultimate reality.

Spirituality

The spirituality of native Americans of the eastern woodlands emphasized medicine. The tribes that populated this area wanted to enjoy a vital existence. They sensed that vitality, energy, and power were signs that they were in harmony with the sacred forces running the world. So they asked their animal familiars to help them ward off sickness and debility and grow in robustness and virtue (the power of good character). Certainly they were concerned with mundane matters, such as ensuring that the corn and squash grew well and trying by diplomacy to avoid war. Certainly they wanted lovely, fertile spouses and strong children. They knew that they had to bury their dead with dignity and courage. They knew that visions were the best way to put a personal stamp on the perennial wisdom of the tribe. But they could subsume most of these duties or concerns under the concept of medicine.

What they put into their medicine bundles (collections of tokens of power, mementos of helpers) cheered their spirits, because these things reminded them that medicine was available. The Great Manitou (Algonquian), the Source of widespread *orenda* (Iroquian for power), had touched their lives through the eagle whose feather lay in their bundle, or the bear whose claw was there, or the bit of charred bark that recalled the bolt of lightning that came shortly after a late afternoon prayer.

The native Americans whom we have considered did not separate their medicines from the sacred power at the foundations of their world. It was not their characteristic to distinguish sharply between an ultimate source of healing or vitality and proximate ones. To be a member of the Shake the Pumpkin society was not to assert that all *orenda* came through its ceremonials. The more deeply one pursued the mystery of healing, the more clearly one saw that "medicine" could become a metaphor for everything that human beings needed. Like virtually all other traditional peoples, native Americans of the northeast woodlands were profoundly aware of their neediness. They had few of the technological intermediaries that modern western peoples have enjoyed (or been harmed by). Nature impinged on them directly, and so the vagaries of nature held their attention. They knew that a dozen things could go wrong, as quickly as a flash flood or a fire started by lightning. They knew that if the sun, the rain, the wind, and the earth did not cooperate, their crops could go to ruin in a week. Present-day industrial societies are also fragile, but it takes considerable shrewdness to realize this. Most days, things run smoothly enough to save most people worries about food and shelter.

The medicine that the various societies that flourished in the southeast woodlands focused upon was a powerful metaphor for the human condition. There is no need to doubt that many of the mature participants in such societies were aware of this fact. In other words, there is no need to think that native Americans believed that shaking the pumpkin was a magical act, in the low sense, that would compel the good forces loosed in the world to help them. Thoroughly, native American culture was metaphorical. In every way, people were immersed in the myths and rituals that oriented them in the universe.

This is not to say that they had no awareness that much in their culture was of human manufacture. People of small-scale societies could be as self-aware as the typical modern, and so they could sense the role of imagination and will in their construals of reality. But this is

The native Americans whom we have considered did not separate their medicines from the sacred power at the foundations of their world.

to say that few native American cultures had the distance that critical reason has introduced into modern and post-modern white culture. Few stepped back and contemplated seriously a nihilism in which all myths and rituals would be deconstructed into arbitrariness. Native American cultures lived so close to nature that their myths and rituals had to make finding food, hunting animals, raising corn, burying the dead, celebrating human fertility, honoring the sun and the moon, and other very concrete, positively primitive forces the stuff of what we call spirituality. If such concreteness could be limiting—no astrophysics, no depth psychology, no theology of the relations among the Trinitarian persons—it could also be medicinal.

There is something healing in deriving what humanity means from the impact of trees and animals, sex and medicine. There is a blessed rootage in the earth, the tribe, the body that keeps the mind from venturing into gnosticism. The native Americans of the southeast woodlands remind us how richly symbolic human existence was, when bodily health and sexual differentiation were strong shapers of culture. As much as we may wish to honor the changes that have come with literacy, modern science, and abstract art, we do well to remind ourselves of the ashes of our grandmothers. They remain a potent epitome of how any healthy culture understands the essentials of the human condition.

Chapter 3

TRADITIONS OF THE
FAR NORTH

Background

Toward the end of an article on arctic religions, Åke Hultkrantz, one of the leading scholars of American Indian religions, offers a useful orientation: ". . . the cultures of the Arctic area are remnants of a Paleolithic hunting culture at the northern fringe of three continents. They preserve hunting customs and religious ideas that have disappeared or become transformed in the southern pastoral and agricultural societies."[7]

The three continents in question are Asia, Europe, and North America. The assumption is that the native peoples who now live in the arctic share a common heritage, even though different groups among them have also been shaped by other forces. For example, the Inuit (a better name for the people often known as Eskimo) have been shaped considerably by the fishing cultures long significant in the Pacific, including the far north. The Finno-Ugric and Paleosiberian peoples, who have had greater influence in Europe and Asia than in North America, appear to have preserved the original Paleolithic hunting culture more purely. To the West, the Saami first came under considerable influence from Scandinavian and then, later, Christian traditions.

The Inuit, who will be our special concern in this chapter, seem to have been shaped not only by the Pacific fishing cultures already mentioned, but also by traditions from the Eurasian steppes. Some of the ways that they treat animals reflect such Eurasian traditions. Much in this description is conjectural, in that it takes into account relatively recent phenomena such as reindeer breeding, a practice that probably

41

only reached the arctic in the eighteenth century. Also, scholars cannot know precisely what kinds of cultural interactions took place
among the arctic peoples, and so what aspects of arctic culture in
North America were the result of relatively recent European or Asian
influences. This is the case, for example, with the important practice
of shamanism, often intense, among arctic tribes. It seems likely that
such shamanism came from the south, due originally to the north-
ward spread of techniques of Tibetan origin. These techniques, in
turn, were probably a blend of native Tibetan practices and Buddhist
practices adopted from India.

All the more so is our sense of the deep background of native
American tribes of the far north conjectural. If it is hard to know
where the Inuit gained the distinctive aspects of their culture in relatively recent times, it is close to impossible to know what influences
molded the first settlers of North America, many of whom who presumably made their way across what was then a land bridge at the
Bering Strait. The most that scholars can hypothesize is that such
settlers brought with them the traditions of the Asian hunting group
to which they belonged. Precisely what rituals, senses of animals or
spirits, ecstatic practices, and the like that entailed is probably beyond
recapture.

Mircea Eliade has written provocatively of the impact that hunting had on the human psyche, and some of his ideas may serve as
useful background to all the hunting cultures that we shall treat, including those of the far north. Working with reports about the cultures of recent hunters (peoples of oral, small-scale societies that long
avoided contact with literate cultures), Eliade has stressed, for example, the magical bonds between hunters and their prey.

In the traditional hunter's world, animals are much different
from what we contemporary westerners take them to be: "Primitive
hunters regard animals as similar to men [human beings] but endowed with supernatural powers; they believe that a man can change
into an animal and vice versa; that the souls of the dead can enter
animals; finally, that mysterious relations exist between a certain person and a certain animal. . . . In addition, certain patterns of religious
behavior are peculiar to hunting civilizations. For example, killing the
animal constitutes a ritual, which implies the belief that the Lord of
Wild Beasts takes care that the hunter kills only what he needs as food
and that food is not wasted. Then, too, the bones, especially the skull,
have a marked ritual value, probably because of the belief that they
contain the 'soul' or the 'life' of the animal and that it is from the
skeleton that the Lord of Wild Beasts will cause new flesh to grow . . .

Eskimo mask.

among certain peoples the soul of the slain animal is sent to its spiritual home . . . [and there is] the custom of offering the Supreme Beings a piece of each slain animal."[8]

The relevance of such a view of hunting cultures to any particular group, including native Americans of the far north, is only generic, yet it remains stimulating. When we read descriptions of Inuit saving the bladders of seals, or keeping taboos so that they do not hunt bears during certain months, or insisting that menstruating women not handle deer, we catch overtones of a millennial effort to establish good relations with the game on which the tribe traditionally depended. The relation between the hunter and the hunted was more mystical than that between a customer and a supplier. The hunter was not merely a customer, and the hunted was not merely a supplier, however unwilling. Rather, the two shared not only a physical habitat but also a spiritual necessity: to live they had to kill. The human hunter stalking the bear knew that the bear itself was a hunter, stalking its own prey. The "economy" in which they were both trying to survive was one in which roles could reverse. The bear could hunt the human being, and even if this remained a remote, unusual possibility, it was not beyond the pale of what human beings could imagine.

The great fact of ancient life, sometimes brought to burning intensity among hunting peoples, was that life was always precarious. Usually life was precarious because the supply of food was uncertain. Especially at the times and in the places where only the hunter's luck and skill stood between the people and starvation, everything depended on the whim of an animal, the strength of a spear. But even when people could gather sufficient food from berries, roots, nuts, and other forms of plant life, human existence remained precarious because some formidable hunting animal—bear, pack of wolves— might move in for the kill.

In the landscape of the ancient hunters of the far north, to be disabled in any way further increased one's peril. If the tribe had to move, it might be impossible for them to take along the disabled. Thus old people (and we have to remember that old age has always been a relative thing; in most periods of human history, people seldom lived beyond 50) could take it upon themselves to go into solitude and freeze or starve. They did not want to burden the tribe, and they preferred to have a say in their own demise.

The close observation of animal life necessitated by the hunter's way of life seems to have suggested that reincarnation might be the way of the natural world. Observing that new members of the tribe came into being as old members departed, hunters could conjecture that what had made the old members alive had passed into the bodies of the new members, animating them. Similarly, hunters were quick to accredit the species they stalked with powerful spirits, full of intelligence and courage. It was not a big step to think that it would be good to possess such a spirit, and so to wonder about the possible transactions between hunters and their prey. Could one help a little child, newly born, grow up to be a good hunter of polar bears by wrapping it in bear skin? Would tossing the bladders of the seals one had killed back into the water help to replenish their store and so provide a good future for the new generation? Questions such as these appear to have woven their way through many customs of traditional arctic hunters. Their mythology became replete with stories about how to deal with the fish, the foxes, the caribou, the wolves that were their natural prey or enemies. The hunting peoples of the North American far north never ceased to be mesmerized by a mystique of animals.

Nature

Two passages from a fine book about the arctic by the American naturalist Barry Lopez may stimulate our appreciation of what it may have meant to live in the far north as a hunting people. The first deals with the emotions of the hunter: "A Central Eskimo shaman named Aua, queried by Knud Rasmussen [a noted early 20th century arctic explorer] about Eskimo beliefs, answered, 'We do not believe. We fear.' To extend these thoughts, it is wrong to think of hunting cultures like the Eskimo's as living in perfect harmony or balance with nature. Their regard for animals and their attentiveness to nuance in the landscape were not rigorous or complete enough to approach an idealized harmony. No one knew that much. No one would say they knew that much. They faced nature with fear, with *ilira* (nervous awe) and *kappia* (apprehension). And with enthusiasm. They accepted hunting as a way of life—its violence, too, though they did not seek that out. They were unsentimental, so much so that most outsiders thought them cruel, especially in their treatment of dogs. Nor were they innocent. There is murder and warfare and tribal vendetta in their history; and today, in the same villages I walked out of to hunt, are families shattered by alcohol, drugs, and ambition. While one cannot dismiss culpability in these things, any more than one can hold to romantic notions about hunting, it is good to recall what a *struggle* it is to live with dignity and understanding, with perspicacity or grace, in circumstances far better than these. And it is helpful to imagine how the forces of life must be construed by people who live in a world where swift and fatal violence, like *ivu*, the sudden leaping shore ice, is inherent in the land. The land, in a certain, very real way, compels the minds of the people."[9]

The land compels the minds of the people. That is very different from the situation of most citizens of the contemporary developed countries. The land is barely something upon which we walk, so covered is it by concrete and asphalt. The violence that seizes our minds is the murder and brutality, the rape and theft, of our inner cities. We are not schooled to walk as though each step might be our last, because the icy ground might tear away under us. We do not depend on the keenness of our senses for our food and survival. If Lopez could find among Eskimos of the last quarter of the twentieth century strong remnants of an immemorial hunting culture, how much more powerful must that culture have been when it was simply the way things were—the human way to exist, without competition from manifest other ways?

The second passage from Lopez's book draws on a Lakota woman: "A Lakota woman named Elaine Jahner once wrote that what lies at the heart of the religion of hunting peoples is the notion that a spiritual landscape exists within the physical landscape. To put it another way, occasionally one sees something fleeting in the land, a moment when line, color, and movement intensify and something sacred is revealed, leading one to believe that there is another realm of reality corresponding to the physical one but different. In the face of a rational, scientific approach to the land, which is more widely sanctioned, esoteric insights and speculations are frequently overshadowed, and what is lost is profound. The land is like poetry: it is inexplicably coherent, it is transcendent in its meaning, and it has the power to elevate a consideration of human life."[10]

The land has the power to elevate a consideration of human life. The land is not inert matter. No matter is inert, at least when beheld by a being of mind and heart, of feeling and spirit. Lopez is saying that people probe their landscapes for further significance. Usually they do not probe abstractly. Usually they follow lines of color and form, moments when the light throws everything into unusual relief and so reveals the constant extraordinariness of existence. The very barrenness of lands like the arctic and the desert turns out to stimulate poetry, mysticism, and metaphysics. In a spare landscape, the human spirit seems stimulated to work harder, and so to suspect, hope for, or create more meaning. Hunting peoples depend on the physical landscape for their survival. They do not believe that food grows in a supermarket. But neither do they believe that the physical landscape is only facts and figures, forms and movements. Neither the plants nor the animals are the predominant players in the landscape of hunting peoples. Rather, the total aliveness of the land, the whole portentous gestalt of the surroundings, is what draws the people's spirit.

Lopez, and others who write about native Americans of the far north, stress their alertness and patience. They are not people who have to solve problems by tables of time-and-motion experts. They are not people who have to talk over every aspect of a problem or project. The land sets them their basic task, which is to observe. The better they observe, the better they will understand—the patterns of the foxes or wolves or seals, the ways of the weather, and even the overall message of the environment. Nothing is static or repetitious in the Inuit world. Each day brings different weather, light, temperature, movement of animals. The typical hunter is afraid because he is so fully aware that he is not in control. He can never get in control. Always the whole in which he is immersed is greater than he: subtler, trickier, more full of surprises. To be a hunter is not simply to wait, to stalk, to pounce and kill. More fundamentally, it is to attend upon the land. Attending, one pours one's human intelligence into a wrap-around-sensitivity. Reflective thought is not the capital talent. The capital talent is so focusing sight and hearing, smell and intuition, that one senses each shift in the atmosphere, the environment. One becomes a fully human *animal*. One's cunning and strength go into wrestling with the landscape, to force it to yield enough secrets to let one survive.

It is this living sense of the land that "nature" ought to convey most of the time we deal with it in this book. As a modern word, "nature" carries mechanistic overtones. It is something that stands apart from us human beings, which we may examine as we examine an automobile, or a piece of art, or a computer print-out. But nature has never been that for hunters and gatherers. Nature continues not to be that for many farmers and naturalists. Nature is not a thing, an objectivity, something we can keep at arm's length. The more accurately we estimate the significance that nature has to have for human beings, the more we realize that nature is our milieu, our environment, our further skin. In nature we live, and move, and have our being. It is always the greater and we are always the lesser. It is always the longer and we are always the shorter. No wonder that nature has been the great symbol for divinity: that before which we simply have to bow, in pure realism, because it is our sovereign.

Certainly the controls over nature that have come with modern science have challenged this description of humanity's relationship to nature. Equally certainly, those controls have brought much psychic imbalance. As occasion warrants, we can contrast the sense of nature that native Americans traditionally have had with those regnant in the current west. At the moment it is more important for us to secure the mysteriousness, in a positive sense, that the land has carried for traditional hunting peoples. They have moved on and through a fullness of significance they knew they would never fathom.

In good times, this fullness of significance has made their lives splendid. To be a native American in good times has been to be a blessed contemplative, surrounded with more beauty, more sights to take one's breath and mind away, than one could handle in a lifetime. In bad times, this has made lives desolate. To whom could people cry out their pain, if the ultimate powers were impersonal and careless? What could their lives signify, if death and violence could be completely casual? Just as native American senses of the land can teach white Christians a great deal about the impersonality of God, so white Christian traditions have much to offer when it comes to humanizing the divine face and making personal love the inmost secret of the creator. The land itself suggests this dialogue.

The Group

During a study of Eskimo children carried out in the 1970s, the psychiatrist Robert Coles came to appreciate how completely the northern land, so challenging in the cold of winter, has shaped Eskimo cultural life. From their earliest years, children are socialized to pay attention to the land—the wind, the ice, the shifts in temperature and light. Much of the task of socializing children in this way falls to grandparents, who have the time to take children on walks, tell them stories, and initiate them in the attitudes that make for survival and delight.

So, for example, the grandfather in the following story has just given his granddaughter a lesson in the joy that seeing a whale wink at an Eskimo and escape from a tight spot can provoke. The lesson then continues and expands: "The granddaughter will not forget the heart of the message—his smiling face, his kindly regard for all life. Later, on the way home, she sees some salmon on a rack, drying under the warm summer sun. She is sad; she wishes, out loud, they had been able to wink at an Eskimo and escape. The old man sighs, agrees. But he tells her not to be downcast. The salmon can take care of themselves; they are quick, daring, persistent, inventive, and yes, beautiful—as beautiful, he tells the girl, as she is. Some die so that Eskimos will live; but most salmon, the old man insists, live full lives, love the arctic waters, and don't at all mind the occasional challenge a fisherman makes for them: how to slip by? And when they do slip by, there is plenty of laughter; those Eskimos, so smart and so patient and so agile—once again they have fumbled, have been no match for an adversary. Surely the salmon are delighted as they move along, safely out of range. By the time the old man has carried on so, the girl is smiling. She knows that salmon don't really 'think' or 'talk' or have emotions like pride; she knows that whales don't smile. She knows that her grandfather has really been trying to tell her about himself and herself rather than about the 'reactions' of nonhuman Arctic life—about the requirements of civility, about the need for modesty and humility."[11]

Certainly all peoples feel the weight of civility, modesty, and humility. Equally all peoples need to find ways to make their landscape, their entire way of life, attractive. But this Eskimo pair, grandfather and granddaughter, show us with special clarity the process of transmitting such values. In part, their discussion may reflect the stark requirements of survival in the traditional Eskimo setting. Coles points out that Eskimos often become moody in the summer, when the living is relatively easy. They indulge themselves in melancholy, allow themselves to show irritation—at the short nights, the mosquitos, whatever else rubs them the wrong way. None of this is possible in the winter. In the winter all energy and attention have to go into battling the elements. From their earliest years, children learn to discipline themselves, so that they remain quiet, pay attention, keep their patience, consolidate their wills to endure. Summer is a brief, passing aberration. Eskimo culture as a whole has been geared to surviving the winter. Whatever could make the land lovable has had considerable survival value.

The personality traits that Eskimo life has demanded include alertness, discipline, and selflessness. There is little margin for carelessness, slackness, becoming so absorbed in one's own problems or feelings that one loses sight of the common task. Thus Coles saw Eskimo adults dealing with children very forcefully: commanding their attention, bringing them into line and making sure that they did not overreach themselves. The Eskimo child raised traditionally grows up most impressed by the vastness of white—the snow, the ice, the bleached sky. Death is ready to hand, no stranger. And yet usually the result of so challenging an environment seems to be an energetic realism. The people sense that the cold and the ice place them on their mettle. They sense that without so formidable an adversary, they would slacken and lose vitality. That is why they are so ambivalent about the summer. The price of relaxation and indolence may be too high. If people become used to lolling around, they may not be able to meet the demands of winter.

Barry Lopez offers some complementary observations about Eskimos. Working with hunters out in the wild, he came away amazed at their practical skills. They could draw maps of virtually any area they had traveled, as though cartography were an inbred talent. They could fix any piece of machinery and rig ingenious solutions to practical problems. Other commentators, reflecting on the speed with which Eskimos can build an igloo at the approach of a storm or the marvelously efficient clothing that Eskimo women have produced from skins and furs, have spoken of an amazing adaptation to a natural milieu. Even the traditional use of dogs for transportation has a touch of genius about it. Clearly these native Americans have learned not only to survive but to thrive. Clearly something in the very hardship of their situation has become congenial—a way of testing themselves and extending their range of courage or ingenuity.

The happiest side of traditional Eskimo socialization comes through in Coles' story about the grandfather and granddaughter. The grandfather is not simply preaching a sermon on the virtues of civility. He is also expressing his delight in the land that he has come to know intimately. And he is telling the granddaughter how she must think about her fellow creatures if she is to live with delight. Finally he is implying that wisdom is finding ways to live with delight in the place that one has been assigned. Who has done the assigning, why the assignment was made in this way—those are questions beyond the scope of the scene that Coles reports. Sufficient for the given grandfatherly lesson was a helpful way of looking at Eskimo life.

"We are a people," the grandfather was saying, "who feel close to the whales and salmon. We are a people who rejoice in the prospering of these fellow creatures—and not simply because we depend on them for food. We share with them this amazing land. As much as we, they have to struggle to survive, muster wit and courage. And so we should toast them, like one survivor to another. We should not stint on our admiration. The more they prosper, the better things will be for all of us. The more beauty they bring into our lives, the more beautiful our own grandchildren will seem."

Much of the goal of any people's processes of socialization boils down to educating its children, not only for survival but also for delight. Much of the test of any given culture is the degree to which it keeps the generations in close contact, so that the young look forward to a challenging, fulfilling life. Traditional peoples such as the Eskimos knew instinctively that they could never give their children an easy life. They knew that the real wealth they ought to try to hand on was a set of skills and attitudes. The skills reduced to making good practical use of the materials at hand in the environment, to ensure physical survival; the attitudes reduced to loving the land, the basic situation and tradition of one's people, the rich meaning that one's culture provided. People needed challenges if they were to feel that they were using their full potential. People not challenged, not feeling that they were growing, could never be full of joy. When they considered the land, traditional Eskimos found endless challenges. Always there was more to learn or appreciate about the wind and the snow. The dozens of names for ice that one finds in Inuit speech suggest the specialized knowledge that Eskimos sought. And even when this knowledge was not scientific, in part because Eskimos were convinced that locales and animals differed as individuals, it was very fulfilling. To contemplate one's world, one's people, one's tradition, one's self— not for scientific knowledge but practically and aesthetically—could be to enter states of spirit that were their own reward. The more that we can glimpse such states of spirit, the more we shall realize how much traditional peoples have to offer us when it comes to fashioning a post-modern spirituality.

The Self

Even though a viable post-modern spirituality will have to be thoroughly ecological, it will also have to engage the self fully. The self is the "place" where tribal values become concrete. The self is the only full sensorium of significance and divinity. At our present stage of evolution, we are far from the "hyper-personal" reality that Pierre Teilhard de Chardin imagined might one day make human beings into something truly organic. So it behooves us to study the ways that traditional peoples have heightened awareness of the self.

Among peoples of the far north of America, the most impressive self has usually belonged to the shaman. Consider the testimony that one Eskimo shaman of the interior (a Caribou Eskimo named Igjugarjuk, who lived near northern Hudson Bay) gave to Knud Rasmussen, the Danish explorer previously mentioned: "We shamans in the interior have no special spirit language, and believe that the real angatkut [shamans] do not need it. On my travels I have sometimes been present at a séance among the saltwater-dwellers, for instance among the coast people at Utkuhigjalik (Back River, or Great Fish River). These angatkut never seemed trustworthy to me. It always appeared to me that these salt-water angatkut attached more weight to tricks that would astonish the audience, when they jumped about the floor and lisped all sorts of absurdities and lies in their so-called spirit language; to me all this seemed only amusing and as something that would impress the ignorant. A real shaman does not jump about the floor and do tricks, nor does he seek by the aid of darkness, putting out the lamps, to make the minds of his neighbours uneasy. For myself, I do not think I know much, but I do not think that wisdom or knowledge about things that are hidden can be sought in that manner. True wisdom is only to be found far away from people, out in great solitude, and it is not found in play but only through suffering. Solitude and suffering open the human mind, and therefore a shaman must seek his wisdom there."[12]

Igjugarjuk had been initiated by his father-in-law. The arduous process had emphasized solitude, fasting, and exposure to cold. He had had to keep taboos concerning food and sexual intercourse. In these ways he was trying to gain the pity and help of a female spirit who would give him the powers that make a shaman. Having been dragged close to death, he gained from this spirit (whom he called Pinga) the power known as *sila*. *Sila* is what courses through the universe and the weather. It is the source of common sense and intelligence. Through *sila* Igjugarjuk could heal his people of their illnesses and discern what they ought to do at critical junctures. *Sila* was what made him useful, and so *sila* was the great treasure in his life. Because he was convinced that he had only gained access to *sila* through suffering, he was very demanding when he initiated other shamans.

Once again part of the explanation for native American behavior comes from the situation in which the people in question find themselves. The central Eskimo lived a very harsh life. Their physical culture was the most primitive that Rasmussen had encountered. Whatever the historical reasons, the fact was that they battled fierce conditions with minimal physical equipment. Perhaps to compensate, they developed a spiritual equipment with few peers in the far north. By taking human endurance to the brink, their shamans seemed to free an unusual potential and tap the powers directing the universe. They seemed to break down human resistance to what we might call the sacredness of the cosmos.

If we remember that the sacred is the holy (in the sense of the most real rather than the most moral or respectable), we may see that a shaman like Igjugarjuk sought to transform his human constitution. He wanted to make his selfhood an instrument of *sila*. To do this, he had to sacrifice much that human beings, including his fellow Eskimos, spontaneously thought the self deserved or required. He had to strip selfhood to its essence, which he found to lie beyond pleasure and pain. It was not what he wanted in the superficial aspects of his personality that would bring him wisdom. It was what he wanted in his depths, where he longed to know the world as it was in itself, with precious little concern for human desires.

Admittedly, this interpretation of Eskimo shamanism draws on the full spectrum of the experiences that holy people report. What is distinctive about the report of Igjugarjuk is the extremity of suffering he sought. On the other hand, there is little indication that Igjugarjuk was a masochist or sadist, and his own disdain for the trickery, as he saw it, of coastal shamans suggests that he did not impose suffering on those he initiated as a gimmick or dramatic technique. He imposed it because he thought it utterly necessary. To gain the power that living wisely in the far northern inland required, one had to be stripped to the bone.

This stripping was both literal and symbolic. For Eskimo shamans, removing clothing in below-zero temperatures was a standard way to force oneself to draw upon extraordinary powers. Indeed, some instructors forced candidates to plunge into icy water. Unless candidates could muster the heat to keep themselves warm, they would perish quickly from exposure. The symbolism of the icy plunge, and the simpler stripping, was of dying to normal consciousness: common sense, prudence, self-protection. Still, this was a calculated dying, not a venture in suicide. From immemorial tradition, Eskimo shamans knew that holy people lived on the far side of the ordinary human fear of death. Shamans had conquered what kept most people from realizing their deeper potential. By suffering the worst fears of their flesh, they had gone beyond their flesh, to gain unusual spiritual powers.

Eskimo symbolism focused on stripping in another way. A typical exercise set before candidate shamans had them contemplate a skull or a skeleton. The idea seems to have been to try to penetrate to the very essence of human selfhood—to what alone outlasts death. A skull or skeleton represents both death and the conquest of death. It shows the human being as both succumbed and persistent. Taking that imagery to heart, by an intense contemplation perhaps like that of Zen students seeking enlightenment by boring into their *koans*, Eskimo shamans could find a profound message for the human spirit. If the human spirit can become skeletal—stripped, plunged into mortality (death to selfishness), existing beyond death in an elemental state—it may find the creative force that is stronger than death. Since this is the same force (*sila*) that runs the world (shapes the weather, changes the landscape, shows itself in physical birth), to find it could be to reach an archimedian point. The shaman cared for by Pinga (who must symbolize an acceptance by *sila*) stands where no ordinary person can. Beyond ordinary limitations, perhaps beyond most fear and desire, the successful shaman becomes an instrument of ultimate reality.

Ultimate Reality

The traditional Inuit of Canada and Greenland believed that a Sea Woman controlled the animals that they hunted (especially, the seals and walrus). One of the main functions of the shaman was to visit this woman, when the tribe had offended her and so caused her to withhold the sea animals. The typical way of offending her was to break one of the taboos that were supposed to govern tribal life. For example, if the people fished out of season, or did not keep menstruating women segregated, or performed an abortion, they broke their moral code. When things turned bad—disease came upon them, or the game stayed away—they tended to think that their breach of taboo was the cause.

The woman who controlled the sea animals, Sedna, lived at the bottom of the sea. In one dramatic version of her myth, she had been a lovely maiden who married a sea bird (a fulmar). For various reasons this marriage went badly. The woman became estranged not just from her bird-husband but also from her father, who had arranged the marriage. The father tried to drown her. As she clung to the edge of the boat, he cut off her fingers. From the pieces came the various sea animals. That is why she is able to command them. The woman got revenge on her father by commanding her dog to kill him. For this parricide she was banished to the depths of the sea. There her dog guards her domicile. The shaman wanting to reverse the ill fortune of the tribe has to travel to the depths of the sea, get by her dog, and appease her. One of the ways he can do this is to comb out her long hair, which tends to get snarled. Also, he must assure her that his tribe will repent of its breaches of taboo and rededicate itself to high morality.

Polar to the goddess of the sea was a male divinity, the spirit of the moon. One of the myths about this divinity says that he committed incest with his sister, who became the sun. Because of their sin, they had to be separated permanently. This moon divinity had a special relationship with women, whose fertility he controlled. Also, he was a great hunter, so those wanting to stalk game would try to bring him to their side. Interestingly, the Alaskan Inuit made little provision for the sun. The moon seems to have impressed them more deeply, perhaps because of its associations with female fertility (menstrual cycles). The sun was so weak, during most of the year, that it commanded little respect.

We have seen the significance of *sila* for the shaman Igjugarjuk. To his mind, *sila* was the force that made sense of the world, the most important power. For the general population of Inuit, *sila* was the spirit or divinity of the air. The most significant way that it manifested itself was through the weather. By extension, *sila* was also the universe—the full span of being—and the intellect. That is an interesting trinity: air, universe, intellect. It suggests a perception that what exists is oriented to the mind, and that the mind and being are as subtle and volatile as the air. In the Inuit landscape, weather was a paramount consideration. To get caught in a storm could mean certain death. As they studied the weather, Inuit must have thought that a strange intelligence ruled there. If they could attune themselves to that intelligence, they might become wise. Indeed, they might come into harmony, phase, with the wisdom of the universe itself. Probably that is why outstanding shamans were willing to sacrifice so much to gain states of consciousness in which they felt united to the ultimate powers.

The traditional Inuit also considered people's relations with animals extremely important. Each animal had its own soul, and also its own "owner," who could be a human being or a spirit. This notion of owners (*inua*) tended to populate the world with souls. Since souls were principles of life, Inuit had to be careful how they dealt with even the least significant animals. If they did not respect the souls surrounding them, they could find themselves out of harmony with the universe as a whole. One of the perils of Inuit life, according to some informants, was that people were always in danger of injuring souls—of plants and animals, necessary for food; even of rocks and special places, which for Inuit could be alive.

These beliefs led to distinctive practices. For example, it was common to offer a drink to a seal or a whale after one had captured it and dragged it ashore. The hope was that by treating such game hospitably, one would encourage their souls to return again to the seas and quicken a new generation of seals and whales. Another common practice was to divide the meat of the first kill of the season among all the members of the tribe. This divided responsibility for the kill. If the spirit of the deceased animal harbored a grudge, it would have to visit it upon a great number of people.

A third practice stemming from the Inuit beliefs in animals' souls concerned polar bears. If the people killed a polar bear, they tended to place the carcass facing the direction from which they thought polar bears usually came. Then they would honor the bear for five days, before eating the kill. The notion was that it would take the spirit of the bear five days to reach its home—the source of new polar bears. The people would bring presents to the bear, close its eyes and nostrils so that it would not be disturbed, and feed it blubber, so that it would feel good.

On the whole, Inuit myth and ritual strike the comparative religionist as relatively impoverished. Compared to the luxurious mythology of some other peoples, and their tendency to ceremonialize all of life, the Inuit religio-cultural complex seems quite spare. India, for example, is a much wealthier area than the American north when it comes to myths and rituals. So is Central America. Perhaps the severity of the environment contributed to a certain contraction of the Inuit mind. People had to focus on what was absolutely essential. Most of the religious interests therefore concentrated on interactions with the animals that the people hunted. Stories about the creation of the world or the origin of death or the appearance of the first human beings were minimal.

Still, we have seen that individuals like Igjugarjuk developed a profound appreciation of suffering. Through their shamanic experiences, they felt that they made contact with the power of the universe, and that was enough for them. The divinity that stands out in the far north of America is a demanding sacrality. It can be as capricious as the storm, as hard as the ice, as blinding as the snow. And yet, if one is able to contend with it courageously, taking all the suffering that it imposes and still striving to live well, one can gain considerable satisfaction. As though many Inuit knew instinctively that simply besting their environment year after year, simply raising children and obtaining sufficient food, were heroic achievements, their deity demanded relatively little of them.

The relationship between a symbol of ultimate reality like Sedna or *sila* and the many souls with which the Inuit had to deal is not clear. Apparently the Inuit did not think it necessary to fashion theological distinctions, such as the Christian one between God and the various angels. Most likely, the different souls partook of the sacredness, the special significance, of the ultimate reality, because those souls localized the mystery of life. The life of the animals with which they were so intimately bound was a presence of ultimate reality in the midst of Inuit existence. When they dealt with such animals correctly, the Inuit were pleasing the *sila* that ran their world.[13]

Spirituality

If we reflect on the implications of this sketch of traditional native American life in the far north, what comes to mind? Perhaps, first, the significance of hardship in the lives of many pre-modern peoples. Certainly our world today does not lack for hardship. Tens of millions go hungry, are ill with terrible diseases, feel abandoned and worthless. But modern technology has made such advances that the physical conditions of human life have changed considerably. The percentage of people who have to battle a fierce, threatening nature nine months of the year is relatively small.

Prior to modern technology, that percentage was much higher. In the days when human existence generally lay at the level of hunting and gathering, perhaps the majority of human beings felt imperiled most of the time. Still, the worst peril confronted the people to whom nature showed the fiercest face. Among them the peoples of the far north are bound to stand out. So, in the struggles of traditional native Americans of the far north to survive, we see a more intense version of the endurance, the call to suffering, that has been a permanent factor in the evolutionary existence of our species. As well, we see how human beings have turned their trials to account, making suffering a passage to dignity, wisdom, and even holiness.

Is this to say that native American spirituality in the far north canonized suffering, or that the record of human striving for meaning shows religion to have usually been morbid? By no means. A shaman such as Igjugarjuk may have thought that suffering was the only way to gain wisdom, but he never confused suffering with the way things ought to be. Ideally, all human beings would be wise, and their lives would run smoothly. Unfortunately, however, few people find their lives to run smoothly. Certainly most traditional Inuit found their lives to be demanding and painful more days than not.

The intuition that human existence should not be as painful as most people find it lies at the heart of myths of a fall. Again and again, people create stories to explain why things are not the way they ought to be. At the beginning, many of these stories say, life was easy. Nature provided an easy living, the plants and animals cooperated, the gods were nearby, obliging and ready to help. But something went wrong.

A messenger from the gods got lost, or garbled what he was supposed to communicate. Or human beings offended the gods by taking them for granted, or by violating their laws, or by choosing unwisely. The mentality in which most stories about a fall are couched is not disciplined enough to sift out the logical problems that the typical scenario creates. It does not see that for human beings to be able to make bad choices, or for messengers to be able to get lost, is already to imply flaws in existence. Manifestly, though, the mythmakers are struggling to coordinate two intuitions. The first is that suffering is unnatural. The second is that suffering is now a constant reality and so has to be dealt with.

Unless we can ratify the intuition that suffering is unnatural, we risk looking at the human condition as something demonic. Whatever the source of this flawed world, it would have to be flawed itself. To create beings bound to suffer is to seem to create beings for suffering, which appears sadistic. So, most peoples have sought to find reasons to affirm the essential goodness of the human condition—the body, the mind, the natural world. They have sought to bolster education, which might cure and fulfill the mind, and to bolster healing, which might cure the vulnerable body. They have sought to encourage peaceful, helpful interactions with the physical environment. Manifestly, native Americans of the far north did this.

Relatedly, most peoples have sought to overcome suffering. In this search they have imagined ways in which the entire human condition might be redeemed. At the end of time the gods would destroy all the sources of suffering and remake the world. In the afterlife, people would enjoy an untroubled, blissful existence. And even in the present phase of existence, people could find solace in the beauty of nature, or the animation of children, or the deep wisdom of the tribe's lore, or the ecstasies of spiritual travel, when one left the vulnerable body behind.

The question of suffering remains, though, and often it develops into the question of evil. Why is there something in human existence that we cannot understand, that works for harm or conflict, that seems to require death and suffering? Why are there malevolent human beings—people so unruly, or selfish, or unwise that they constantly cause trouble? "Evil" brings to mind all the things that should not be: natural disasters, cancers, blood feuds. One of the significant weaknesses of native American traditions of the far north is their inarticulateness about evil. The story of Sedna suggests that evil lies in the very roots of existence. The tensions between Sedna and her father seem to lodge at the joint between the generations. The tensions between Sedna and the birds (who rally to the side of the spurned fulmar-husband) suggest friction between human beings and nature from the beginning. Certainly human beings and animals are close. The marriage of Sedna to the fulmar dramatizes that. But they are also different, and frequently their different tendencies or needs bring them into conflict. Why is the world ordered so that this conflict seems inevitable? Why is there disorder within order?

The epitome of what ought not to be, as human instinct perceives things, is death. Death is the evil that overshadows the entire human, indeed created, condition. Yes, many peoples have intuited that endless life in a vulnerable body would become hellish. And many other peoples have realized that life and death are coordinates: the corpse fertilizes the earth for a new round of life. Yet the human spirit resists the notion that death is correct. Even when it recognizes the wisdom of accepting the body's return to the earth, it imagines ways for the "real" part of the human personality to continue on. The Inuit world filled with souls testifies to this tendency. What is most significant about any entity is the force that animates it, and this force continues after the whale or seal appears inert.

The lesson for any present-day spirituality may well be that certain basic problems never go away. If native Americans of the far north show more ecological awareness than most modern groups have, and if their lives have been more powerfully shaped by physical hardship, they are very much our kin in having to contend with evil and death. Imperfection, life not being what we think it should be, is built into the human condition, as all peoples have experienced it. The Inuit shaman's willingness to confront this fact is realistic and astringent. The question for our own spirituality is whether we are willing to be similarly realistic.

Chapter 4

TRADITIONS OF
THE PLAINS

Background

The geographical area that we have in mind in this chapter is vast indeed: about 1.25 million square miles—a third of the land of the United States. Its boundaries are the Mississippi River to the east, the Rocky Mountains to the west, the central Canadian provinces (Alberta, Saskatchewan, and Manitoba) to the north, and the Gulf of Mexico to the South. Over thirty different native American groups lived in this area at the time of contact with whites. In the time since such contact seven different linguistic families have divided those groups.

In alphabetical order, these linguistic families are the Algonquian, the Athapascan, the Caddoan, the Kiowa-Tanoan, the Siouan, the Tonkawan, and the Uto-Aztecan. Tribes speaking Algonquian included northern Arapaho (Wyoming) and southern Arapaho (Oklahoma); Atsina (Gros Ventre); Blackfeet (several tribes); northern Cheyenne (Montana) and southern Cheyenne (Oklahoma); Plains Cree; and Plains Ojibwa (Chippewa). Tribes speaking Athapascan included the Apache (Kipan and Kiowa) of Oklahoma and the Sarsi of Alberta (though they were part of the Blackfeet Confederacy, where the main language was Algonquian).

Tribes speaking Caddoan included the Arikara (Ree), the Caddo, the Kichai, the Pawnee, and the Wichita. These tribes used to be scattered from North Dakota to Texas. Now the Arikara live in North Dakota and all the others live in Oklahoma. The only tribe speaking Kiowa-Tanoan is the Kiowa, who now live in Oklahoma. The largest linguistic family in the Plains consisted of tribes speaking Siouan.

These included the Assiniboin, the Crow, the Kansa, the Omaha, the Osage, the Ponca, the Quapaw, the Hidatsa, the Iowa, the Oto, the Missouri, the Mandan, the Dakota (Sante), the Lakota (Teton), and the Nakota (Yankton). Many of these tribes now live in Oklahoma. Others live to the north, in Montana, Canada, or the Dakotas. The Dakota, Lakota, and Nakota are closely related and sometimes are called the Sioux. The Mandan, Arikara, and Hidatsa are affiliated and sometimes share reservations.

The Tonkawan speaking groups belong to the Tonkawa of Oklahoma, while the Uto-Aztecan speakers belong to the Comanche of Oklahoma. One sees, then, that Oklahoma has the richest representation of plains native Americans. In historical times many were forcibly moved to Oklahoma, because of white desire for traditional tribal lands.

The central plains by nature constitute a huge, uninterrupted stretch of grasslands. At the time of encounter with whites, the native Americans who lived there mixed hunting and farming. The main animals they hunted were buffalo and deer, while the main crops they farmed were maize, beans, squash, and various fruits. Native American culture changed considerably in the seventeenth century, with the introduction of the horse. Archeologists have found evidence of human habitation for perhaps twelve thousand years, but, with the advent of the horse, tribes assumed a nomadic life based on hunting the buffalo. Indications are that prior to this cultural change, a more sedentary life, based on agriculture, had been the rule. Indeed, the Mandan, Hidatsa, and Arikara in the north, and the Pawnee in the south, preserved this older way of life. Their custom was to build earthen houses and work fields nearby. The tribes that changed to following the buffalo lived in portable teepees, using horses and dogs to carry their few goods. They also built round "bullboats" to travel by water.

One estimate is that the current population of native Americans in the plains area is about what the population was at the time of contact with whites: nearly a quarter of a million. Contact led to a significant decline in population, due to both wars and new diseases. In recent generations, however, population has increased. The pressures of white culture drove the natives together, producing some cultural homogenization. Even prior to white presence, however, tribes interacted significantly, especially for trade. When they met people of a different linguistic group, they could employ a sign-language invented for barter. Such tribes appear to have enjoyed a great variety of cultural and religious differences. (Regularly, signifi-

With the advent of the horse, tribes assumed a nomadic life based on hunting the buffalo.

The main animals hunted by the Central Plains Indians were buffalo and deer.

cant differences in language tend to spearhead significant differences in basic customs and ideas.)

If one compares the linguistic groups mentioned for the plains with those mentioned for the native Americans of the eastern woodlands, several overlaps are obvious. Many woodlands tribes also spoke Algonquian or Siouan languages. This suggests that plains natives probably shared some basic religious beliefs with woodlands natives, and investigation shows that the suggestion has merit. In the recent period, three major complexes of religious beliefs have been found across the entire plains area: the sun dance, the ghost dance, and the Native American Church. We discuss all three later. Many tribes have also employed the vision quest and the sweatlodge ceremony, adding to the religious homogeneity of the plains peoples. Because all five of these phenomena have received much attention from scholars, the religious features of the plains natives sometimes have been considered nearly synonymous with "native American religion." (We should note that individual tribes may consider these features unique to themselves, either because of small variations in their local traditions, or because of convictions that the rituals in question arose with them.)[14]

When one reflects on the general background that geography, linguistic diversity, and history provide for native American religion in the central plains, perhaps what emerges first is the psychological effect of living on an apparently unending prairie, with few obstacles to the movement of either people or the weather. Cold winds could sweep down from the north, or warm winds could move up from the south, changing weather conditions significantly. The clash of cold and warmth could create dramatic thunderstorms, even destructive tornadoes. The sky lay vast overhead, partnered to the expansive land. Overall, this was an area open to easy traveling. Even before the introduction of the horse, tribes could move after game without great difficulty. The buffalo were so numerous, and so useful, that hunting them was attractive, even when farming was relatively easy and inclined tribes to a sedentary life. Relatively easy movement also meant that tribes could resolve hostilities either by separating from one another or by rushing into battle. After the advent of the horse, both separation and warfare became equestrian.

Most plains mythology associated both the origin of maize and the coming of the buffalo with an archetypal female figure. Apparently these two great resources of plains life connoted fertility so directly that they suggested female beginnings. Male symbolism attached to hunting and horsemanship, but the buffalo continued to be a gift of an original lady, as did corn. Certainly, women worked with

Male symbolism was attached to hunting and horsemanship, but the buffalo was linked to primeval femininity.

the buffalo that men brought home, much as Inuit women worked with the seals and walruses. Buffalo skins became a staple source of clothing and housing, while buffalo bones were turned into useful implements. Women prepared the buffalo meat, too. But probably it was the richness, the bounty of good things, that the buffalo symbolized, rather than these practical associations, that linked them to primeval femininity (Mother Nature, in localized garb). The sky was usually a grandfather figure, source of sun and rain. The earth, and all that came from it, carried a grandmotherly motif.

The openness of plains life also encouraged a special awareness of the different directions of the compass. The weather that one could expect from each direction was different, as was the influence on light. So each direction had to be treated differently, with a reverence and affection all its own. The people lived fully aware that their fate owed much to the weather. Their rituals therefore tended to call upon each kind of wind to provide its good gifts and hold back its bad (for example, freezing cold from the north, withering heat from the south).

Nature

An old Omaha Indian, reflecting on how things had been in his youth, expresses the sense of nature that formed traditional native Americans of the plains: "When I was a youth, the country was very beautiful. Along the rivers were belts of timberland, where grew cottonwood, maple, elm, ash, hickory, and walnut trees, and many other shrubs. And under these grew many good herbs and beautiful flowering plants. In both the woodland and the prairies I could see the trails of many kinds of animals and could hear the cheerful songs of many kinds of birds. When I walked abroad I could see many forms of life, beautiful living creatures which *Wakananda* [the divine] had placed here; and these were, after their manner, walking, flying, leaping, running, playing all about. But now the face of all the land is changed and sad. The living creatures are gone. I see the land desolate and I suffer an unspeakable sadness. Sometimes I wake in the night and I feel as though I should suffocate from the pressure of this awful feeling of loneliness."[15]

Originally the land was hospitable, full of living things that gave delight. Yes, they also gave food and shelter, but in this recollection delight is to the fore. We miss much about traditional native American spirituality if we overlook the role of natural beauty. Native Americans grew up attuned to the colors of the plants, the graces of the animals. Their senses were formed by a natural landscape, one largely unaltered by human interventions. Human beings did not dominate nature or transform it. They reacted to it more than they altered it to fit forms in their minds. The loneliness that the old man feels is instructive. He has lost some of his best friends. The animals in whom he used to delight have disappeared, or been greatly diminished, and with their going his horizon has emptied. His mourning is as though for part of himself. A love, an enjoyment of beauty, that once pulsed in him like a heartbeat now has no object upon which to fasten. It throbs like the beat in a missing limb, like the phantom sensations that continue after an amputation. Schooled in beauty, accustomed to feeding upon it as food for his soul, the old man feels starved, abandoned, stripped and left bereft.

Nor is this all. The living forms that he now remembers with nostalgia were more than beautiful. Their beauty was a mark of their holiness, their divinity. That they came from *Wakananda,* the ultimate creative power that was both beautiful and divine, meant that they mediated ultimate reality. In rejoicing in them, treating them well, offering thanks for the manifold gift that they comprised, the old man had prayed in what Christians might call a eucharistic mode. His first thought had been that the world is a wonderful benefaction, a limitless blessing. Who was he that so much beauty and usefulness had been poured out in front of him, for his admiration and profit? Certainly he might not always have sustained this mood. Admittedly some of his compatriots abused the nature that he appreciated and loved. But, on the whole, his culture encouraged him to treat nature well and be grateful. Nature was much more than a warehouse of utensils created to meet his needs. More primordially it was the offspring of a holy, generous, beautiful ultimate reality—a sacrality before whom human beings always ought to bow.

The aesthetic component of native American spirituality can be a salutary shock. It can remind pragmatic people that, long before things are useful, they are wonderful in their simple being. The first thing to be said about trees and grasses, deer and chipmunks, is that they reflect their creator. In their variety, suppleness, abundance, grace, power, and so much more, they tell us about the source of being and life, the mysterious fullness from which all species must come. Traditional native Americans struggled to grow more and more sensitive to the presence of this mysterious fullness of being. Thoroughly, their lives were geared for contemplation. They listened more than they spoke. The great book in which they read the significance of their lives was nothing set down by human hands. It was the ever changing horizon of nature.

Compared to the full-bodied, three-dimensional, vividly sensuous revelations of the natural world, what white people offered on parchment seemed a terrible diminishment. Why trade a vast, wrap-around world of wonders for dry, abstract notations on a page? What was the gain in shifting one's spirit away from the physical presence of the Great Spirit into a purely mental zone where reality became ideas and flickerings of imagination? Eventually many native Americans came to appreciate the cultural power of literacy and abstraction. In the beginning, through the middle, and even in today's end, however, a nostalgia for the days when nature was relatively simple, immediate, trustworthy and sufficient has filled many native American hearts.

Of all the plains tribes, the Pawnee have gained the reputation of having developed the most creative sense of the world. In the cosmological mythology of this people, the supreme being, Tirawa, lived in the heavens, married to the vault of heaven. Among the lesser deities that Tirawa, who was completely spiritual, tended to use to convey his messages to embodied human beings was Teuperika, the Evening Star. A young maiden, she kept the garden in the west from which came all the food that creatures needed. Assisting her were wind, cloud, lightning, and thunder. From her marriage to the Morning Star (Oprikata) came human beings. The Morning Star was a great warrior who cleared the sky each day. Occasionally the Pawnee would sacrifice a young girl to the Morning Star (a practice suggesting the influence of religions of central Mexico).

If we pause to reflect on just these few symbols (Pawnee cosmology has had many others), we find several motifs of note. The first is an orientation to the heavens, as though the human spirit were bound to think that its best prospects lodged on high. The world over, something in the inclination of the human mind to "rise up" when developing its best thoughts leads it to associate divinity, its source and goal, with what is above. Even when people are adamant about sacralizing the earth, source of material fertility, they tend to grant the heavens greater dignity. Thus, the Pawnee gods who dwell in heaven are spiritual beings. Human beings are so different from them that the gods have to enlist messengers when they want to communicate with earth. And yet all this mythology subsists within the orbit of the natural world. Nature is not purely material. Native Americans have tended to find spirituality within creation, not apart from it. They have tended, naturally and spontaneously, to be sacramentalists—people inclined to find grace mediated by physical things. Certainly, they have sensed that only purely spiritual beings could stand apart from death and ignorance. Yet their sense of "spiritual" has been quite physical. The spiritual has been a force, an energy, a vivid reality as obvious as a body that had to eat and sleep. The spiritual has not been effete or evanescent. The more deeply one entered into the spiritual realm, the more fully human one became.

We should note the prominence of heavenly phenomena related to the weather, and also to the origin of human beings from Evening Star and Morning Star. Wind, cloud, lightning, and thunder are powerful forces on the plains. They bring the weather, and the weather seems to color all human existence. Indeed, human beings are so deeply influenced by the weather that their moods and personalities cloud over or clear, grow stormy or calm. The lovely Evening Star can stand for feminine grace and delicacy. The Morning Star, thought to clear the heavens for the work of the day, can stand for masculine strength and decisiveness. To be a child of delicate evening and vigorous morning was to be something wonderfully compound. Humanity depends on the gentle and the strong. It depends on endings and beginnings. And always it hopes that its endings and beginnings will be sources of light. For traditional native Americans, the variety and beauty of nature were the main sources of hope that human existence would prove well worth enduring.

The Group

The old Omaha man whom we quoted derived most of his sense of nature from his upbringing. However distinctive the depth or sensitivity of his personal longing for the creatures now gone away, what he had been taught as a youth, how he had been socialized, had much to do with his love of nature. As most scholars of religion note, group rituals have been among the most powerful socializing forces. Two rituals important on the plains can suggest how most tribes taught their members to think and feel about their place in the world.

A ceremony called the Hako is among the best documented rituals of plains Indians. The goal of the Hako was to secure tribal prosperity: increase in numbers, good health, strength, longevity, happiness, peace. An old man venerated for his wisdom would lead the ceremony. He was the keeper of the traditions—the songs and dances, prayers and gestures, handed down from the past. Something magical attached to these traditions. It was important to perform them exactly, because otherwise they would lose their efficacy. This reminds us that

COKESBURY LANCASTER
04/12/94 09:22   E   2   2423

1 @ 10.95 0819251953 20%$ 8.76
SPIRITUAL JOURNEY
1 @ 14.95 0809134047 20%$ 11.96
NATIVE AMERICAN RELIGION
SUBTOTAL $ 20.72
TAX @ 6.00% $ 1.24
TOTAL: 89 COKESBURY BOOKSTORE   21.96
TENDERED DISCOV R$21.96 DISCOV R$$ $21.96

COME TO OUR CUSTOMER APPRECIATION SALE!!
25% OFF IN STOCK MERCHANDISE APRIL 30TH!

COKESBURY LANCASTER
04/12/94 08:25   E   2   2423

COME TO OUR CUSTOMER APPRECIATION SALE!!
25% OFF IN STOCK MERCHANDISE APRIL 30TH!

63105000186454150001
63105000186454150001   BATCH 227

                COKESBURY BOOKSTORE
                  555 W. JAMES ST.
                LANCASTER, PA 17603
TRANSMIT VISA DAILY
DATE 04/12/94   0431

ACCT # 6011002167502871   EXP 1094
DV T05 REF 0473   A70PROVAL 01215
2

PURCHASE
AMOUNT $21.96

    I AGREE TO PAY ABOVE TOTAL AMOUNT
    ACCORDING TO CARD ISSUER AGREEMENT
    (MERCHANT AGREEMENT IF CREDIT VOUCHER)

SIGN X _Veena H Beerman_
        RETAIN THIS COPY FOR YOUR RECORDS
    TOP COPY-MERCHANT BOTTOM COPY-CUSTOMER

many traditional peoples have considered rituals to be ways of molding the world. In oral cultures, the most solemn words take on a life of their own. For instance, Hindu theory of the ancient sacrifices makes clear what many traditional peoples have thought: words can never be called back. Once uttered, they embark on fated journeys, becoming part of the karmic realm that shapes the future.

How deeply native Americans shared this attitude is questionable, but the solemnity of many of their rituals suggests at least analogous instincts. The breath that human beings expel in words is their own vitality. Words carry the human spirit, physical and mental. It is crucial that the human spirit interact with all the other realities of the natural world honestly, rightly. One of the best ways to ensure this is to remember the words hallowed by long usage and utter them mindfully, carefully, so that they become holy arrows into the mysteries of nature and the future. The mysteries of nature and the future are where the next chapters in the tribe's story lodge. The more beautifully, appropriately, a people approaches these mysteries, the more likely it is to receive their blessing.

The Hako would be celebrated in the spring or the fall, when the birds were nesting or flocking. Perhaps the tie to the birds expressed an intuition that human thoughts rise best when they fly like birds, full of life and grace. The participants in the ceremony, divided into "fathers" and "sons," represented the past and future of the tribe, now joined in the present. After a lengthy series of rituals, usually lasting three days, during which the people rehearsed their traditional tribal lore, the fathers would bless the sons with sacred feathered wands (more avian symbolism). The wands came to represent the entire significance of the Hako, so to offer them to enemies became a way of making peace. Students of Pawnee lore suggest that this is how the wands and the Hako passed into Lakota culture.

A second ritual that tells us volumes about the self-understanding of plains tribes is the sun dance. Ordinarily groups celebrated this in the early summer, in conjunction with the buffalo hunt. The essence of the ceremony was for men to dance for several days gazing at the sun (or the heavens). The dance became an expression of willingness to sacrifice oneself for the well-being of the tribe. The sacrifice was to the heavenly powers, who held the fate of the tribe. In addition to offering their endurance (the constant dancing), participants might cut their breasts so as to pass leather thongs through their flesh. They would then tie the thongs to poles set in a circle (representing the hoop of the tribe) and consecrate the blood and pain that resulted to the protection of the tribe.

In offering their pain, their flesh, to the Great Spirit, the sun dancers expressed a belief that everything else in the world belonged to the Great Spirit. It made little sense to sacrifice other creatures (though one might set aside a pinch of tobacco or a part of an animal slain in the hunt, as a way of remembering whence all good things derived). Human beings' only real possession was their own bodies, their selves. So this is what the dancers offered. That they offered their bodies in the context of symbols of the tribe's collective identity must have increased their motivation. The emotions that we sometimes lump (or dismiss) under the heading "patriotism" can be very powerful, especially when the group has intense bonds. Nothing stood higher in native American conception than the well-being of one's people. All personal gifts were valuable in the measure that they protected the tribe and helped it prosper. Certainly native Americans differed as individuals and possessed individual virtues and vices. Certainly tribal existence did not eradicate selfishness. But traditional native Americans depended on one another so constantly and obviously that "individualism," as we may now lament it, was not a serious temptation. The sun dance helped to articulate the conviction, pervasive on the plains, that suffering for one's people was the most religious of acts.

The United States government banned the sun dance in the 1880s, thinking it barbaric. Northern tribes continued to practice it secretly, but it fell out of use in the southern plains. However, in the mid-20th century it emerged from hiding, and in the last decades some northern tribes have made it part of their regular religious observances.

Perhaps this is a good occasion to reflect on two questions. The first is whether one people ought to interfere in the traditional ways of another. The second is why pain, self-mortification, shows up regularly in the ceremonies of pre-modern peoples the world over. In the days when whites thought they had a superior culture, and that the religious roots of their superior culture (Christianity) ought to be accepted by all other peoples, whites thought little of changing native ways. In the name of overcoming benighted paganism, they might ban practices like the sun dance and pressure native peoples to accept Christ.

Nowadays, much missionary theology embraces virtually the opposite position: leave native peoples alone, look for the expressions of grace in their traditional ways, and offer them Christian ways completely freely, emphasizing how Christian faith is consonant with their best native traditions and may fulfill them. This newer missionary theology seems quite wise, as long as it does not mean that one becomes completely uncritical about native ways. Ideally, natives and outsiders would discuss their beliefs as equals, full of mutual respect. Ideally, only when natives were truly persuaded that the religion of outsiders offered them a depth and beauty, a salvation and divinization, that they wanted to embrace because of their own best traditional instincts would one speak of conversion. The sun dance might serve as a concrete focus for such a discussion.

Second, it seems clear that pain shows up in many traditional rituals because human beings realize that doing what is difficult can both strengthen them (so that they fulfill their ordinary responsibilities generously) and intensify their awareness of ultimate reality. Human existence is difficult. To live well requires asceticism: doing what we ought to do, not what our selfishness or laziness prompts. When we sacrifice to live well, as we ought, we realize the demands of ultimate reality. To love God for himself, we can want to put aside God's gifts, material or spiritual. This is a delicate business, especially for people not yet mature. The key would seem to be avoiding sadism, masochism, and the other ways that pain can become twisted into something supposedly good in its own right.

At its worst, the controlled self-mutilation of the sun dancers is relatively harmless. At its best, it seems a moving petition of God. But real mutilation, to say nothing of human sacrifice, shows the dangers of focusing rituals for the preservation of the tribe on suffering and pain. In the extreme case, people can construct an angry, sadistic God, and so seriously warp their souls. The true God, a cloud of witnesses from various traditions insists, is far better than what we can imagine. The sacrifice that the true God most wants is of our fear, doubt, self-concern, so that we can let God love us as the divine goodness makes God desire. This is the position that knowledgeable religious outsiders would bring to a dialogue with native Americans about the significance of the sun dance and the nature of God.

The Self

Among the rituals that plains tribes traditionally found precious, we should note the use of the sacred pipe and the sweatlodge. Both were communal possessions, but in this section we focus on their impact on individuals. The pipe, usually filled with tobacco, mediated intercourse with the Great Spirit. The smoke that drifted heavenward could carry the thoughts and the intentions of the smokers. Lakota lore has it that the pipe was a gift of a lovely young maiden. The maiden was holy, as the following story shows, and in giving the pipe she offered the people a way to epitomize their whole existence: "Early one morning, very many winters ago, two Lakota were out hunting with their bows and arrows, and as they were standing on a hill looking for game, they saw in the distance something coming towards them in a very strange and wonderful manner. When this mysterious thing came nearer to them, they saw that it was a very beautiful woman, dressed in white buckskin, and bearing a bundle on her back. Now this woman was so good to look at that one of the Lakota had bad intentions and told his friend of his desire, but this good man said that he must not have such thoughts, for surely this is a *wakan* [holy] woman. The mysterious person was now very close to the men, and putting down her bundle, she asked the one with bad intentions to come over to her. As the young man approached the mysterious woman, they were both covered by a great cloud, and soon when it lifted the sacred woman was standing there, and at her feet was the man with the bad thoughts who was now nothing but bones, and terrible snakes were eating him . . . she [the mysterious woman] took from the bundle a pipe, and also a small round stone which she placed upon the ground. Holding the pipe up with its stem to the heavens, she said: 'With this sacred pipe you will walk upon the earth; for the earth is your Grandmother and Mother, and She is sacred. Every step that is taken upon Her should be a prayer. The bowl of this pipe is of red stone; it is the earth. Carved in the stone and facing the center is the buffalo calf who represents all the four-leggeds who live upon your Mother. The stem of the pipe is of wood, and this represents all that grows on the Earth. And these twelve feathers which hang here where the stem fits into the bowl are from *Wanbli Galeshka,* the Spotted Eagle, and they represent the eagle and all the wingeds of the air. All these people and all the things of the universe are joined to you who smoke the pipe—all send their voices to *Wakan-Tanka,* the Great Spirit. When you pray with this pipe, you pray for and with every-thing."[16]

The pipe, like the buffalo, the corn, and the other staples of plains life, is a gift from the holy powers running the world. The lovely maiden who brings the pipe is a figure of divine wisdom, holy and pure. She comes in benevolence, and only those who will not receive her purely have anything to fear. The pipe, like most of the other gifts that feature in Lakota rituals, becomes an epitome of native American belief. What it is made of, what is carved on it, what it burns, where its smoke rises, what adorns its stem, and all the rest draw into the rituals in which it is employed the whole of creation.

In fact, Lakota Indians used the sacred pipe on many different occasions. In fact, it served social uses, reconciling enemies, uniting tribal members, and expressing good fellowship, as well as naturalistic uses. The pipe reminds us of the mythopoeic mentality of traditional peoples. Their tendency was to invest the items they used again and again in their rituals with cosmic significance. Thus the clay of the pipe could stand for the earth, and the earth called to mind all the bounties of creation. The buffalo calf and the spotted eagle stood for all the animals and birds who shared the world with human beings. To walk on the earth, one's Mother, was ideally a prayer. Every deed and thought ought to ascend to the heavens, where the Great Spirit dwelt. The smoke of the pipe represented this ideal ascension. In smoking it solemnly, plains Indians were expressing their desire to have everything in their lives ascend to God.

When people have a will to see the world as sacramental—full of gifts of God that ought to stimulate a complete return of self—they can turn a smoking pipe, or water, or bread, or wine into epitomes of their human condition. For they intuit, however dimly, that everything is grace, and so that anything can summarize the bounty of God, the complete dependence of human beings, and the call to worship that sounds whenever they acknowledge the realities of their condition gratefully.

The ritual use of the sweatlodge was another way that plains Indians acknowledged the realities of their condition gratefully. The physical foundation of the ceremony was the experience of building an enclosed space, heating stones to high temperature, pouring water over the stones to generate steam, and feeling one's body cleansed by perspiration. This physical cleansing became a metaphor for spiritual cleansing and renewal. As the body felt emptied of all impurities, so the mind and heart might be emptied of everything defiling, might be turned again to the holiness of the Great Spirit.

Though this was the simple gist of the ceremonies that transpired in the sweatlodge, native Americans tended to embellish it considerably. The materials from which they constructed the lodge, the stones from Mother Earth, the steam arising to Father Sky, the pipe that might be smoked, the bonding with brothers (and sometimes sisters) in the lodge, and much more entered into the ceremonial attitude, so that, once again, all of life and creation was caught up into the participants' prayer. Certainly, the main motif remained purification. Certainly, in the "sacramental" system of the seven Oglala Sioux rites, *inipi*, the purification in the sweatlodge, was akin to other religions' penitential rites. But the complete immersion in such symbols that one finds in Black Elk, a narrator of the traditional Oglala rites, made any of them a summary of the entire Lakota way of life. So the purifications of the sweatlodge could not be separated from the gift of the sacred pipe, or the gift of the buffalo, or the rite for consecrating a young woman just come of age, or even the sacred ball game through which the Ogala represented human beings' place in the universe. Always and everywhere, Oglala thought was holistic and cosmic. In every case, people prayed, or danced, or sacrificed with a profound sense of association with the four-legged and winged "persons," as well as with others of their own kind.[17]

This is to say that the self of the typical native Americans of the plains was ritualistic, cosmic, and social through and through. As well, it was metaphorical: primed to see everything in its ambience as a symbol of the divine mystery. The remarkable note running through Black Elk's account of the Oglala rites is the gratitude that breaks out again and again. The world is full of wonders. Human beings are privileged to live in such a world, to have minds and hearts able to appreciate it. The bounties of the Great Spirit are beyond recounting. The longer one lives, the more one finds reasons for praise. Human beings are not alone in the world. On all sides, they have humble yet wonderful helpers. From the grasses that stoke the fire, to the four-leggeds who provide food and the winged persons who are reminders of heaven, fellow creatures do human beings many good deeds. Thus the center of human existence, as a holy interpreter such as Black Elk sees it, is worshiping the creator. While human beings have to do many practical things to survive, the essence of their being is not pragmatic. Rather, the essence is contemplative: appreciating the splendors of creation and rendering proper return to the Great Spirit responsible for them. In native American perspective, the core of the self is a capacity for worship.

Ultimate Reality

We have seen that the Lakota oriented their lives toward a holiness that they called *wakan*. Other plains tribes held similar notions: the Algonquian *manitu*, the Comanche *puha*, the Ponca *xube*. Although Christian missionaries sometimes equated native concepts of a creator who possessed great *wakan* or *manitou* with a monotheistic deity, further study makes it clear that most plains tribes distributed holiness among various possessors. Holiness was not the sole possession of the creator. He was at most first among a field of deities (largely personifications of natural phenomena—wind, sun, stars, earth). Holiness could come to expression anywhere. It was a kind of power, but other kinds of power were not holy—power to destroy and power of witches, for example.

Plains Indians believed that their prayers and rituals could influence the flow of holiness and power. The deities whom they petitioned could change the human condition, improve human fortunes. What white observers often collected in the term "medicine" was the totality of natives' efforts to bring holy power to their side. Correlatively, natives realized that much depended on the dispositions with which human beings regarded the world. Thus many of their rituals sought the transfer of human beings from a profane to a sacred state of consciousness. Medicine bundles, and ceremonies concerned with strengthening the tribe, worked both sides of the divine-human relationship. They petitioned the holy powers, but they also called human beings to repentance and renewal.

The question of the relationship between the holiness that plains natives found in the depths of existence and the different deities on whom they focused—Grandfather Sky, Grandmother Earth—invites considerable interpretation. On the whole, the safest view is probably one that underscores the pervasiveness of the metaphorical quality of the native mind. For a metaphorical mind (all minds are metaphorical, but pre-modern minds tend to have little distance from their metaphors—to be pre-critical), it is hard to separate the ultimate from the proximate forms in which it manifests itself. It is uncongenial to speculate about holiness or divinity in itself. Much more interesting is how *Wakanda* appears in the Spotted Eagle, or through the Maiden who brings the sacred pipe. These are comings of holy power that rivet the whole personality: senses and imagination, intellect and will.

Now, it is not simply that vivid representations of holiness seem easier to understand and take a stronger hold on human attention. It is also that this vividness makes them seem more real than more abstract forms of divine power or existence. Holiness seems more present, efficacious, challenging, when it dazzles the eyes or turns the heart ablaze. Eventually contemplation suggests the limitations of all forms, but contemplatives who come to prefer the *via negativa* (the path that avoids images) are relatively few. So the native American tendency to proliferate scenes of holy power, like the Hindu tendency to multiply the limbs of the gods (to suggest their super-human powers), is a shrewd estimate of what the majority of human beings need, if they are to think, and even more feel, that their lives are instinct with holiness. In fact, the proliferation of presences of divine power turns out to have the same goal as traveling by the *via negativa:* finding divine ultimacy in all things. Yet the initial psychology is different. Native American thought on the plains seems much more affirmative than negative. Intimations that all metaphors fail, and so that divinity can seem nearer when one remains in a darkness unlit by metaphor, are relatively few.

What we might call an "intermediate" functionary in plains thought, the trickster or culture hero, shows the vagueness of the boundaries that native Americans have set around holiness and divine power. Many myths about the origins of distinctive features of tribal life feature the trickster, often making him a bungler. He becomes responsible for the limitations in the human condition, as well as a negative example. Children especially enjoyed the tales about this mischievous, roguish creature, but they also got the message that they were to avoid the mistakes the trickster had made. He was a cautionary figure. To do as he had done, or (more profoundly) to think and feel as he had felt, was to risk ruin. Trickster had a great appetite—for food, sex, play. The message therefore was to curb one's appetites, live under discipline. On the other hand, myths about trickster tended to breed into plains culture a tolerance for human folly. To have an exemplar who messed things up regularly was to say that perfectionism is not realistic. It could also be to say that laughter at human foibles is healthy, even necessary for mental balance.

Trickster suggested the ambiguities of creation and so of ultimate reality. So did the various taboos that plains Indians enforced. Sexual intercourse, menstruation, and eating could all be fenced about with limitations. Much depended on seasons and circumstances, but the mere fact that natives felt the need to give these activities a potentially dark side is instructive. Clearly sex and food are central to human existence. Clearly both are also the subject of strong appetites. Whether it was the centrality of procreation and love that caused taboos, or the strength of sexual appetites, is hard to say. The same concerning food: was it sustenance or hunger that created the need to complicate behavior in this area? Probably both aspects were at work.

Menstruation is easier to explain, because the two sides revealed in native taboos are relatively clear. On the one hand, blood is associated with trauma and death, so a monthly discharge of blood could seem unnatural, a kind of regular sickness. Also, men, who did not bleed in this way, could focus upon menstruation as the essence of what made women different. All these associations offered reasons for segregating menstruating women, lest they "pollute" other people, especially men. On the other hand, it seems equally clear that the segregation of women was a positive tribute to the creative power tied up with their bleeding. Women brought forth life, and to honor this capacity it was good for them to withdraw at times of bleeding. Practically, this gave women a break from their usual round of chores. Spiritually, it gave them a chance to reflect on their wonderful role of bearing life and deepen their appreciation of women's mysteries. So, in the case of menstruation, "taboo" is not wholly negative. Perhaps that was also true of fences around sexual intercourse and eating. Perhaps the need to complicate sex and food was in good part a tribute to their power and beauty.

Last, we should mention that plains Indians have tended to have strong ideas and practices concerning the dead. Many tribes have thought that the human person has at least two souls: one to animate the body, and one that functions like an aura. This second soul easily, naturally becomes a ghost. Thus it has seemed important to treat the dead with respect, lest their ghosts turn ugly. The traditional method of dealing with the dead was to place them in trees, so that they might decompose. Relatives would prepare foods for the deceased and pay them attention. Women would mourn and relatives might place favorite tools alongside the deceased, or even sacrifice their favorite animal (horse, dog). The Lakota mourned their dead for a year, often keeping a lock of the deceased person's hair and "feeding" it each day. At the end of the year a ceremony proclaimed the end of mourning and the fixing of the ghost in the afterlife. Prior to that time, the ghost could wander, as a partial participant in human affairs, and so had to be placated. The afterlife was a vague replica of earthly existence, not a place of full peace and perfection. There was enough pleasure and joy to make entering it attractive, but its ambiguities suggested that one ought to live earthly life to the full.

Spirituality

Two important developments, the ghost dance and the Native American Church, can stimulate our reflections about the spirituality carried in plains traditions. The ghost dance was a phenomenon of the nineteenth century. A Paiute Indian living in Nevada, Wovoka, had a vision that took him to dead relatives and promised that soon the whites would vanish from the face of the earth. Wovoka had been raised as a Christian, but native instincts were strong enough to oust his Christian beliefs. His vision promised that there would soon be a cataclysm in which the earth would overturn and all the dead Indians, along with all the dead buffalo, would return. No longer would native Americans be subject to whites. The ghosts with whom he visited taught Wovoka a dance to hasten the cataclysm. Wovoka proclaimed what had happened to him and passed the dance along. The ghost dance spread so rapidly, and seemed to cataclyze such opposition to white rule that the U.S. government banned it. This created a crisis on the plains, where the greatest number of adherents had grown. In 1890, at Wounded Knee in South Dakota, ghost dancers clashed with federal troops and about 260 Indians were massacred. This ended the movement, though the hopes that lay behind it continued to live underground.

The Native American Church is a phenomenon of the twentieth century. The remote origins of this movement lay in pre-Columbian Mexico, where many tribes used a hallucinogenic mushroom to facilitate visions and intense experiences. Known as peyote, this mushroom, or similar plants, became a sacrament—a way of communing with ultimate reality. The Native American Church is a pan-tribal organization dedicated to celebrating the powers of peyote to reconnect native Americans with their religious traditions. Most of the members come from the southern plains, but scatterings live elsewhere.

Although the Native American Church seeks to preserve and revitalize native traditions, in fact many Christian notions have entered into its beliefs and rituals. So, for example, one branch of the Native American Church, the Cross Fire, uses the Bible in its ceremonies. Still, native symbols, such as feathers and drums, adorn the rituals, and prayers ascend to such deities as the Morning Star. In some branches, worshipers wear blankets of red and blue, red standing for day and blue for night. Singing and dancing, the participants revere "Chief Peyote," who brings their spirits to life and quickens their dreams. Members may also pray to Christ, and their consumption of the peyote buttons is likened to a communion ceremony. Native American Church communities tend to celebrate at least once each week, from sundown on Saturday to sundown on Sunday. They may also hold ad hoc services for curing illness, celebrating birthdays, conducting funerals, and otherwise dealing with special occasions.[18]

Both the ghost dance and the ceremonies of the Native American Church testify to the strong hold that native traditions have maintained. Many American Indians who apparently had capitulated to Christianity or secularism found that when they had a chance to re-enact traditional ways they could not resist. The appeal seems obvious on some levels, yet mysterious on others. Naturally it felt good to enter into the traditions that had inspired one's people in the past. And, equally naturally, it felt good to oppose the traditions of the whites, who had taken so much from natives and were bound to seem brutal conquerers.

Third, there was the beauty of native ceremonies, especially their instinctive veneration of nature. The majority of native Americans were still living on reservations, and dismal as life there could be, they remained in contact with plants and animals, the spirits of the hills and the prairies. White religion had little to say about the beauties and vitalities of nature. Its divinity stood apart from the world and seemed concerned only with human beings. Natives who tried to practice white ways often felt there were many gaps. When presented the alternative of a religion that would return them to nature, they could sense that part of them had been starving.

The traditional love of visions suggests why the Native American Church made significant progress. Peyote opened new horizons, many of them reminiscent of traditional shamanic experiences. People could argue whether it was good or bad to induce visions by "artificial" means, but in fact many tribes had used peyote-like substances for centuries. For them peyote was not a common article, akin to a rock or even a tree. It was fully living, and the more deeply one experienced it, the more one realized it strengthened one's ties to all creatures.

Psychologists have made it clear that people who ingest hallucinogens such as peyote tend to have visions that fit their cultural assumptions. If animals figure prominently in their worldview, animals are likely to appear. If they have thought about the world in artistic terms, realizing that much in our perception is arbitrary, their visions tend to underscore the flux of external reality, the chance that plays in how matter arranges itself. Drugs amplify not only the sensitivity of normal sense organs but also the subject's feelings about sensual imagery. Emotions as well as perceptions intensify. Native Americans therefore tended to find that peyote enhanced the beauty of the world. With such enhancement came an endorsement of the old, traditional ways. In the past, people had lived close to nature, communing with plants and animals, alert to a variety of spiritual forces. Modern, white ways had deadened native American sensitivity. To revive people's love of nature, their sense of being bonded to other members of their tribe, their openness to spiritual influences—all of that resurrected a way of life that held great appeal.

Spirituality is a matter of finding ways to life—alertness, gratitude for creation, strength to dream dreams and endure sufferings. The basic assumption in spiritual discernment is that a regime or outlook may be known by its fruits. What happens to people who dance the ghost dance or take peyote ritualistically is the best indication of the goodness or badness of such practices. When people feel retied to their roots, strengthened to care for the earth and bear one another's burdens, it is hard to reject their spirituality. If they act more humanely—creatively, selflessly, lovingly—they bear signs of what native Americans have called the Great Spirit and Christians have called the Holy Spirit. Until those signs fail, or turn into something negative—destructive of individuals, the community, or the natural milieu—prudent observers will urge that the practices generating them continue.

That is not to say, of course, that outsiders have to agree with all of the interpretations of human nature that a given spirituality, apparently quite positive, may put forward. It is not to say, for example, that Christians have to set aside their conviction that the incarnation of the Word of God has given the world its most humanizing wisdom. It is simply to say that prudent observers look more to practice than to theory. Important as right thinking can be, right action is rounder and fuller. The ways of naming God are nearly infinite. The ways of trying to reach out to God, or open one's self to God's Spirit, are many. But the crucial signs of God's presence are relatively few. Love and peace, joy and integration, are the decisive, incontrovertible signs. When these persist despite severe trials, external or internal, one can be confident that the grace of God is nigh. To take a contrary position is to deny that human beings have any access to divine wisdom, any way of discriminating between good and evil.

Chapter 5

TRADITIONS OF THE SOUTHWEST

Background

This grouping of native Americans concentrates on the area from the southern end of the Rocky Mountains in Colorado southward to northwestern Mexico and the Gulf of California. The bulk of this area lies in what is now New Mexico and Arizona. The topography varies considerably: mountain regions, high mesas, deep canyons, and low-lying deserts. The combination of mountains and deserts is most characteristic. Water has usually been a problem, because only the Colorado and Rio Grande rivers have been available to offer generous supplies. A great variety of tribes and languages have populated this area, but the Pueblo, Navajo, and Apache people have received the most scholarly attention. One reason is that they have apparently preserved more of the traditional religious ways. Other groups have been greatly influenced by Christianity, so much so that often it is impossible to determine what their original, pre-contact myths and rituals were.

Linguists speak of four major families of languages in the southwest, but of course in fact there has been greater diversity: dialects, and isolated languages (peoples hard to place in larger families), created more distinctiveness. The four major linguistic families are the Uto-Aztecan, Hokan, Athapascan, and Tanoan. Zuni and Keres seem to represent isolated tongues that scholars cannot locate in a larger family. Thus, the thirty-one settlements (pueblos) of New Mexico and Arizona have included speakers of six mutually unintelligible languages. There is a rough correlation between differences in language and differences in culture (economy, religion, sociology), but within

The topography of the region of the Southwest Indians varies considerably: mountain regions, high mesas, deep canyons, and low-lying deserts.

larger linguistic families groups have varied considerably. So, for example, the Shoshoneans, who have lived in the northern parts of this area that we have designated as the southwest, practiced hunting and gathering. The large Aztec civilizations in Meso-America, to the south of our southwest, were what we might call fully developed states. Yet both fall within the same linguistic group: Uto-Aztecan.

One typology of economic arrangements in the southwest lists four major patterns at the time of contact with Europeans. The first, called the rancheria, was a form of agriculture suitable for arid areas. People tended to farm in small, isolated communities, which in effect were extended families working small ranches. Their main crops were the staple trio of native North American agriculture: maize, beans, and squash. The rancheria economy existed in several different areas: the Sierra Madre of Chihuahua (northern Mexico), southern Arizona, the Sonoran coast of the Gulf of California, and some valleys and lands close to rivers. The groups that lived this way had fixed settlements, but they were willing and able to move fairly easily.

A second economic classification is that of villages—truly permanent, sedentary communities, large and long-standing enough to develop fairly intimate social patterns. The Pueblo peoples represent this arrangement. They built permanent villages in stone and adobe, farming the surrounding area for centuries. The Anasazi culture of the twelfth and thirteenth centuries featured some large-scale constructions that apparently allowed complex social relationships. Even though the size of the typical Pueblo was much smaller in the sixteenth century, when natives first encountered whites (about 1540), Pueblo culture has continued for over four hundred years. Whatever the influence of white Christianity, it seems that the Pueblo peoples have retained much of their traditional religion.

Pueblo-dwellers fall into several different linguistic groups. Tribes speaking Tanoan include the Towa, Tiwa, and Tewa, who have lived along the upper Rio Grande in New Mexico. Groups speaking Keresan dialectics have lived in the same area, while Zuni-speakers to the west, across the continental divide (along a tributary of the Little Colorado River), have also been Pueblo-dwellers. At the far west of the Pueblo area have lived the Hopi groups, whose language (Hopi) belongs to the Uto-Aztecan family. Thus it is clear that constructing fixed villages was not the prerogative of any single language group. Many of the western Pueblo-dwellers practiced what would now be called dry farming. To the east, where water was more available, villagers employed various means of irrigating their crops. Pueblo peoples can probably claim the distinction of having the oldest continual settlements in North America: some Hopi and Acoma villages seem to date from the twelfth century.

The third economic style, according to the typology that we are following, is that of people who formed bands. They were more mobile than either the village-dwellers or those living on rancherias, and their way of life tended to be more eclectic. They might modify traditional hunting and gathering, add farming, and also raise sheep. The Navajo and Apache fall into this category. They adopted use of the horse from the Spanish, and the likelihood is that they had only migrated into the southwest shortly before the arrival of the Spanish in the sixteenth century. Prior to that, they had lived on the plains. The main language of the people who organized themselves in bands has been Athapascan, and they have shown a facility for adapting cultural features of other peoples, rather than clinging steadfastly to long-standing traditions of their own (unless we should count adaptability as a long-standing tradition).

The fourth economic group has been non-agriculturalists whose bands have been somewhat nomadic. Their basic economy has been one of hunting and gathering, and their main representative has been the Seri, who have lived on the northwest coast of Sonora (Mexico). Traditionally they fished, hunted small game, caught sea turtles, and gathered plants. Their area was largely desert, and their way of life was quite sparse.

The religious lives of native Americans of the southwest sort themselves into two main groups, though of course there are many exceptions and meldings. The agriculturalists have tended to sponsor communal rituals geared to the cycles of nature. The Pueblos developed a hereditary caste of priests to preside over such ceremonies, and some of them integrated individual concerns, such as for healing, into their communal, cyclical rituals. Among the Pueblos, the Hopi stand out for varying this pattern, inasmuch as they retained a place for individualistic shamans (in contrast to priests based in the community), both male and female, who were much concerned with healing.

The second cluster, of groups less fully involved with agriculture than the Pueblos and more involved with hunting and gathering, tended to base much of their religious lives on shamanistic activities. Their ceremonies tended to be less communal, more individualistic. Shamans were especially concerned with curing sickness, but "sickness" could carry fairly wide connotations. Just as the agriculturalists found ways to integrate individual concerns into their ceremonies celebrating the natural seasons (the cycles of the fertility of the land), so the non-agriculturalists found ways to pray for the well-being of the entire group. Some peoples (the Pima, the Papago, the Havasupai) explicitly mingled the two base-line forms of southwestern religion, holding both shamanistic ceremonies and ceremonies for the agricultural cycle.

On the basis of what we have seen of other native American peoples, we can feel confident that natives of the southwest found little contradiction between honoring nature and seeking cures for sick individuals, between shamanistic activities that depended on ecstatic techniques and priestly activities that depended on traditional lore and ceremonial learning. A given group might have a strong predilection for one or the other way of dealing with the mysteries of the cosmos, but all groups sought harmony with the natural world, peace with the spiritual beings moving in their milieu, and good use of such spirits. The antiquity of many pueblos allowed the development of a conservative, complicated sense of the world, and a parallel complexity or sophistication about ritual. But everywhere there was great sensitivity to the cycles of nature and the impact of spiritual beings, if only because people thought that human prosperity depended on harmony with the powers running the natural world.[19]

Nature

The Papago of southern Arizona, who were largely vegetarian, can remind us of the intimacy that traditional peoples have felt for their own part of the bountiful earth. The crops on which such people subsisted became fully living, personified beings. Thus the Papago would sing to them: "Evening is falling. Pleasantly sounding will reverberate our songs. The corn comes up; it comes up green; here it comes upon our fields, white tassels unfold. The corn comes up; it comes up green; here upon our fields green leaves blow in the breeze. . . . Blowing in the wind, singing, am I crazy corn? Blowing in the wind, singing, am I laughing corn? . . . All together, all together they sing—the red beans. All together, all together they sing, the white beans. Am I not the magic tobacco? Here I come forth and grow tall. Am I not the magic tobacco. The blue hummingbird finds my flowers. Above them softly he is humming. . . . Truly most comfortably you embrace me: I am the blue corn. Truly most comfortably you embrace me: I am the red corn."[20]

First, the singer sings of the crops—corn, beans, tobacco. The crops are part of the audience hearing the song. Then the singer identifies with the crops: blows in the wind with them, wonders whether he, or she, has become crazy with the corn, then laughs with the corn. Third, the crops sing back. The beans, red and white, all sing together. Last, when the stalks of corn lie in the harvesters' arms, the crops sing with contentment: they are embraced by the people (whom they shall feed). So the song becomes a duet. Both parties to the relationship express themselves. Certainly the singers are all "really" human beings, but the wind moving in the fields can seem to give the plants voice, while the native American mind is sophisticated enough to identify with the crops and offer them another voice.

When people did identify with their crops, or the animals that they hunted, or the woods or deserts or coasts where they walked, they could not treat these natural beings casually. They had to deal with them personally, and to imagine that such beings had rights. At the least, such beings had the right to respect and appreciation. The Papago conceit at the end of the song is that the corn is delighted to be in the embrace of the harvesters. Behind this is the conviction that it is the nature, the destiny, of corn to nourish human beings. Human beings help corn to fulfill its destiny. When human beings do this gratefully, with proper respect and discipline, their songs become blessings. The world is moving as it ought to move; nature's children are offering one another mutual respect and mutual service.

The Hopi have made corn central to many of their religious services. Their mythology tells them that at the time when human beings were to emerge into the present, fourth world order, the creator assembled various peoples and asked them to choose from among a wide selection of different types of corn: "The people made their choices. Some took the large ear, some the long, some the fat. Only the small, short ear was left. This the Hopis took because it was like the original humble ear given them on the First World, and they knew it would never die out. Growing in small ears on short, stunted stalks in sandy fields and rocky hillsides with only an occasional rain to nourish them, Hopi corn is still an agricultural miracle and a dependable staple that has earned for the Hopis the name of Corn-Eaters among neighboring meat-eating tribes. The Hopis have never forgotten their choice of the smallest ear. Every year at Harvest time a man goes into his cornfield and selects first the smallest ears on the stalks, saying, 'Now you are going home.' Singing softly, he carries them home in a basket and gives them to his wife. She, without setting them down, carries them to her storage room, where she stacks them on the floor as a base for all the larger ears in the crops, saying, 'Now, seed, you have come home.' "[21]

Hopi accounts of the creation of corn stress the cooperation of mother earth and father sky (rain). As the other animals lived on grass and other plants stemming from the union of earth and rain, so human beings were to live on corn. Both kinds of creatures took to the fruits of mother earth the way that children take to their mother's milk. Corn is like the milk of mother earth offered to human beings. The Hopi find in sacred corn the concrete presence of both principles of divinity, female and male. The motherly and the fatherly have joined to produce this food. The Hopi see the leaves of the growing corn bend toward the earth, and this reminds them of a child reaching out its arms to its mother. The first tassles of corn seem to them signs of masculine power, while the first ears strike them as feminine. The interaction of these two in what they take to be the fertilization of the plant is like a sexual union, and the browning and bending of the mature tassles seems to them like the onset of old age, after the time of fertility.

This ability to invest the commonplace, staple features of their natural environment with rich symbolic significance tells us volumes about the mentality of native Americans. Regularly they show a great desire to find beauty or care in their world, and to express gratitude for it. Food is not something that comes from the supermarket. It remains miraculous, as do the other manifestations of life. Life is miraculous: since death can occur so easily, how is it that things live? The life moving through other natural beings must be like the life that human beings know from within. All forms of life share something precious. "Life" is a common property, and so all living things are brothers and sisters. All depend on the providence of the creator, and when natives have imagined this providence they have tended to picture it as the care of parents for their children. At times native Americans did destroy life casually, but on the whole that seems untypical, rare. More typical was the inclination to sing to the crops, show respect for the animals, because they were kith and kin.

A Navajo hogan (house) song suggests another aspect of native American feelings about nature in the southwest: "Far in the east far below there a house was made; delightful house. God of Dawn there his house was made; delightful house. The Dawn there his house was made; delightful house. White corn there its house was made; delightful house. Soft possessions for them a house was made; delightful house. Water in plenty surrounding for it a house was made; delightful house. Corn pollen for it a house was made; delightful house. The ancients make their presence delightful; delightful house. Before me may it be delightful; behind me may it be delightful; around me may it be delightful; below me may it be delightful; above me may it be delightful; all (universally) may it be delightful."[22]

A similar song, taking up themes from the west, complements this song to the east, and then the people work out songs to the south and the north. The word "delightful" (*hozho*), which occurs as a refrain, also carries the connotation "beautiful." The point, clearly enough, is to assimilate human dwellings to the natural environment and the homes of other creatures who share the earth with human beings. May they all dwell happily, in a beautiful, delightful, atmosphere. May human beings share in the delectation that runs through nature.

For it seems that, left to itself, not injured by the barbarious assaults of human beings, nature and its directions, its dawn and dusk, its corn and water, are simply beautiful, peaceful, self-possessed in delight. In times of religious insight, native Americans such as the Navajo could feel such delight. They could want, as the most central urge of their being, simply to praise the beauty of the world and commune with it. "Let us just be part of your delightful dwelling," is the subtext of these prayers. "If only our dwellings could be as beautiful, as blessed, as yours." Nature seemed more fortunate than human beings. The beings who did not have to think about their blessedness, did not have to plan, build, plot, seemed closer to the sky and the earth, the sunrise and the sunset, the world in which delight was natural and easy.

The Group

The Hopi traditionally have celebrated a cycle of festivals designed to assist the crops to maturity. In describing how the Hopi regularly reassert their ties to the land, the myths of their origin, and their relations with the world of spirits, we may suggest the ritualistic self-definition that occurs among most southwestern tribes.

The Hopi are a typical pueblo-dwelling people inasmuch as they have organized their social life in terms of various religious societies. The typical society has both priests and lay people. Men's societies seem to receive more attention, but women's societies may be equally important, for the usual theme of the rituals that the different societies enact is fertility, which requires both sexes. In praying for the fertility of their crops and families, the Hopi call upon the forces of the earth, the spirits of the plants, and the rain above to play their proper roles. Hunting and curing sickness are lesser but still significant aspects of the Hopi concern with fertility (productivity, strength, flourishing).

Peter Whiteley has distinguished three levels of religious societies among the Hopi.[23] The lowest-ranking groups are the Kachina and Powamuy societies. These are open to all children aged six to ten, regardless of sex. The kachinas are spirits whom masked dancers represent in a variety of different celebrations. The Powamuy society focuses on the bean festival celebrated in February. Neither of these groups is exclusive (though usually children enter either one or the other, not both), and membership in one of them is a requisite for joining a second-ranking society.

The second-ranking groups include four societies for men (Blue Flute, Gray Flute, Antelope, and Snake) and two for women (Maraw and Owaqol). Young people who wish may enter these societies before the age of sixteen. At about sixteen they are eligible to enter a manhood or womanhood society, which deals with the third, highest rank of Hopi ritualistic life. Only males initiated into a manhood society can participate in the very important Soyalangw society, which carries out the holiest ceremonies (but has no special initiation of its own).

These various societies are active in different parts of the annual ritualistic cycle, which·is geared to the germination of the main crops. The Hopi year begins in the fall (October to November, according to the lunar calendar). Activities of the manhood societies predominate at this time. Members retreat for eight days into the *kivas* (underground chambers, significant in view of the Hopi mythology of how human beings emerged from the earth [in four stages, represented by the four levels of the *kiva*]). After this retreat, two manhood societies parade around the village. Called *Wuwtsim*, these groups of men sing songs about various aspects of tribal life, including songs that poke fun at women's ways. The four men's societies distribute the different tasks that together make up men's sense of Hopi life. For example, while two groups process around the village, the two others continue with ritualistic activities in the *kivas* that regenerate the people's ties to the myths of origin. Among the other tribal concerns for which the men's societies are responsible are the fertility of the crops, hunting, the fertility of the game, dealings with the dead, and dealings with the supernatural forces necessary to protect the village.

The Soyalangw ceremony occurs at the winter solstice. All of the important priests participate, and the rituals are the most complex of the Hopi year. They amount to a sacred planning for the coming year, as well as a concerted effort to reverse the course of the sun, so that it will come back north and eventually bring spring and summer. A major motif is the restoration of harmony in all aspects of creation. Following the Soyalangw occur "animal" dances designed as both social occasions and ways of keeping ties with animals important to Hopi life or traditions.

The Soyalangw ritual is also the beginning of the long season (roughly January through July) during which the kachinas perform. There are more than three hundred different kachinas in the Hopi repertoire of masks, in tribute to the variety of functions that the kachinas execute. In general, kachinas are spirits influential in Hopi life. They represent both plants and animals. The dances tend to occur at night from January to March and to take place in the *kivas*. From April to July the dancers appear during the day in the village square. This latter part of the kachina season is the time when unmasked clowns may accompany the kachinas. The commentary and satire of the clowns tend to express criticisms of how village life has been going, as though to hold up a mirror in which those who should reform themselves may get the message.

The ceremonial highlights of the kachina season are the Powamuy ritual that occurs in February and the Niman ritual that occurs in July. The Powamuy, as mentioned, is concerned with beans. It features processions designed to purify the earth for the planting of beans. People germinate beans in the *kivas*. Kachinas distribute bean plants, which are stewed. They also distribute baskets to girls and arrows to boys— symbols of the fertility associated with each sex. So the bean stands not only for itself, a central food, but also for the broader fertility to which it contributes. The people express their dependence on beans—the many interrelations between the fertility of the earth and the prosperity of the tribe. The Niman is a "homegoing" ceremony at the end of the kachina season. It sends the kachinas back to their homes in the mountains. The dancers representing the kachina spirits are commissioned to take back to the kachina community the prayers of the Hopi.

Following the kachina season, the second order societies dance unmasked. This is the time of the year (late summer) when the crops are well under way but a little more rain is necessary for optimal growth. The snake, antelope, and flute societies dance to bring this about. They also re-present aspects of the traditional mythology, especially that concerned with the origins of particular clans within the whole tribe.

The last phase of the annual liturgical cycle involves the women's societies. Their dances tend to be circular and dominated by baskets. Women run in and out of the circle throwing gifts to men, who dispute over the gifts. For nine days images of women's fertility and roles

dominate the village plaza, and the women poke fun at male characteristics, often by performing burlesques of male dances. The two
women's groups, Maraw and Owaqol, divide the ritualistic tasks, the
former dealing with themes of war and the latter with harvest themes.
Both deal with fertility.

It is clear that the Hopi manage to fill most of the calendar year
with ritual dances. Their religious activities are not a part-time, peripheral aspect of their cultural life. What they have to do to maintain
their homes and work their fields, to care for their children and hunt
or cure, weaves in and out of their dealings with the spiritual forces at
work in all aspects of tribal life, as the "other" side of each venture.
The half of the year when the kachinas hold sway brings home the
message that each person is as much involved with spirits as with
earthly comrades.

This is a dramatic way of socializing people to think of their real
identity, both communal and individual, as intimately tied to unseen
forces. The kachinas are seen, of course. Hopi dancers tend to resist
describing themselves as masked, because that might imply that the
kachinas were not real. When dancing, the traditional Hopi become
the kachinas. The result is a tendency in Hopi psychology that Europeans might describe as divinizing the self. The self goes so deeply into
the mysteries of the supernatural, has such constitutive ties to the
spiritual or sacred world, that one cannot define the self apart from
the kachinas. This implies that culture and social life are always filled
with sacredness, making the Hopi a people always contemplating the
mysteries and wonders of the world in which the creative powers have
placed them.

The Self

We may approach the ideas of native Americans of the southwest
about the self through some considerations of Navajo characteristics.
First, concerning physical appearance, Bertha Dutton has written:
"The Navajo tend to be taller than the Pueblo Indians, and most of
them are slender. They have long, somewhat raw-boned faces and a
number of the men have mustaches. Back of the heads are flattened
by cradleboards on which infants are carried. A typical Navajo woman
might be described as having small arms, hands and feet, with thin
legs; long face, nose and chin; and thick lips. The slanted, oriental eye
is fairly common among women and children. Their particular style
of walking and their manner of making gestures are identifying char-

acteristics of Navajo people. A few old Navajo men still wear the attire of earlier days, at least in part. But in the main, clothing, like that of other Indian men, has come to be that of the western stereotype: blue denim pants worn with an ornamental belt, cowboy boots or heavy shoes, colorful shirts and kerchiefs, large felt or straw hats, or maybe a bright headband, coat or leather jacket. Particularly on special occasions, silver and turquois jewelry is worn. . . . The female attire has shown less change through the years. Until recently, most women and girls wore garments reflecting the style of the 1860s, when the Navajo women began to wear long, full skirts of calico or some other colorful material, and velveteen blouses. . . . In their homeland, Navajo traditional moccasins of deerskin and cowhide are still in evidence to some degree. The Pendleton blanket, or one of similar manufacture or appearance, is a favorite of older men and women, worn about the shoulders or folded over an arm."[24]

Looking more to the interior of the Navajo self, Clyde Kluckhohn wrote what became a famous study of witchcraft. Among the most useful features of this study are appendixes in which Navajos speak about different aspects of witchcraft, revealing how riddled their speech was with rumor and supposition. For example, "When witch people get together they talk about things. One person will say to another man, 'When I was out there at the people, one man got mad at me or one woman. And what I want to do about that man or woman. I want to kill that man.' One reason the other witches will be glad to kill this man is after they kill him they'll make more medicine, fresh medicine. When they kill him they go out and get him and bring him inside to this bad hogan. For a man he can be made into that medicine. If they kill a woman, a good woman, they'll bring her down here inside the hogan and one man can have intercourse with her. Maybe two, maybe three, maybe all of them can have intercourse with her. Put a little pot or something underneath her and catch the stuff. Make medicine out of that too."[25]

Even before one imports categories of social scientists to study how peoples deal with their fears of evil, sickness, and death, it is clear that talk such as this is either put on for white investigators or used as a safety valve. People gossip about witches—sources of evil fortune. They imagine how such wicked people must live. The "medicine" that witches use to work their foul purposes must be like the potions that healers concoct. But wicked medicine ought to come from wicked sources. Thus the people gossiping (whether just to pass the time of day, or to exorcise their fears of unknown forces that do harm) imagine that witches kill people and concoct their medicines from their victims.

Indian infants are carried by cradleboards.

A typical victim would be someone who had offended a witch, however witlessly. (This compounds the eeriness of witchcraft: How can innocent people ever know when they have offended the wicked?) If the victim were a female, of course the witches would abuse her further, having sex with her corpse. The objective of this imaginative exercise seems to be to make witchcraft as repulsive, nefarious, heinous as possible. Murder and necrophilia furnish witches their medicine. Blood and genital emissions are the stuff with which they work.

When he gets to cultural interpretation, Kluckhohn begins to imagine how a Navajo child might be socialized into believing in witchcraft: "The child, even before he is fully responsive to verbalizations, begins to get a picture of experience as potentially menacing. He sees his parents, and other elders, confess their impotence to deal with various matters by technological or other rational means in that they resort to esoteric prayers, songs and 'magical' observances and to esoteric rites. When he has been linguistically socialized, he hears the hushed gossip of witchcraft and learns that there are certain fellow tribesmen whom his family suspect and fear. One special experience of early childhood which may be of considerable importance occurs during toilet training. When the toddler goes with mother or older sister to defecate or urinate, a certain uneasiness which they manifest (in most cases) about the concealment of the waste matter can hardly fail to become communicated to the child. The mother, who has been seen not only as a prime source of gratification but also as an almost omnipotent person, is now revealed as herself afraid, at the mercy of threatening forces. The contrast must be uncommonly great between the picture of the world which the child had during what psychoanalysts call the period of 'oral mastery' and the picture of the world which he gets from the words and acts of his elders during the period when he is being obliged to give up the 'instinctual gratifications' of unrestricted urination and defecation."[26]

Kluckhohn's book, first published in 1944, shows how much baggage early investigators of native American culture tended to bring. What Freudian views of the development of children have to do with Navajo witchcraft is not at all clear. The superficial tie might be the tendency of those gossiping about witches to make the witches' activities "dirty." The rest—how the child thinks about toilet training, how snatches of adult conversation about witches might mix into such thoughts—is highly speculative, to say the least. Kluckhohn is on safer ground when he muses that learning that the world has its irrational or uncontrollable aspects is sobering, whether the learner be a child or an adult. When such uncontrollable aspects seem to do real harm—

cause sickness or death—they can rise up as threats to the possibility of a meaningful, good life. All cultures have to find ways to defang the monstrosities conjured up by "evil." All religions are religions of salvation, inasmuch as all struggle to find states of soul, casts of mind, that help people hope that death and evil are not the last word.

Navajo ideas about witchcraft naturally relate to Navajo myths, ceremonies, and judgments about human nature. In the traditional Navajo world, sickness or misfortune could not be purely accidental. The more likely explanation was a malevolent spiritual force. As they enlarged their imaginations to deal with such a force, the Navajo tended to associate it with marginal, outcaste people. The assumption was that, as marginal, these people were likely to carry grudges. If such people built up occult powers, they might easily turn them to bad account—unleash them to hurt their enemies. Or they might put their evil powers out for hire, serving "normal" people who had run afoul of a neighbor or suffered an injury and wanted revenge.

One could consider all this concern with imagining witches relatively harmless, even healthy, as long as it remained a way to handle inexplicable sickness, misfortune, or evil. (Kluckhohn seems naive to think that "technology" could ever wipe these away.) Just as Christians have blamed Satan for bad things in their world, so Navajo could blame witches. Navajo lost their mental balance, however, and became sick selves, when they let witchcraft preoccupy them. (One can say the same about Christians preoccupied with Satan.) So the real question is not whether traditional Navajo believed in witches, but what place (central or peripheral) witches occupied in traditional Navajo culture.

Kluckhohn was dealing with people who had already suffered much at the hands of white people. Their way of life had changed beyond recall, and not for the better (most of them would have said). That made them vulnerable to worries about evil influences: witchcraft. In better times, one suspects, witchcraft had less psychological clout. Nature showed itself more helpful than harmful, so traditional Navajo thought tended to control images of evil-doers within a larger picture that stressed the benefactions of the good spirits responsible for the earth.

Ultimate Reality

The Zuni, a Pueblo people quite different from the Hopi, have a full cultic life involving at least six different societies. Let us examine this cultic life, en route to reflecting on the view of ultimate reality representative for native Americans of the southwest.

First, the Zuni revere a priest whose main responsibility is the cult of the sun. This priest has political as well as religious power within the tribe. Only men belong to the religious society that he heads, and their main responsibility is to hold rituals at the winter and summer solstices. The sun is a powerful presence in the southwestern sky. Some of the Pueblo peoples have thought that contemplating the sun was to contemplate the most brilliant image of divinity. Others have thought that their ceremonies moved the sun through the heavens each day. Without their prayers, the sun might not rise and set, and so the earth might not have heat and light. Such thoughts could give Pueblo life much dignity. If the people played a vital role in the economy of the cosmos, they had to have great worth.

A second Zuni religious group, gathered for the cult of rainmaking, has been composed of twelve small-scale societies. Membership in these groups is hereditary (through one's mother's line). Prayers, songs, and dances for rain are not public among the Zuni but private. The priesthoods that make up the group hold retreats for their members during the summer months, when the question of rain becomes critical. Once again we find a Pueblo tribe responding to a natural need. Crops need rain, as well as sun. By assuming that human petitions can make a difference in the cosmos, the Zuni gave themselves considerable significance. How they dealt with the times when their prayers apparently failed is a further question (to which any people who petition ultimate reality are vulnerable). The most we can say is that they considered it better to try to influence the world, and risk disillusionment, than to stay aloof, as though they could not make a difference. The further, speculative point is that when individuals or groups begin to feel that they cannot make a difference, that they are of no account, they come close to losing their pride and reason to be.

The third Zuni religious society enlists those who perform in the kachina dances. While the Hopi admit women into their kachina dances, the Zuni do not. The Zuni divide the world into the familiar six directions (north, south, east, west, above, below), so they have six different kachina groups. Each has its headquarters at a different *kiva*. The kachina groups dance at least three times a year: summer, late fall, and winter. The symbolism of Zuni kachina dancing differs somewhat from Hopi, but the basic idea is the same. Through the masked dancers, the spirits to whom the Zuni are partnered in all their significant activities can assume palpable form. The dancers can take on the identity of given spirits, and so the spirits can gain a regular, semi-permanent residence in the spiritual world.

While the general run of Zuni kachina dancers participates in ceremonies for rain, the fourth Zuni society, composed of kachina priests, deals with matters of fertility. In their hands is the ritual responsibility for the increase and health of both human beings and the animals with whom the Zuni interact. Some of their costumes and dances are spectacular (the Shalako kachinas are birdlike figures ten feet tall). They are also the group that presents the "mudhead" kachinas, who are both clowns and fearsomely powerful spirits. The effect of the ceremonies of the Zuni kachina priests is to distribute the allure and challenge of ultimate reality throughout a number of points (temporal, geographical, and symbolic) of Zuni culture. The kachinas make present the wonder of ultimate reality, feeding human beings' sense that the fully real must be more alive, powerful, and significant than what dusty, limited human beings can manage to produce or even appreciate on most days.

This "distributive" quality of Pueblo ultimate reality reminds us of how rituals tend to run parallel to views of the cosmos. The ultimate reality that one finds in monotheisms such as Judaism, Christianity, and Islam is not spread out the way that it was traditionally in the native American southwest. For the biblical monotheisms, God was everywhere, but divinity did not arrive, take shape, in such discrete forms as the kachina dancers. This difference had its advantages, but also its disadvantages. Among the latter was the difficulty of making divinity as near, dramatic, and absorbing as the kachinas could make it.

The fifth Zuni religious society was composed of priests whose concern was war. Initiation into this society required one to bring the scalp of an enemy. In effect, members of the war society served as the military leaders of the people and as their police. They were also the executives in the Zuni system of government, charged to carry out decisions that the tribe had reached. One of their executive responsibilities was to execute witches. The war society reminds us that the Zuni considered the supernatural world to be populated with evil as well as good forces. Native southwestern culture as a whole seems relatively stark about evil. Perhaps the starkness of the landscape contributed to its mentality. People had to be on guard. Even when witches served more as symbols of what might go wrong than as a strong practical force in Zuni society, their significance was considerable. The Pueblo picture of ultimate reality did not describe a God who was pure Light, in whom there was no darkness at all. Negative forces could seem as ultimate as positive forces, even when it was clear that positive forces had to be more populous and powerful (for the world to function at all).

The sixth and last Zuni group that we treat has been composed of both male and female healers. Their distinctive trait has been dedication to a particular predatory animal (bear, mountain lion), whose lore figured in their curing ceremonies. The totemic quality of this medicine seems plain, and once again we are reminded of the intimacy that native Americans have felt for the animals with whom they have shared their habitat. Even in the southwest, where animals were relatively scarce and hunting was less significant than farming or herding, native Americans remained convinced that their fate was tied intimately to that of the four-leggeds.

Perhaps that is the most salutary reminder: native American culture, in both the southwest and elsewhere, did not separate human beings from the rest of the natural world as sharply as modern western culture has. Human beings had to find their health and wealth through harmonious relations with the animals, the crops, the forces of the weather, and all the other natural "beings" in their habitat. They could not treat the rest of creation as mere grist for their mill, raw material for their technology. They had to honor the spiritual force of other creatures—the impact that other creatures made on the human psyche, when the human psyche was healthy: contemplative, not absorbed with itself but lost in the wonders of creation.

Spirituality

Among the Pueblos, the path of an individual's life is set at birth. The ceremonies surrounding birth petition that the newborn enjoy a long life, full of good things, and a peaceful death. That is the Pueblo conception of earthly blessedness. The rituals in which a person may engage throughout the life-cycle aim at incorporating the person more fully into the world. The world is conceived as determined by spiritual forces. In ritual activity, people have the opportunity to interact with such forces: incorporate them in kachina dances, petition them for rain and fertility, come to know their ways.

When one joins a religious society, this interaction moves up a notch in intensity. Occasions for intercourse with the spirits become more frequent, and the person tends to make ritual a more substantial part of his or her identity. At puberty, marriage, and other significant moments in the life-cycle, rituals invite Pueblos to contemplate their place in the cosmos. Fertility is not a purely private matter. Sexual activity and procreation tie one into patterns of the entire natural world, and the more that one can appreciate such patterns, the more responsible and spiritually fruitful one's sexual activity will be.

For most Pueblos, death marks a transition to a new phase of existence, but one that remains within the boundaries of the natural world. The dead remain within the orbit of nature or the cosmos. There is no heaven or hell transcending the world that human beings know on earth. The dead, the clouds in the heavens, and the kachinas form a triad. Relations among them vary from tribe to tribe, but in general the dead are considered to be part of the cloud-people, and to be involved with the kachinas. Pueblo mythology has the breath of the dead person (the sign of life) return to the site of emergence (during the creation of human beings), which is symbolized in the *kiva*. This breath then becomes part of the clouds (heavenly vapor).

Social status has much to say about one's afterlife. Priests tend to have more significant post-mortem existences than ordinary, lay people. The kachinas, as spirits, move in the general orbit that the dead (liberated from their bodies) inhabit. Significant deceased people may return as kachinas, though the majority of the kachinas are physical forces or personifications of social powers.

For Pueblo people such as the Tewa, only those who have become priests (people deeply involved in religious rituals) are fully human or "complete." Ritual activity is the process through which one is made human. Lay people remain somewhat incomplete. They have not immersed themselves in the activities—the contemplation of the forces of nature, the identification with the kachinas—that bring human potential to climax. Of course, this is a very provocative view of human nature. If people do not mature fully without religious ritual, then a secular life is ipso facto retarded or underdeveloped. The Zuni and Keresan peoples hold a similar distinction between priestly, ritualistic people and those whose participation in ceremonial life is minimal.

In Robert Coles' interviews with Hopi children, the hallmark is their attention to the natural world, especially the rocks and clouds that stand out in the Arizona landscape. So, for example, a Hopi girl initiates her little sister into the wonders of the world into which the youngster has been born: "She stops to point toward the sky. The baby has watched her, listened intently, even if unable to understand the specific words. The baby has remained still for a few minutes. Now the baby lifts her head upward, tries to capture with her eyes the moving bird—but no luck. The eyes, too—the head, for that matter—are not ready. The baby sits down, at the same time lowers its head. The older girl sits down, also begins to look at the ground. She spies a small, flat stone, picks it up, feels it in her hands, holds it tightly between her palms, moves the palms toward the baby's face, holds them transfixed, almost as if in prayer, in front of the little girl, and suddenly: 'Here you are! This is one of many; this is a Hopi stone. Do you see the lines on it? Someone made them. I do not know who it was, but they are here to remind us that before us there were others.'"[27]

Native Americans like the Hopi strike a white observer like Coles as slower, more attentive, than the ordinary white person. Their culture has attuned them to the natural world as white culture has not attuned its children. The clouds passing above, splendid in the usually clear blue sky, are not merely meteorological phenomena. They carry a spiritual significance, perhaps that of venerable ancestors or kachina spirits. The stones that predecessors have marked are mementos from the past, reminding the present generation that, long before them, forebears walked this way and cared for the land.

To "care" for the land has at least two connotations. A traditional native American provides for the land, tries to ensure its prosperity, avoids what we might call "unecological" activities that seem to hurt nature. But he or she also has a tender regard for the land. The land lies on the people's heart, is a constant concern, like a much-loved child or parent, even like a lover, distant yet near, a source of joy and also a source of worry.

Traditional American peoples like the Hopi were wedded to the land. They had an intercourse with the land that made them pregnant in several ways. Not only did they draw their living from the land, they loved the land. It was their delight, as well as their fate and habitat. The land (the sky, the birds, the stones) never failed to interest them. It varied every day. No spot was identical to any other. Where an outsider might find only barrenness, natives could find constant cause for wonder and thanksgiving. Much is always in the eye of the beholder. From infancy, Hopi children were taught to behold carefully, wonderingly, with a tender love and gratitude.

It is tempting to see an entire redemptive ecology in this attitude. If we and our contemporaries were taught to treat the land like a parent, a lover, the best of friends, would we not change our destructive ways drastically? Those who attack the biblical religions as anthropocentric tend to neglect the sense of God's presence in nature that rings throughout the psalms and the prophets, and that hovers in Jesus' notice of the lilies of the field, how they grow. But it is hard to deny that Christianity lost something precious when it took over the biblical polemic against the fertility gods of the Canaanites and separated God from the cosmos. Certainly this "secularization" encouraged human beings to develop modern science and technology, which are both wonderful achievements of the human spirit and the sources of significant cures for human ills (poverty, sickness, helplessness before natural disasters). But it also brought enormous losses. Indeed, this kind of secularization, which demystified nature, not only opened the door to the abuses of natural systems that have given us our current ecological crisis, it also shrunk the human spirit.

For a human spirit that does not wonder about rocks and clouds is smaller, more restricted, than the traditional Hopi spirit that did. And with such shrinking has come a loss of dignity. For traditional, native Americans, to be human was to play an important role in the maintenance of the cosmos. The world of sacred forces needed human participation if it was to function well. Our contemporary alienation from nature, ourselves, and God derives in good part from our doubts that we play a significant, necessary role in the cosmos. If the heavens are but icy wastes, however beautiful, and the human being is but an interesting collection of chemicals, then the existence of our species is insignificant. A spirituality that would make human beings whole and happy in the twenty-first century has much to learn from traditional peoples of the American southwest. Only when we are able to integrate the gains of western science with age-old contemplative attitudes like those of the Hopi will we begin to think of ourselves as whole or trustworthy stewards of creation.

Chapter 6

TRADITIONS OF THE FAR WEST

Background

The native Americans of the northwest coast were one of the most diverse groups. The area we are calling the northwest extends north from the mouth of the Columbia River to Yakutat Bay in Alaska. It is a narrow strip of land, bordered by the Pacific Ocean, which had the greatest influence on how the tribes lived. The mountains to the east tended to separate these peoples from those to the west of the plains. To the south, California Indians also enjoyed the bounty of the sea, but lived under sunnier, drier weather conditions.

The tribes of the northwest clustered in three sub-areas. Tlinglit, Haida, and Tsimshian inhabited the northern regions. Bella Coola, Nootka, and Kwakiutl lived in the central area. Coast Salish and Chinookan occupied the coast of what is now Washington and Oregon. Each geographical area housed tribes more alike to one another culturally than to tribes outside their area, but a great variety of languages and customs obtained everywhere. So diverse were these peoples, in fact, that scholars postulate considerable migration, acculturation, and cultural borrowing. Only in the late eighteenth century did white culture begin to make an impact. Until whites had completed their migration westward and reached the Pacific coast, native Americans lived according to the patterns that had evolved through millennia in which their own interactions had determined the beliefs, economies, and political structures of the area.

The bounty of the sea and the forests made life in the northwest quite easy. People could fish for a variety of species (salmon was the most important), hunt sea birds and seals, and gather shellfish. The woods housed caribou, deer, bears, and smaller animals. The people did not farm. They could gather seeds, berries, and roots to balance their diet of fish and meat. The woods also furnished plentiful material with which to build—houses, canoes, implements. Extended families tended to winter in wooden houses, to carry their possessions in wooden chests, and to be buried in wooden coffins. The famous totem poles of the northwest, carved on tall trees, suggest how the woods furnished materials on which to employ religious imagination. Native Americans built magnificent dug-out canoes, capable of carrying thirty or forty men, and they used the sea or the rivers for easy transport. The typical site for a northwestern village was the mouth of a river. Villagers could come and go easily, and such a site tended to offer protection against raids by enemy tribes.

Warfare was frequent in the northwest, and so skill in fighting was important. Tribes tended to raid those most different from themselves in language and customs. The raids sought to remove enemies and potential conquerors. They were also a way to gain wealth, including human slaves. The Haida, living on the northern islands of this area, were least involved in warfare. Profiting from their relative isolation, they became greater carvers in wood and stone. Other tribes suffered more from warfare, but the natural bounty of the entire area was so great that material prosperity seldom suffered.

The lure of trade in fur brought whites into the northwest in the nineteenth century, and from that time native traditions began to decay. Population declined, trade and intermarriage among tribes increased, and many groups abandoned their ancestral villages. Pressure came from the U.S. government to abandon traditional customs, including native religious practices. Eventually the government displaced many natives, because of white desire for their land. The old social and religious forms no longer fit the people's circumstances, so what can only be called a cultural death occurred.

The basic social unit traditionally was the extended family, which tended to occupy a middle-sized wooden house. During the summer the people lived much of their lives outdoors, but in the winter they needed shelter. Winter tended to be the time for celebrating religious festivals. Taking advantage of respites from hunting and fishing, tribes would rehearse their mythologies and celebrate the rituals that told them about creation, their self-understanding as Haida or Kwakiutl, the mysteries of birth and death. One distinctive focus of ritual activity in the northwest was food. Natives of the area tended to think that the forces driving the world were all competing for a limited

The bounty of the sea and the forests made life in the northwest quite easy.

The lure of trade in fur brought whites into the northwest.

supply of food. Equally, they were competing for a limited supply of souls.

The food chain focused this competition. Creatures lived in their special niches along the food chain, and ritual was necessary to balance or adjudicate their competing claims. Why such a sense of competition should have arisen in an area unusually rich in resources for easy subsistence is hard to say. Perhaps observing the mutual devouring of the many species of the sea and the woods stimulated the native sense that everything was a matter of eating or being eaten. Seals devoured fish, and bears or human beings could devour seals. Large fish fed on small fish. Small animals were the prey of large animals, but small animals in turn fed on mice or berries.

Whatever the reason, native Americans of the Pacific northwest tended to celebrate ritual meals that required deliberate control of hunger. This control was twofold. On the one hand, by providing generous amounts of food, the people hoped to avoid greediness. On the other hand, by tabooing hunger as a destructive or polluting desire, they sought to develop restraint from within. The point may well have been to stay independent of the motivation they saw driving the other species in the food chain. If human beings could avoid voraciousness, they could affirm their unique identity and dignity. A typical feast, for example on the occasion of the first salmon run of the season, would require the participants to treat the salmon as though these were chiefs of high rank. The hope that was by treating the salmon well, their souls would inform other salmon that serving the needs of human beings was not a bad fate. Such ceremonies took place under the direction of the head of the extended family. Behind them lay the conviction that continued success in hunting or fishing depended on preserving good ritual relations with one's prey.

Their location by the sea influenced the spiritual imagination of many tribes. The Kwakiutl, for example, tended to depict the spirits moving in their milieu as *sisiutl*, double-headed serpents characterized by wetness and fluidity. By extension, the *sisiutl* were associated with tears, blood, the sea, the rain. The Kwakiutl worldview stressed constant motion or fluidity. The different spirits, which could become visible to human beings, symbolized the lability of meaning in the cosmos. Human beings could stop the world sufficiently to perceive it as material and deal with it pragmatically, but in itself the world was always moving on. Decay, death, and rebirth expressed some of the world's transiency. Changes in life, losses and gains in memory and riches, represented more. When human beings received visions of spirits, they gained insight into the manifoldness of the cosmic flux.

California and the Intermountain Region

In this chapter, we also cover ethnographic areas south of the Columbia River. For present purposes "California" means the lands west of the Sierra Nevada crest to the Pacific Ocean. What is now Oregon is the northern border, while our California extends south of the present U.S.-Mexican border to include northern Baja. A great variety of tribes lived within this geographic region, but one can distinguish them, as a cultural group, from tribes of two geographic regions often called "Intermountain," those of the great basin and those of the plateau.

The intermountain region lies between the Rocky Mountains of the U.S. and Canada to the east and the Cascade and Sierra Nevada Mountains to the west. The northern portion of this area is the plateau, bounded to the north by the forests above the Fraser Plateau of British Columbia and to the south by the Bitterroot Mountains of Idaho, the arid highlands of southern Oregon, and the highlands of northwestern Montana. Ethnographers customarily include in the plateau area the drainage of the Columbia River in Washington, Oregon, and uppermost northern California.

The southern portion of the intermountain region, the great basin, is a steppe desert, most of which falls into present-day Utah and Nevada. It also includes portions of southern Idaho, western Wyoming, and western Colorado. Beginning in the north with the Salmon and Snake rivers in Idaho, it runs south through the Colorado Plateau to the Colorado River. The interior deserts of southwestern California also fall within the great basin.

Languages, tribes, and so cultures were most uniform in the great basin. There the languages were all Numic. There was greater variety in the plateau, and wild diversity in California. Understandably, this meant that religious practices were most diverse in California and most uniform in the great basin. The great basin was also the least populated area, due to its ecology. The land simply would not furnish enough food for large populations.

Until the eighteenth century, change apparently was slow in all three areas. Interactions among different cultural groups sparked a steady evolution, especially in California, but nothing dramatic or traumatic intruded from the outside. All of the peoples shared the general suppositions that we have found among native Americans thus far: a mythopoeic mentality, great influence from local physical conditions, a keen sensitivity to animals and plants, a rich sense of the spiritual world, and a tendency to represent the world, and frame human responses to it, through ceremonial singing, dancing, rites for curing, coming of age, burial, and the like.

Beginning in 1789 Catholic missionaries sought to control native groups in California, with the result that many native cultures changed drastically. While some natives converted to Christianity voluntarily, others were pressured into baptism. Living under missionary rule, in mission communities, destroyed the way of life that many tribes had practiced for centuries. White diseases reduced the native population, while crowded conditions in some missions and hard labor also exacted a high toll. On the other hand, contact with Christianity seems to have stimulated natives who did not convert to incorporate features of Christian theology or ritual into their systems of belief, bringing about something new and hybrid. For example, the Gabrelino people of southern California developed a new high god, Chingichngish, who seems much like the Christian God in his call for strict morals and his omniscient character. Other tribes of that area, such as the Luiseno-Juaneno, the Ipai-Tipal, the Yokut, and the Chumash, also adapted their native sense of God, to accommodate Chingichngish and so Christian notions.

In the nineteenth century Protestant missionaries worked in California, the basin, and the plateau. On the whole they converted few natives, but they did stimulate new religious forms. The plains Indians, who had adapted their cultures to accommodate use of the horse, stimulated natives of California, the basin, and the plateau to follow their lead. Along with the horse, and so new possibilities for hunting and travel (and so a more nomadic existence), came military groups, the sun dance, and related aspects of plains culture.

In the late nineteenth century Christian ideas of prophecy interacted with native discontents to spawn a series of millennial movements, the most famous of which was the ghost dance. Western Indians had previously developed ghost societies, for dealing with matters related to death, and some grafted the ceremonies and ideology of the ghost dance onto the social structures, rituals, and beliefs of such groups. Prior to the ghost dance, which emerged in both 1870 and 1890 (affecting California and the basin in 1870, but only the basin in 1890), other prophetic movements had sought religious revival, especially in the plateau. The prophet dance sprang from these movements in the 1830s, and in the 1870s the prophet Smohalla revived this dance and expanded its influence.

Generally the prophetic movements drew on Christian inspiration, and employed some Christian theology or symbolism, but put both in the service of reviving native hopes that present sufferings (cultural dislocations, due to white influence) might pass away and a new era of peace and prosperity appear. A Salish Indian, John Slocum, founded a native Shaker church that spread through the plateau in the 1880s. In the early twentieth century the use of peyote (peyote way) grew in the basin. Since the 1960s natives of all three areas have worked to re-establish authentic traditions: dances, shamanistic activities, and renewal ceremonies. These have had political as well as religious overtones: the effort to reassert a native identity.

Among the general features of the religious systems that native groups in California, the basin, and the plateau shared traditionally were an interest in acquiring power. This power was spiritual: the force that sustained and directed the cosmos, was out of kilter in sickness and rebalanced in healing, made women fertile and men able to hunt and fight. The myths that explained the origins of the world or features of tribal culture dealt with power, inasmuch as they not only recalled dispersions of power in the past but mediated such power into the present. (To rehearse a myth or ritualize an account of creation is to bring the forces named in the myth or dramatized in the ritual to bear on the present.) Shamanic exercises were ways of seeking and finding personal power. Shamans might use their powers for good or evil. In itself, power was neutral, a force like electricity or magnetism. All depended on the will that directed it. The greater their powers, the more that shamans were feared, in effect being suspected of witchcraft. Indeed, the general attitude toward shamans prevailing in the areas we treat in this chapter appears to have been more negative than what we have seen in other chapters.

Among other general, background features of these ethnographic areas we might note the widespread presence of secret societies, the seclusion of women at puberty and menstruation, and the use of sweatlodges. The secret societies initiated people into special lore, offering a way to deepen their wisdom, their understanding of how the world in fact worked. The seclusion of women, in tandem with the rituals for puberty, gave females an equivalent of the "spirit quests" open to males. Menstrual blood was ambivalent: highly powerful, but therefore both dangerous and wonderful. To come in contact with it could be polluting, but on it depended the fertility of the tribe. Hunting peoples laid more stress on menstrual seclusion than did gathering peoples, which suggests a fear that the killing power of men and the life-giving power of women might collide destructively. The sweat lodges were frequented by men and considered holy places for purification. In some ways they ran parallel to the places of seclusion set aside for women.

Nature

As always, myths tell us much about the convictions of native Americans, in this case of the far west. Consider, for example, the story of Bear Mother, told by the Haida. Princess Rhpisunt, daughter of the chief of the Wolf Clan, was out one day picking berries. By accident she stepped into bear dung, which displeased her greatly. For the rest of the day she complained about the dirtiness of bears, who had inconvenienced a lady of her high standing. At the end of the day of gathering, she found herself separated from her companions, because she had stopped to fix the straps on her basket.

· Before the princess could become distraught, she met two handsome youths. They volunteered to help her, so she followed their lead gladly, barely noticing that they took her away from the sea, where her own people lived, and into the mountains. After some time, they reached a village with a large house in the center. The youths led her into it, promising to introduce her to their father. It turned out that he was the chief of the Bear People, whom she had offended greatly by her complaints at stepping in their dung. Around the house the princess noticed many people who moved like sleepwalkers. From a mouse woman she learned that these were slaves, captured because they too had offended the bears, either by making fun of them or by mutilating them after hunting them down. The mouse woman asked gifts from the princess and promised to help her. She advised the princess always to make her toilet outside and to put a piece of her copper bracelet on top of her excrement. The bears were always spying on the princess, so after observing her relieving herself, they rushed to her spot. Finding a piece of her copper bracelet, they exclaimed that she was right to call their own excrement dirty, since her leavings were shiny, valuable metal.

The princess was married to the son of the Great Bear. She learned the customs of the Bear People, including their tradition of wearing their bear skins whenever they went outside. The Bear People would move their dwelling from time to time, and about the time that the princess found herself pregnant, soon to become Bear Mother, they moved close to her own people's village. Her people had searched constantly for her, killing many bears in the process. The princess gave birth to twin cubs, who were lively and beautiful. Her Wolf brothers gradually closed in on the cave where she was living, and her husband, the Bear Prince, became reconciled to losing her and being killed. He told the princess to make sure that her brothers did not mutilate his body, and he promised to use good magic to turn their children into humans who would be great hunters.

The princess and the brothers went along with the wishes of the Bear Prince, and eventually his coat became a source of great blessings to their father, the head of the Wolf People. The cubs turned into handsome little boys, and their new grandfather built them a high pole, from which they could see their old home among the Bear People. When the princess grew old and died, the boys put on their bear skins and returned to the Bear People. Ever after the Wolf People and the Bear People considered themselves relatives, and the Bear People helped the Wolf People to hunt well.[28]

This story reminds us of the deep immersion of native Americans in the world of animals. Living by hunting, natives of the northwest felt that their lives were intwined with the game on whom they depended. Equally they felt that how they treated the game, even how they thought about the game, made all the difference in their fortune. The fault of the princess was pride. She thought herself aloof from the bears whom her people hunted. She was able to dismiss the bears as dirty, inferior, when she stepped in their dung. This attitude was bound to bring disaster. The moral of the story is that the princess had to pay for her pride. Indeed, she had to become the subject of the Bear People, submissive to their desires.

On the other hand, the story shows that native Americans found much ambiguity in relations among the different species. The Bear People were not simon-pure. They kept slaves, and a small, quick-witted creature like the mouse woman was able to spy out their weaknesses. In fact, they were less confident than they appeared to be, as their willingness to accept the princess' estimate of their dirtiness shows. Why the story should be so scatalogical, fixated upon excrement, is difficult to say. No doubt one reason is to introduce humor—it is funny for people to be obsessed with the humblest of their activities. A sign of the native American insight into the ambiguities of social relationships is the happiness of the princess' marriage. Even though she had been forced into marriage with a stranger, she came to love her husband, who treated her well, and was fruitful by him. Perhaps this motif reflects the cultural situation of captured brides, encouraging them to think that even though they had joined a new family against their will, they could find love and fruitfulness.

Apparent also in the story is the native American use of totems. The Wolf People and the Bear People both cross the line between animals and human beings, moving back and forth. Are they wolves and bears, or human beings in wolf and bear "skin" (clothing, attitudes)? This ambiguity reflects the native conviction that all animals are "people": intelligent, willful creatures who deserve respect. It also reflects the native sense that human beings do well to aim at the virtues of estimable creatures like wolves and bears, identifying with them.

Finally, a clear theme is the value of reconciling enemies, who might well be tribes associated with different totems. Wolf People and Bear People might find themselves having to get along. The best way to achieve peace would be for both groups to put aside their pride and realize that the other group had its good points. The willingness of the Bear Prince to sacrifice his life so that the Wolf Princess could return to her home and bring up her children there shows the magnanimity that good tribal relations could require. But the Bear People also receive their reward, for in the end the offspring of the Wolf Princess and Bear Prince return to the Bear People.

Themes from California

As we have noted previously, a good clue to how people think about nature is their mythology of creation. The Maidu of northeast California represent a group who depicted the process of creation as the work of a heavenly being in concert with a being able to dive to the bottom of the sea. "Earth-initiate," as the Maidu called the heavenly being, shone so brightly that none could see his face. The sun was his sister, and after making the earth he put the stars in place. He came from the heavens and met turtle, who nagged at him to create good things. Above all turtle wanted some dry land, because he was tired of always having to swim. He wanted a place to rest. "Where am I going to get earth to make dry land?" Earth-initiate asked.

Turtle volunteered to dive to the bottom of the sea and bring up some earth. They tied a rope to his arm, and he was gone for six years. When he returned, the only earth that he brought up was a tiny bit of mud under his nails. Earth-initiate molded this into a little ball, which grew—slowly at first, and then with a rush—into a great roundness, the earth. Earth-initiate promised to make human beings to populate the earth. Observing all this was the Father of the Secret Society, who cried out and chanted at appropriate occasions. The two who assisted Earth-initiate, turtle, and the Father of the Secret Society, had floated in on the water (whence is never explained), using a raft. At that time, before the establishment of the sun, the moon, and the stars, there was no light, no land, only water. At the end of Earth-initiate's work, however, there was dry land and light. That was how the cosmos began, with dry land below and light in the heavens above.

X   This story is touching in its simplicity. It doesn't care where turtle
and the Father of the Secret Society came from. It is only interested in
imagining how a supernatural power drew earth from the sea and
established light where previously there had been only darkness.
Clearly the intuition at work is that darkness and the sea are primordial, light and the land are things that come in a second phase. "Creation" is not a making from nothingness. It is merely separating or
clarifying things contained in the primordial situation, though not
obviously so. Turtle nudges Earth-initiate to get to work, do some
good. The presence of the Father of the Secret Society suggests that
something ritualistic was going on at the very beginning. We may
interpret the shouts of the Father as a ceremonial counterpoint to the
prosaic dredging and shaping of the earth that turtle and Earth-
initiate worked out.

     Other northern California tribes tended to represent creation
with greater sophistication, picturing a divinity who thought the world
into being. Some such accounts are quite metaphysical, providing for
the different kinds of beings that one now finds in the world. The
intuition seems to be that everything lodges in a divine mind. The
Luiseno of southern California describe a step by step process in
which creation arises out of a void. This is not precisely "creation from
nothingness," but it represents an awareness that the most fundamen-
tal question is: Why is there something rather than nothing? In postu-
lating a void in the beginning, the Luiseno imply that matter is not
eternal. They do not explain, however, how one gets something from
nothing. Indeed, their clearer interest is the steps through which the
cosmos passed, in its coming into being. The main agent, Wyiot, transformed the first, crude forms of being into more developed shapes.
He came on the scene after there was an earth (a stuff to transform),
and when his work was finished he left the scene. This is typical of the
forces who mold the world in California mythology. The work of
running the world is distinct from the work of first fashioning it, so
after fashioning the world, the "transformers" have nothing to do.

     Tribes of the basin and plains show even less interest in begin-
nings than California tribes. The focus of their myths about origins is
rather the different kinds of beings that the world now houses. Their
stories tell where the heavenly beings, the animals, the important
spirits, and human beings themselves came from. Frequently the central figure is a trickster (Coyote is a popular one) who arranges things
(but also bungles them on occasion, or turns mischievous).

     In the Maidu collection of stories, Coyote tries to work along with
Earth-initiate (in a later phase of creation, when men and women

come into being). In the beginning human beings were very white (they darkened over time), but they had no hands. Coyote suggested to Earth-initiate that they have paws like his, but Earth-initiate preferred to give them hands like his own. When Coyote asked him why, he said, "So that, if they are chased by bears, they can climb trees." Coyote thought that Earth-initiate had made human beings very easily, so he decided to imitate him. Earth-initiate had told him not to laugh at human beings. He made a couple, easily enough, but in the morning, after their creation, the woman of the pair poked Coyote in the ribs. This caused him to laugh and turned the couple's eyes to glass. Earth-initiate accused Coyote of having laughed, but he denied it. That was the first lie to enter the world.

The Group

We may examine the social structure of northwest coastal peoples by studying the potlatch, their most distinctive ritual. Interpretations vary, but most analysts show that the potlatch possessed both social and religious motifs. Socially, the most overt function of the potlatch was to transfer hereditary titles and rights. Northwestern groups were highly conscious of social rank, and to be a chief was a great distinction. Chiefs led their extended families, representing them to the outer world, including the world of supernatural beings, and in turn representing to the extended family the gods relevant to its special history.

At the potlatch, those claiming power (having their accession to leadership or their inheritance of familial rights legitimated) had to show a mastery of the family's (mythic) history and traditional rituals. The context for this display of competence was a ritual feast, at which the leader or celebrant distributed considerable wealth. It was important to distribute this wealth correctly, in accord with the status of each guest receiving a gift. Thus, the potlatch not only established the rights of the new claimant (new chief, child coming of age, person marrying into the tribe, or other person-changing state), it also reaffirmed the hierarchy of social relations (status, degree of tie) that the family saw as objective reality.

The potlatch could also occur at times of change, when social relations might seem to be coming under pressure. If a person were to receive a new name (perhaps as a result of a vision, or the death of a relative [who had to be memorialized]), or a family were erecting a new house, or a person had died and a funeral was in order, or there was a marriage that would change social relations, it was felt necessary to reassert the family's traditions and smooth away any possible frictions by redistributing material wealth. The fact that the leader of the potlatch could command the respect of his family and guests enough to get them to the feast, that he could run the ceremony competently, and that he would distribute his wealth generously legitimated his claims to dignity and leadership. (It could also thwart the claims of rivals.)

As a recent study of the potlatch suggests, anthropologists and students of religion, although coming to this phenomenon with different interests, have shown both its richness and its complexity. Concerning the former: "Anthropologists have focused on the secular, social aspects and functions of the potlatch—on the way in which potlatches maintain social equilibrium, consolidate chiefly power over commoners, provide for the orderly transfer of wealth and power, provide a measure of group identity and solidarity, redistribute surplus wealth and level economic imbalances, provide outlets for competition without recourse to violence, and provide an occasion for aesthetic expression and dramatic entertainment. Concerning the latter: Irving Goldman has suggested in his *The Mouth of Heaven* (1975) that, since in northwest coast philosophy all status, power, and wealth are considered to be a gift from the beneficent supernatural beings who provide the materials that human beings need to survive, the potlatch is inherently a religious institution, fundamentally endowed with a sacramental quality."[29]

The stories constituting the family's lore tended to explain how the supernatural beings had provided for its ancestors, giving them the right to hunt or fish in a given area, to collect roots of a given type, and so forth. As well, the supernatural beings had given ancestors of the family the right to impersonate them (especially in religious ceremonies), bear aristocratic titles (by the leave of heaven), and call upon them in times of need. The reciprocal responsibility of the tribal leaders (or the entire tribe or family, through its leaders) was to hold the potlatch ceremony, offering the supernatural beings an occasion in which to come into the group's midst dramatically and so be revitalized. Thus we may speak of a covenant between the family and the supernatural beings, and of the potlatch as the ceremony that renewed the covenant.

The chief, who led the potlatch ceremony, was himself the locus or nexus of these various intentions. He represented the family to the supernatural beings, and they became incarnated in him. The tendency of oral peoples everywhere has been to use their rituals as an occasion to let the gods come into their midst, and to let themselves leave ordinary existence, becoming gods. The person representing a supernatural being becomes that being. For the duration of the ceremony, the person is the god, and something of such a divine identity is bound to linger after the ceremony is done. This is not schizophrenic, nor does it occur with no awareness of the psychological manipulation involved. But it is dramatic and ecstatic. It does raise the intensity of the people involved and expand their horizons. In the final analysis, it is an exercise in incarnating divinity, and so Christians should find it congenial to think of it as something intrinsically sacramental.

A very challenging view of material wealth emerges from the potlatch, when we take it as a sacramental rendering of the gods' intentions for human beings. The distribution of wealth reflects northwestern convictions that selfishness is the root of social evils. If the world is not to lapse into chaos, human beings have constantly to give away their wealth (give away their selves, symbolically). We have noted the concern in this cultural area for the moral aspects of creation. People were more interested in how to establish good relationships, just arrangements, than in how the world had originated or what its ontology (being) might be.

In some creation myths, the world had no order until the culture heroes (the beings responsible for human arrangements) began the process of distributing wealth. At the potlatch, participants reaffirmed not only the proper social hierarchy, with the chief at the top and commoners supporting the chief from below. They also reaffirmed the obligation of the chief, and all others, to stand free of their wealth and make it circulate for the common good.

Several further motifs make unavoidable the conclusion that in creating the potlatch native Americans of the northwest expressed a kind of genius—the ability to epitomize their entire existence in a sacramental ceremony (much as the Christian eucharist does for followers of Christ). The supernatural beings incarnated in the ceremony bring power and knowledge, but they also give themselves as the food for human beings. The supernatural beings usually are present in the form of animals, and when human beings eat an animal for survival, they take in the spiritual essence of the animal, which is a supernatural being. The paraphernalia of the potlatch—animal flesh and skins, large plaques (representing souls waiting to be reincarnated), and dishes (coffins for the animal's spirit)—symbolize the entire "economy" of relations among supernatural beings, humans, and animals. In the presence of the (willing) sacrifice of animals so that human beings might survive, it seems clear that human beings ought to be willing to sacrifice themselves (their wealth, their tendencies to rebel against proper social order) for the sake of one another (and to maintain cosmic order).

Themes of the Intermountain Region and California
Social life in the great basin took shape from the poverty of the material conditions. Because food was scarce (the desert areas were never lush), people had to form small, mobile bands. The essential social unit was merely the extended family. In good times this unit might join with one or two others, but a band of three extended families was a large group.

Consequently, organizational problems were few. People did not have to work out elaborate social codes, with careful rosters showing status and titles, because their numbers were so small that common sense dictated a politics of quick, informal ways of doing business. Relatedly, since resources were scarce, people tended not to sponsor extended occasions for ritual (long-playing festivals). For example, compared to the winter activities of the natives of the northwest coast, the ritual life of natives of the great basin was simple, even crude. In California and the plateau, however, material resources were more plentiful, so both social and ritual lives were more complex.

That is an interesting correlation: a sparse ecological situation tends to generate a small-scale social life and a spare ritual life. Confirmation comes from the fact that religious life in the basin was more individualistic than what obtained in California and the plateau. Shamans dominated religious life, and events crying out for celebration, such as girls' coming of age, tended to become family affairs, rather than large public gatherings. The largest festivals that occurred in the great basin were the harvest times, when several bands of Washo or Paiute would come together to celebrate a temporary sense of bounty. Tribes might also cooperate, in both hunting and ritual, on occasions such as tracking antelope, a seasonal venture.

Such cooperative activities seem to have generated the need to celebrate religiously on a larger scale. The simple fact of cooperation, focused on hunting, tended to expand a tribe's horizons. Having to consider what the coming together of several tribes implied, especially in conjunction with an especially dramatic demand on the animal world (for food and the satisfaction of the millennial need to kill), tended to pressure tribes into creating more profound, elaborate rationales for their activities—both their hunting, and their entire cycle of rituals.

On the plateau, winter was the time for ritual, and the highlight of the winter season was a series of "spirit-dances." This area sponsored spirit-quests, for both boys and girls, at the time of puberty. The goal was to secure a personal spiritual helper. Children were removed from the group, sent out to fast, bathe in cold streams, endure solitude, and in general afflict their bodies so as to prepare their spirits for revelations. This could be a kind of boot-camp or rite of passage. But the goal was not merely to survive. The goal was to offer the priming that the ascetical preparation created to the spirits, so that they might grant one a vision by which to direct one's life. The vision might come in a dream, and usually it was of an animal spirit who became one's guardian or helper. Typically the young person who received a vision encoded it in a distinctive song and/or dance. This song and/or dance became a personal signature. The winter festival offered the chance to express this personal signature and watch it blend into the overall self-expression composed by all the signatures of members of the group.

Some groups counseled the young person to forget the dramatic experience of consummating the spirit quest, hoping that it would go underground and return at the threshold of maturity (about age twenty-five), when new responsibilities came into play. Men could become sick about that time, apparently as a way of gaining a moratorium on ordinary activities, so that they might contemplate their responsibilities as adults. Shamans would help such sick people remember the vision they had received at the time of puberty, easing the way for the vision to take possession of the adult with full vigor (now that the person might understand more of its symbolism and implications). On the plateau the spirit dances frequent during the winter months allowed many people to update or reinvigorate the visions that had formed them since their youth.

The rituals that grew out of these concerns on the plateau were closely controlled. Among many groups, members of a society with the totem Bluebird served as police during ceremonial occasions, to keep good order. The idea was that the spirits invoked in native ceremonies were wild and needed to be both placated and reassured. Much that we said about the rituals of natives of the northwest coast applies to traditions in the intermountain region. Those participating in the rituals incarnated the gods, and it was important to distribute wealth to those looking on or participating on the margins, as a sign of both generosity and commitment to helping the spirits bring moral order into the cosmos.

In California secret societies or sodalities were well established (in the great basin and plateau they were rudimentary). California natives embraced at least four different ritual foci, each of which generated different ceremonies. These were not sealed hermetically from one another, but the fusion of social, economic, biological, and other aspects of human life with a given tribe's ritualistic focus was so strong that few native Americans risked losing their identity in a vague, pan-native movement with generalized ceremonies.

The Toloache portion of California culture was one of the four significant sub-foci of ritual life in that area. This ritual sub-set could sponsor the use of psychotropic drugs such as jimsonweed (*toloache* in Nahuatl), which was ingested to facilitate visions of animal helpers. Toloache tribes could also sponsor severely testing physical ordeals, and the artistic among them might become fascinated with painting, as a way to represent complex tribal lore in vivid symbols reminiscent of what they had seen under psychotropic influence. Toloache people formed special groups or guilds, focused on such projects as learning the drift of the heavenly bodies. The drugs approved for religious use tended to heighten the prestige of astrologers, who had ready explanations for what was going on in the tribe, based on supposedly inside knowledge of current social tensions and the other factors shaping how people tended to fashion their ideas about God. However, some Toloache groups stressed dreaming more than taking drugs.

Other California tribes focused their ritual lives on one or more of three other concerns. First, some tended to underscore anniversaries of death, and other occasions where cosmic birth and death could come into focus. Second, the *kuksu* cult developed in northern California focused on a culture hero impersonated by masked dancers. Other, contiguous areas had similar rituals named for other culture-heroes. Festivals provided occasions for larger gatherings than usual, and so also for special games, contests, banquets, and other ways of establishing social bonds. Third, numerous tribes held complex, extensive ceremonies thought to renew the world. In effect, these ceremonies rehearsed the entire mythology of the tribe, which was implied in how the world had arisen and was presently constituted. The world depended on the songs and dances, the rememberings and rededications, of the singers and dancers to keep it going, so their celebrations were immensely important.

The Self

We may gain some sense of how northwest coastal natives thought about the self by examining their ideas about shamanism, witchcraft, and ghosts. Shamans were important functionaries, whose main job was to cure disease. However, disease was considered a result of a malign or malfunctioning spirit, so shamanism involved a complex of relations with the world of the spirits. Shamans could inherit their office or acquire it through a vision. Generally, shamans came into their vocation involuntarily, receiving it as a task imposed upon them by fate or the gods. Their duty was to bear this fate generously, for the sake of their people. Being a shaman did not make one a chief, give one an impressive title (in the social hierarchy affirmed at potlatches), or bring one wealth. But it did carry prestige: one was a spiritual person, fighting a good fight for the sake of one's people.

Shamans tended to work their cures by going into trance and extracting the foreign substance (bit of bone, or stone, or the like) that had caused the disease. This foreign substance represented the body of the spirit who had caused the illness. The implements that shamans used and the movements they made during a curing ceremony represented their efforts to direct good spirits to cure the disease. The good spirits, guardians to the shaman, would fight the evil spirits responsible for the disease. The typical shamanic curing session was a theatrical performance, complete with singing, dancing, and even feats of illusion.

In a broader perspective, shamans were intermediaries between their people and the spiritual world. Most people thought shamans had special powers: to foresee the weather and the future, secure success in hunting or battle, restore souls stolen by witches, and above all cure sickness. They interacted with their retinue of helping spirits, both obeying and controlling them. To retain their powers, shamans had to stay in fighting trim: maintain their contacts with their spirits, follow a regimen of sexual and dietary control, keep their psyches able to travel into trance, sustain moral power—good reputation, good conscience.

Witches were evil shamans. Probably few actually existed, but any ill-fortune or fear could raise suspicions of witchcraft. Witches could function for enemy tribes, who were trying to weaken one's people so as eventually to defeat them. Or they could be kinspeople motivated by jealously or envy. Native American thought tended to personify natural events, as we have seen. Illness or bad luck was not simply a casual, accidental conjunction of impersonal forces. Someone had willed the bad event, and shamans existed to overcome such bad will. Witches could act from sheer evil, nothing being unthinkable to them, or they could act in the employ of an enemy, for base gain. People accused of witchcraft could be tortured, either to purify them of their evil or to test whether they were in fact witches (put them through an ordeal). Often none of this was conclusive, and occasionally people died simply because of prejudice or paranoia.

A Kwakiutl story about ghosts suggests how coastal Indians thought about the composition of the human being and the afterlife. A woman was crying for her dead father. For four days she cried at his grave. Now, ghosts live in four houses, each one deeper than the other. A voice called her to come down from the grave-site, into a house on the first level of the nether world. The voice belonged to a ghost, and when she had followed him into his house she found an old woman sitting by the fire. This woman bade her sit down and started to roast some salmon for her. Just as she was about to eat it, another ghost came and invited her to descend to a deeper house. The old woman told her to go along, because the deeper house was more prestigious. In the second house, a similar scene unfolded. An old woman bade her sit down and began to prepare a meal for her. Once again, just before she was to eat, she was invited to go to a deeper house, and so she went. A similar scene unfolded in the third house.

When she was about to enter the fourth (deepest) house, she saw her father sitting inside. He became angry with her and asked why she had come: nobody ever returned from the fourth level. The first three houses could be entered without a definitive commitment. So he advised that she eat nothing in the fourth house and go back, ascending to the earth. At his bidding, ghosts came to lead her back.

To those observing her at the grave-site, the woman had been lying (in mourning) as one dead. The story implies that her travels to the nether world had been in spirit, while her body lay inert on the surface. She came back to the surface on a board, with the ghosts singing a song, to alert the living that she was returning. But the living never saw her. So they took the board into their winterhouse, and they made the ghosts' song part of their tribal collection.[30]

The implication is that the Kwakiutl thought of the afterlife as a continuance of earthly life. Still, the negative reaction of the father to the daughter's arrival suggests that the afterlife was not a happy, desirable state. One who had the chance to continue to live above, on the earth, ought not to squander it. The father does not seem gratified that the daughter would pursue him. That does not seem to be a winning demonstration of love. So perhaps the Kwakiutl were also saying that grief has its limits. The girl stepped over them, identifying herself so deeply with her dead father that even though he ordered the ghosts to take her back, she was not returnable. Probably the story also has the aim of explaining the origin of mourning boards and a particular song (the myth specifies the song that the ghosts sang, to announce the return of the girl, which did not happen).

Themes of California and the Intermountain Region

A myth of the Diegueno of southern California describes the two phases of the cosmogony—the process by which the current world order was born. The first phase is described in a spare account of the creation of the present tripartite world: earth, water, heaven. In the beginning there was earth and water. Earth, a woman, lay under water, a man. By him she bore two sons. They wanted to escape their containment under the water, so they stood and pushed hard against the water, raising it over their heads. That is how they formed the sky. One of the sons was blind, but he worked alongside the other, sighted son. They worked to make the sun, the moon, and the stars. Then the question arose: Where should they put these creations? The blind brother threw the sun into the western portion of the sky, but it fell down. The same thing happened when he threw it up to the south and to the north. Only in the east would it stay, so the east has always been its home, where it starts out from.

The sighted brother complained that the sun made things too hot, so three times they rearranged its height, until it cast just the right amount of light and heat. They had the same problem when they positioned the moon, having to adjust it several times until they got the right amount of cold. They had made the sun and the moon from discs of clay. To make the stars, they scattered small bits of clay. Then they made human beings out of clay. Soon the human beings stirred and came to life. All of this happened at Mount Wikami, the site of creation.

In the beginning, then, things were rather simple. The basic stuff of the world was clay—earth moistened by water. Children of the union of earth and water did the shaping of the heavens. A second phase began, however, when human beings, looking for something to do, planned a ceremony. They built a large enclosure from brush and invited the great serpent who lived in the depths of the sea to attend. He arrived and wrapped himself inside the enclosure, but he was too big to fit. Still, once he had gotten as much of himself inside as he could, the people set fire to him. His body heated up and exploded. In it had been all knowledge, so all languages, rituals, magic secrets, and customs were scattered over the earth. People pick up different bits, and so they develop different cultures.

With human beings, the process of creation shifts from something natural or merely cosmic to something involving consciousness, knowledge, and so culture. The serpent is a common symbol for the dimension of culture, perhaps expressing the ambivalence that people feel about knowledge. Along with knowledge came awareness of death, differences, sexuality, and pain. The creatures not privy to the knowledge created by the explosion of the serpent do not have to worry about these things. Their world is still largely the simple world of earth, water, and a heaven populated by only the sun, the moon, and the stars.

Shamanic ecstasy, whether by dancing, the use of drugs, or dreaming, gave the self access to a wider world. So did the other practices that peoples of the basin, the plateau, or California used to heighten or purify consciousness. Certainly, the self was social, a member of the tribe, a male or female fitting into expected roles. But individuals varied considerably, and their variety produced diverse ways of dealing with natural forces, social roles, and even the spirits who drew near in religious ceremonies.

Both the *toloache* groups and those interested in mourning ceremonies underscored death. Death was both personal and cosmic. The universe was a living thing, and so subject to death and rebirth. Individuals were mortal, had relations with people who had died, experienced anticipations of death and rebirth in sleep, dreaming, the decline and return of physical powers. The tribe saw puberty rites and other celebrations of fertility as a way of confining death. Individuals would die, but the people could go on. Thus the native American self was not sexual as the modern western self has been. Men and women felt a greater impress from nature and the group. Their maleness and femaleness was the flowing through them of coordinated powers that kept the whole animal world going. This did not mean that their attractions were not personal rather than generic. It did not mean that native life had no romance. But it did mean that sexuality was not the private, titillating preserve that it has often become in modern cultures. People could be modest about their sexual interactions, but the power of fertility was more important than their individual daydreams or blushes.

Only rarely was anyone celibate, though people could abstain from sexual relations to increase their sense of power or purity. After menopause or the decline of male potency, the polarization of men and women lessened. They tended to draw closer together, as figures of wisdom. Their social roles loosened, so that they could interact more freely. The self became more androgynous, and more defined by the approach of death. Previously, in young adulthood, the self had been defined by vigor: female potency to conceive and give birth, male potency to impregnate, hunt, and fight. Aging therefore suggested variations in power. Wisdom was a power in its own right. Perhaps the world ran as much by wisdom, or guile, as by vigorous fertility. Perhaps the significance of the serpent was as much the coil of the life cycle as the slither of sexual attraction.

Ultimate Reality

The sense of ultimate reality that one finds among native tribes of the northwest is more diffuse than what we found among eastern and central plains groups, where *manitou* or *wakan* suggested a generalization of sacred power. In the northwest sacred power was diffused throughout a spiritual world, where the main actors were the spirits who could be incarnated during human ceremonies (and otherwise were associated with traditional activities such as hunting, fishing, and gathering). In addition many myths focused on "intermediate" figures, half-animal and half-human, who had brought principal features of native life or stood for the native sense of the powers that moved beyond human control or reckoning.

In closest approximation to naming deities, people spoke of a Chief of the Sky People, who fulfilled in the heavens the role that earthly chiefs fulfilled for their people, but little suggests that this Chief was a supreme deity who attracted much of the people's prayer. We also find references to an Old Woman living under the sea, an image that may stem from psychological associations between birth and water. The Sun and the Moon receive some notice and reverence, but not such that one should speak of worship of them.

Of greater interest were trickster figures such as Raven, who concretized the people's sense that cosmic order was slippery, fluid, canny—something best dealt with carefully, with detachment, attention, and humor. For example, one story of Raven tells how he stole the moon. Originally the moon belonged to an old fisherman, who lived alone with his daughter. The fisherman kept the bright, shining, beautiful moon in a box. Desiring the moon, Raven changed himself into a leaf growing on a bush on the path where the daughter would go to pick berries. Sure enough, she came to pick berries and he was able to fall off his bush and enter her body. There he grew like a child, and in time was born, a strange looking baby: dark complexion, long, hooked nose. When he began to crawl, he would go toward the box with the moon in it, knock on it, and cry, "moon, moon." Eventually his grandfather noticed this, asked the boy's mother about it, and suggested that they give him the moon to play with. The mother unpacked the box, which turned out to be a nest of boxes, one within another, in the center of which lay the moon. Unpacked, it spread a wonderful glow. The boy delighted in playing with this luminous ball.

After a while, however, he began to cry. Once again his grandfather, who was kind-hearted, intervened to get him what he desired. As his mother interpreted it, the boy wanted to see the stars in the dark sky. The grandfather therefore told her to open the smoke hole over the stove, so that the boy could see out. However, as soon as the roof opened, the boy became a raven and flew out of the house, carrying the moon. He went to the top of a mountain and then threw the moon up into the sky. That is why the stars are no longer alone and there is now light in the sky.[31]

This story shows the tricky quality of the forces that have determined how the world should be ordered. Raven did not create the heavens, with their stars and moon, by divine power. He maneuvered to get his way, robbing the fisherman of the moon. Perhaps the implication is that, as a black bird, he loved the idea of illumining the heavens, his habitat. The story suggests that supernatural powers can come into the human world, lodge in the center of human beings, and take up residence. The moon can seem like a bright ball—something that would attract a young child. But Raven manipulates this innocent association, becoming a child in order to achieve his own purposes. So it seems clear that human beings ought to be cautious when dealing with natural forces. They should realize that birds and animals follow different logical and moral codes than they do. It is fine to smile at Raven's trickery, but everyone knows that to imitate him would be to make social existence impossible. People have to be able to rely on one another. To put a tricky, unreliable force into the very design of creation is to suggest how inhuman, or more than human, are nature and the overall cosmic order.

Another story about Raven may have been told as much for entertainment as for instruction about the nature of the cosmos. Raven was wearing a red feather when he met the wife of a fisherman. She admired his feather, and asked how she could get one for her hair. Easily enough, he said. He would take her husband to hunt for robins on a nearby island. Going on ahead, Raven gathered old pieces of wood and changed them into robins. He then released the robins so that they flew deep into the woods and encouraged the fisherman to pursue them. With the woman's husband working in the woods of the island, Raven took the canoe and went back to where the couple lived. He changed himself so that he looked just like the husband.

Welcoming him back, the woman took no special note of his going to the fisherman's favorite pond and hauling out some of the finest fish. Raven, in the guise of the fisherman, then made himself a wonderful meal. When the fisherman returned, he was disgusted. The beautiful red feathers he had collected from the robins had changed back into old pieces of wood. He fell upon Raven, beat him senseless, and threw him into the water. A large fish swallowed the body of Raven, and inside the fish Raven revived. He tormented the fish so that it swam ashore, where some fishermen caught it, cut it up, and so freed Raven to jump out.[32]

Once again Raven is a trickster—an amoral being, bent on fun and the satisfaction of his appetites. He does not commit heinous crimes, but he does disturb human beings and have his way at their expense. Occasionally he may get his come-uppance, as when the fisherman beats him senseless, but usually he lands on his feet, too nimble to control once and for all. It is also apparent, from both myths, that Raven is a changeling. He transforms himself from a bird to a baby and then back to a bird; from his own shape, to that of the fisherman, back to his own shape (in the belly of the fish). This suggests that superhuman reality, the powers running the world for their own amusement, assume whatever shapes serve their purposes. The spiritual world is like the world of dreams, where one may find changes, juxtapositions, fusions of forms not found in nature. Birds can talk in dreams, they can take the shape of human beings, they can be swallowed by large fishes and regurgitated on land. The spiritual world is not confined to the rules, the logic, the order that obtains either in the natural world or in the world of rational human arrangement. It is in good part uncanny, its own master.

Themes of California and the Intermountain Region

Åke Hultkrantz, who has become the dean of western scholars specializing in native American religions, has discussed the thesis, common in the early years of the twentieth century, that California tribes exhibited a natural sense that creation had come from nothingness, and so that they demonstrated a primitive monotheism at the depths of traditional human culture. This thesis is associated with Wilhelm Schmidt, a pioneer in the history of religions, but it is discredited nowadays. Hultkrantz's precis of the theology of traditional California tribes shows why: "Some of the north-central California high gods are distinctly creator figures, and their creative process may furthermore be described as *creatio ex nihilo*. The high god of the Maidu is Ko'doyanpe ('the earth-namer'). After prolonged, intense thought he constructed the canoe in which he and his antagonist, the Coyote, floated about on the primeval sea at the beginning of time. Among the northern Pomo it is said of Dasan, a peculiar hybrid of high god and ancestral father, that he 'came out of the ocean and turned into a man. He intended to build the world. He talked, and by the power of his words, the world came into being. After this he made the first people.' This 'biblical' notion of cosmogony was certainly not very common. Some eastern Pomo Indians have even objected to the Christian doctrine, saying that it lacks common sense since its divinity created the world from nothing, whereas indigenous creators had materials from which to work."[33]

We have intimated that the natives of California and the intermountain region have tended to be less interested in cosmic origins than in "later," culturally conditioned questions about how the world has been organized. Still, the theology, in a strict sense, that emerges from a given people is always worth probing: What does this group make of ultimate reality, the really real, the holy? How does it imagine creation to have occurred, and what relations with the ultimate reality does it envision, in consequence of creation? Theology, in the strict sense, is the science, the probing, of God. It is intriguing that, although most western tribes did not worry much about theology, groups such as the Maidu and the Pomo did. Apparently, native Americans varied, from group to group, in their passion to pursue understanding of ultimate reality. Whether we get this impression simply because the early investigators happened to interview an intense member of the Maidu and a lackadaisical member of another tribe is hard to determine. In principle, it seems clear that to speak about a tribal, generic understanding of divinity one ought to have interviewed a representative sample of the tribe in question, if not a majority. Be that as it may, it seems that some native Americans did try to imagine how the ultimate, the highest deity, lived.

For example, the Maidu conceived of ultimate reality, the creative deity, as engaged in intense thought. To their mind, the world owed its origin and shape to a primeval, divine mind. No doubt, they admitted that the divinity of this mind made it quite different from human minds. On the other hand, the Maidu, as virtually all other peoples who have had the wit to speculate about ultimate reality, have thought that divinity was both like and unlike humanity. Technically, the best name for this likeness-yet-difference is "analogy." Between divinity and humanity there is an analogy, a proportionality, such that human beings may be images of divinity without losing their created character and being absorbed into divinity. In fact, the closer they come to God, the more they affirm their individuality.

Thus the "thought" of the Maidu high god is instructive. In making the world through thought, he allows human beings (who can also think) to expect that they will be able to understand the world, at least enough to survive. Still, this Maidu god goes about the work of creation accompanied by Coyote, who seems bound to introduce imperfection and humor into the origins of the world. The image of the Earth-namer and Coyote floating about on the primeval sea at the beginning of time is rich beyond explication. To an outsider it is something worth contemplating for years, because it says that the two orders, nature and culture, were implied from the beginning. The divinity thinks the world into being. Coyote acts irrationally, subject to the desires of his great will. The suggestion is therefore that natural creation proceeded serenely. The divinity had only to think ("throw") the stars into place and there they were.

We know instinctively that Coyote is going to complicate things. All the stories that the different tribes tell about him suggest that he was the trickster par excellence in their mythological worlds. Coyote, the "little wolf," is a marvelous symbol of the cunning of animal nature, now come into the midst of a new level of beings, the humans, to offer help but also to work mischief. Trickster is not fully rational. That is both his appeal and what makes him dangerous. For him to be riding in the canoe with the first cause, at the beginning of creation, is to suggest that the order of creation as we now know it is greatly influenced by guile. The world is not a machine. Neither is it wholly irrational, only a field of mindless wills. For most native Americans, the world is the work of the gods, beautiful yet vulnerable to corruption.

Many other tribes in the basin, the plateau, or California had vaguer ideas about divinity. For the majority of them, divinity, the sacred, was a diffuse field. Spiritual beings operated in every significant aspect of the world. Whenever human beings found something meaningful, one could speak of "spiritual" forces. Sickness was a dramatic instance of spiritual force, one requiring direct contact with invisible powers. Less dramatic instances dotted the landscape, ambled through everyday experience. The beauty of the physical world bespoke the presence of spiritual beings. The exaltations and depressions of the average person proved (to the native mind) that relations with relevant spiritual beings were going well or badly. Much of what we experience as "divinity" native Americans therefore experienced as "spirits." Much that we gather into a single focus and attribute to God was dispersed among a variety of spiritual beings.

Why did native Americans show little passion to unify their religious experience by referring everything to a single God? Why did they not follow the seers of India who produced the Upanishads? The answer has to be speculative, but one reason may have been the satisfaction that native Americans found in particulars. If people are content with their sense of the world, they don't have to reject the significance of separate experiences of sacredness or supernatural power. They don't need to fuse all such experiences into a single testimony to a single God.

Spirituality

We may gather momentum for our analysis of spirituality in the far west by reflecting on two groups of ceremonies. The first is the *kuksu* dances that were important in northern California. The second is the world renewal ceremonies that flourished in northwestern California.

The *kuksu* dances were the province of secret societies and had their strongest influence at puberty. Some tribes limited them to males, but others admitted females. In addition to the bonding that participation created among the initiates, the main benefit was a chance to contemplate (indeed, to return to) the primary condition of the world—its original state, as the myths described it. *Kuksu* was the creator or hero whose exploits concretized the original condition. Under the names *Hesi* and *Adi,* a similar figure dominated the dances of tribes in other parts of California (Sierra foothills, Sacramento Valley). As they danced out the stories about *kuksu,* young men and women experienced how the world had been originally, and so, to some extent, would be today, if people saw correctly. In an ideal initiation ceremony, people coming of age experienced visions, emotions, that never left them thereafter. They could renew their experience by dancing again, but usually the first experience remained a template.

The world renewal cult, which also flourished in northern California, had ties to the *kuksu* dances. Both aimed at engaging participants with the deepest structures of creation. But the world renewal ceremonies tended to extend for as long as ten days, and the main effort they expressed was to make sure that human failings did not cause the cosmos to fall out of balance so badly that it crashed. Rituals such as the jump dance and the deerskin dance helped to reset the balance

Native American Indians led a simple and dignified life.

that seemed to be wobbling. The implication was that human beings were the odd species out. They alone could act against their given nature or place in the cosmos. So it was important for them to repair on a regular basis the damage that they had done to the world.

These ceremonies, and analogous ones that we could note from the basin or the plateau, sometimes were tied to annual events like the run of the salmon or the new year festival. Often they entailed a rehearsal of the tribe's traditions: where the dances had come from, how they had been handed down. But the most important aspect of the ceremonies was the chance to interact with the structures, the spiritual powers, of the cosmos, which gave human beings their sense of order and significance.

What is most impressive about the spirituality of the native peoples of the northwest is their ability to develop myths and rituals that expressed the complexity, tensions, and interrelatedness of the forces governing human existence. All of daily life entailed an interaction with spiritual forces, and there was constantly the need to help the universe stay on the side of morality (solid sense) and avoid slipping away into chaos. Generally, northwestern tribes divided the year into two portions. During the summer they worked hard and were active outdoors. Throughout this season, their activities were sacramental— full of spiritual implications—but not deliberately, focusedly, ceremonially so. The winter months were the time for deliberate, focused, ceremonial concentration on the meaning, the spiritual implications, of human existence. Indeed, the main activity of the winter months, when the people lived indoors, was celebrating ceremonies that both recalled the given tribe's convictions about the structure of the cosmos and gave the forces running the cosmos occasions to operate dramatically (and so make clear to all members of the tribe what such forces were always doing).

Many of such ceremonies fell under the jurisdiction of dance societies. These groups tended to be secret, performing most of their dances only for their own members. In effect, such private ceremonies constituted an ongoing process of initiation. Like African and Australian societies that led their members deeper and deeper into the mysteries of human existence and the cosmos, preparing them for the ultimate revelation to occur at death, these northwestern groups played more and more intricate variations on the themes of how the spiritual forces ran the world, what human beings had to do in response, where wisdom lay, and how death and life ran together, intermingled, and separated throughout the life cycle. For four or five months each winter, the bulk of the day's energy went into ceremonial rehearsals of the tribe's views of reality and how to live, most of them conducted under the auspices of the closed, private dance societies. Such ceremonies tended to grow more and more elaborate, as generation after generation both preserved them and added to the traditions. Often they became highly elaborate performances, especially those ceremonies that were not private but were enacted for the general public.

The Hamatsa and Myth

A main theme throughout northwestern ceremonial was how the spiritual forces want to feed on human beings and yet also sustain and nourish human beings. The Kwakiutl winter ceremony called the Hamatsa dance is often considered the quintessential northwestern ritual. The myth that it ritualized dealt with the *hamatsa*, a human being who had been carried off by the spiritual beings. These beings preyed on the flesh of human beings. (The explicit sense was that this was a physical devouring of human substance, but the implicit sense was that the divinities depended on human awareness and celebration for their continued existence.) The *hamatsa* learned the ways, the rituals, of the supernatural beings while in captivity, and he took on many of their attributes. When he escaped, he brought back to human beings the rituals of the gods, but also their frenzy. As though his old human forms were too small or weak to contain his newly found, divine energy, he would go beserk on ceremonial occasions and require a dozen ordinary human beings to contain him. The symbolism is clear: there is an immense power afoot in the world, and it is more than what human beings can control, unless they cooperate and bend might and main. This power is at one and the same time necessary for human existence (it is the power that keeps the world going, the power of vitality and destruction alike, in their symbiosis) and a threat to annihilate human existence. To deal with the supernatural beings is to play with fire. One needs it for warmth and light, but it can blaze forth destructively.

The *hamatsa* is dangerous not only because he has supernatural power, but also because he has become saturated with the bloodlust of the supernatural beings. They live off death. They live to kill and kill for a living. Probably the imagery here is an expression of the intrinsic mortality of human existence—indeed, of all created existence. The powers that bring the world into being and sustain it are inextricable from the powers that destroy all creatures. Being and non-being, life and death, are twins, the quintessential dualism of the world that human beings know. One can spread their play, their effects, through a variety of divine actions (all the forces of nature, all the influences—sex, hunger, play, war, etc.—that shape existence and tend to become personified or mythologized), but they remain at the center. The *hamatsa* dance goes to the core of native concepts of the divine flux of power and rivets attention onto what is most interesting to a human audience: how human vitality arises, perishes, and is threatened each day.

The central winter ceremonies had features of the potlatch because they used food to focus the play, the warfare, of the forces that they were dramatizing. The bloodlust of the spiritual beings expressed itself in feeding. Relatedly, in the ecology of creation that the tribes of the northwest favored, the spiritual beings themselves were fed upon, inasmuch as they were the inmost identity of the animals and plants on which human beings depended. Existence itself therefore became an economy of taking life and giving it back. Food, eating, became the principal symbol of this economy. It was the action that accomplished the physical transfer of animal, and so spiritual, power to human beings. The feeding on human beings was less physical. The spiritual beings nourished themselves on human substance at death, but also through all the expenditures of energy that human beings laid out in their rituals. When human beings danced the traditional myths and took on the personas of specific spiritual beings, they "fed" those beings. The beings gained a larger reality, for the duration of the ceremony, and one could think of this increase in being or sustenance as a feeding.

When people express themselves symbolically, through myths and rituals that seek to engage the whole personality, imagination and feelings as much as intellect, in their vision or truth, they tend to make associations in every direction. Metaphor becomes a cast of mind, and metaphors extend themselves, ramify, reticulate so as to cover the entire "ecology" of creation. Thus eating becomes a many-leveled, many-sided metaphor, with extensions to the left and the right, above and below, like a cog in a machine built of tinker-toy parts or legos. For instance, eating regularly overlaps with, enters into the system of, metaphors connected with sex. Sex is both the differentiation of male and female and their fusion. Sex is not only physical but mental, emotional, spiritual. People make human life through sex, and they nourish human life, continue their procreation, through feeding. So there is something sexual about eating, and there may be something nourishing, consuming or devouring about sex. Lovers want to "eat one another up." The end of sexual intercourse is a satiety like that at the end of a full meal. Back and forth the experiences travel, pollinating each field of action and fantasy with images of the other.

For the native mind, such a cross-pollination is natural and requires no quick constraining. Human metaphors, embodied in song and dance, elaborated in rituals, will never match the complexity or richness of cosmic reality itself. Always the mental world that human beings fashion is running to catch up. In fact, it is an oversimplification to separate the mental world from the physical world of cosmic reality. In fact, the two reach into one another, the mental energy of human beings giving them access to the cosmos and bringing it alive, the cosmic world sustaining the mental world, providing its fundament, food, and ballast. The spirituality of native Americans of the northwest sought valiantly to honor this wonderful interrelation of the physical and the spiritual, the human and the non-human, the more-than-human, the uncanny and mysterious and sacred.

Chapter 7

TRADITIONS OF MESOAMERICA

Background

The area that most scholars have in mind when they speak of Mesoamerican religions extends "roughly from the Panuco River in Mexico to parts of Honduras and Costa Rica, and includes all of Guatemala, Belize, and El Salvador. Some fourteen language families have been isolated in the area with upward of twenty-five different Maya languages currently spoken. A number of cultural groups, most of them still poorly understood, had long been established in Meso-america by the time of the Spanish conquest in the sixteenth century. Among the most important were the Zapotecs in the eastern part of the Mexican state of Oaxaca and the Mixtecs in the west; the Tarascans in Michoacan; the Huaxtecs and Totonacs in northern Veracruz, various Maya groups in the Yucatan Peninsula and in the highlands of Guatemala; the Otomi to the north of the Valley of Mexico; and the Nahuatl speakers around the lakes of the valley and in Tlaxcala."[34]

Human beings were probably present in Mesoamerica as early as 27,000 years ago (about 25,000 B.C.). Their way of life was the hunting and gathering that is the familiar, staple economy one finds among paleolithic peoples the world over. Remains of artwork left on rocks, dating to perhaps 10,000 B.C., suggest that the earliest Meso-americans had religious concerns. At the least, it seems that they engaged in imagining the animals, fish, and plants on which they depended as the focus for propitiating the forces running their world. Whether we should call this art "sympathetic magic," and assume that it arose in the context of rituals designed to assure fertility and prosperity, is debatable. The artwork found in paleolithic caves in France and Spain has generated considerable discussion of such possible rituals. Arguing from what we know about hunters and gatherers of historical times, many scholars have postulated such rituals. At any rate, we can suspect that as soon as human beings appeared in the new world, they put their rational consciousness to work trying to figure out how to survive, and that this effort involved imagining the powers that they assumed ran the environment in which they found themselves and trying to draw those powers to their side.

Around 6000 B.C. the Mesoamerican hunters and gatherers began to shift from a nomadic social organization to at least semipermanent villages. This went in tandem with their growing mastery of agriculture. One digest of the progress of Mesoamerican culture from datable beginnings around 8000 B.C. to 1000 B.C. runs as follows: "The epic of Mesoamerican culture played out its course across a terrain that ranged from towering ice-clad volcanoes to steaming tropical jungles. It began well before 8000 B.C., when the cool, moist landscape of the lofty Mexican Plateau became home to small bands of ice age hunters in search of mammoths and other large game. By about 6000 B.C. a warmer, drier climate had transformed the land and its bounty. And for the next 4,000 years people in Mesoamerica progressed gradually from hunting and gathering to true agriculture.

"Seeds, pollen, and corncobs preserved in the dry caves of central and northern Mesoamerica reveal this evolution to have been a complex process of accident and experiment. The principal crops of the land—maize, beans, and squash—probably were domesticated simultaneously in several regions.

"Between 2000 and 1000 B.C. Mesoamerica became a farmer's world. Rustic hamlets of small thatched houses dotted the landscape wherever the magic trio of crops would grow. These communities provided the setting for Mesoamerica's earliest pottery, soon to become a minor art form with an astonishing variety of shapes and decoration. Solid clay figurines—usually of naked females—have been found through Mesoamerica in living sites and refuse piles. These figurines may have served as household fertility fetishes, tangible evidence of early religious customs."[35]

The Olmecs

Around 1200 B.C. the Olmecs, the first dominant people, produced a significant culture centered just south of the Gulf coast (about 94–95 degrees west, by 18 degrees north) at sites in Tobasco such as San Lorenzo, La Venta, Laguna de los Cerros, and Tres Zapotes. We shall deal with the Olmecs in some detail, but for preliminary background we can note now some of the basic characteristics of their

The principal crops of this land were maize, beans, and squash.

culture: "At ceremonial centers like San Lorenzo and La Venta, large artificial platforms and mounds were sometimes arranged around open plazas. These and other constructions suggest a society in which massive amounts of labor were directed by an elite few. The Olmecs practiced bloodletting and human sacrifice and probably played a ritual ball game as well. As a metaphor for cosmic motion, this game would become a hallmark of Mesoamerican civilization [and the remote ancester of present-day lacrosse]. Olmec art emerged in both monumental and portable sculpture that depicted revered rulers and at least ten major gods. Its influence probably spread rapidly and soon the pervasive motifs of what seem to be snarling jaguar deities and depictions of battle and sacrifice appeared throughout southern Mesoamerica. Olmec-related reliefs, carved at Monte Alban in Oaxcaca about 600 B.C., include short hieroglyphic texts that reflect the earliest known use of the Mesoamerican calendar and a limited system of writing. About 200 years later Olmec culture died out as mysteriously as it had begun. But by then it had set the basic pattern for virtually all the civilizations that would rise and fall in Mesoamerica over the next 2,000 years."[36]

The archeological remains of sites such as La Venta provide much of the basis for scholarly reconstruction of the earliest (Olmec) phase of Mesoamerican religious culture. La Venta featured pyramids plastered with mud, earthen mounds in circular or semi-cylindrical shapes, altars, tombs, and stelae carved of stone, and many stone sculptures. When archeologists compare it with later, larger Mesoamerican cultural sites, they find it to be what we might call a primitive miniature of later conceptions. The interesting aspect of La Venta, then, is that it suggests much of what was to follow. Either the traditions that it expressed had roots deep in earlier Mesoamerican psychology, or later eras tended to be quite conservative, clinging to the first patterns that gave form to native Mesoamerican genius.

One hypothesis is that the Olmecs used centers such as La Venta to express the quite new culture—social forms, sense of the natural world, religious images—that came with the shift from hunting and gathering to agriculture. The more settled life that agriculture allowed prompted people to specialize in arts and crafts, trade, government, defense, and (probably) religious ritual. It appears that the pantheon expanded, and (arguing from later theocratic patterns) it is likely that those who mastered the new theology were the leaders of Olmec society.

We deal with the Olmec gods, the religious calendar, and other aspects of this main stratum of pre-classical Mesoamerican culture in

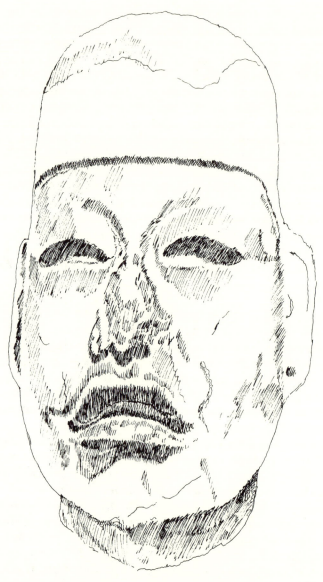

Olmec art emerged in both monumental and portable sculpture that depicted revered rulers and at least ten major gods.

later sections. Here we should mention that sites important during the classical period, such as Monte Alban (a center of Zapotec culture) and some Mayan sites, arose during the pre-classical period, and so were contemporaneous with the dominance of Olmec culture. In other words, we have to remember that the phases into which we have broken Mesoamerican religious history are fluid, one running into the next.

The early history of Monte Alban (to the southwest of the state of Tobasco, in Oaxaca) suggests that between 200 B.C. and 100 A.D. about 10,000 people resided there. They constructed large walls, apparently for defense, and they made their tombs of brick. Numerous stone monuments carved with themes from the calendar and military life suggest that the heavens and warfare were primary interests. There are remnants of hieroglyphic writings and vessels that seem to be decorated with effigies of various gods. Distinctive are nude figurines in distorted poses, apparently associated with rituals for sacrifice. One theory is that they represented people captured in war who may have been put to death to nourish the Olmec gods. (These themes reappear many centuries later in Aztec culture.)

As the Zapotecs prospered, they apparently supported full-time priests and expanded their population significantly. Their pantheon also expanded. They stratified their society into distinct social classes, and they exercised great influence (through trade and warfare) outside their own area. Their architecture increased symbols of astronomical phenomena, and their temples included inner chambers, probably reserved for those who dominated the cult. By the time of the classical period, Monte Alban had become covered with sculptures. Its plazas expanded, probably to accommodate an increased population (sometimes estimated at 30,000), and in addition to a professional priesthood it seems to have created a high priest, to control its ceremonial life.

The Classical Era: Teotihuacan

We have surveyed aspects of the Olmec culture that most scholars consider the best representative of the genetic basis of Mesoamerican religion. Next we must deal with Teotihuacan, the city in the Valley of Mexico that represents a, if not the, peak of classical Mesoamerican religious developments. We must also deal with the Mayan religion that flourished in the Yucatan peninsula. Although the usual dates for the classical period as a whole are about 300–900 A.D., some scholars locate the beginnings of classical achievements in the Valley of Mexico around 150 B.C.

Teotihuacan declined, somewhat mysteriously, around 750 A.D. Nonetheless, for about nine hundred years it was a major center of Mesoamerican culture, so virtually all treatments of the classical period give it pride of place. Mayan religion, the other great achievement that scholars applaud, covers the period of 300–900 A.D., virtually defining the classical period in the Yucatan peninsula. Descendants of both cultural traditions, that of Teotihuacan and that of the Maya, live in Mesoamerica to the present day. While their culture has assimilated many Christian themes, enough of the pre-Christian ways of thinking remain to suggest how powerful a hold they have had on native Mesoamericans.

The classical period was the time when Mesoamerican cultures expanded creatively in art, government, and religious ideas. Culture became focused on cities, even though the economic base continued to be agricultural. A pattern of regular trade developed, and this led to clearly defined trade routes. Along with the exchange of goods that trade involved came exchange of ideas. Because people were traveling and interacting, the influence of a cultural center such as Teotihuacan spread far beyond its own borders. The basic sources for information about the classical religious culture of the Valley of Mexico are archeological. In the absence of written documents, scholars have to reconstruct daily life, and religious belief, in Teotihuacan from the remains of buildings, murals, statues, and other expressions of belief and style.

Many scholars also use later, Aztec documents to formulate hypotheses about earlier cultures such as that of Teotihuacan. In many cases, studies comparing the artworks of the Aztecs with those of earlier people suggest considerable continuity. The scholarly consensus seems to be that ancient Mesoamerica constituted a unified, though perhaps not uniform, cultural area. Unlike an area such as the Mediterranean in its classical period, classical Mesoamerica was not a zone in which quite diverse cultural traditions contributed and competed. The differences among the different peoples were relatively slight. From the Olmec, through the Teotihuacanos and the Maya, to the Toltecs and Aztecs, basic themes and symbols probably remained quite constant.

Among such basic themes and symbols were the convictions that the forces of nature are personal and alive, that it was crucial to measure time and orient human existence by the movements of the heavenly bodies (thus the concern with the sacred calendar), that ritual ceremonies were the staff of cultural life, that such ceremonies ought to be adorned with beautiful, meaningful art and physical settings, and that tradition (oral, mythological), acted out in religious ceremonies, was the guarantor of the people's identity.

What we know of classical Mayan religion, from hieroglyphs on monuments at ceremonial sites, does not contradict such Mexican themes, but it seems to suggest a deeper immersion in the mysteries of time. The Maya apparently associated the passage of time with the unfolding of fates set by the heavenly forces. They seem to have thought that the more accurately they could determine the passage of time, the better they would be able to deal with their fate—know it, and respond to it. Thus, associated with astronomical observation came prophecy: what would probably unfold.

Mayan remains reveal more than an obsession with the religious calendar, however. Some of the inscriptions from the classical period apparently identify actual Mayan rulers. Indeed, the Maya seem to have composed dynastic histories, of a sort, to record the flow of time through the rule of the family dominant around a particular site. This interest probably dovetailed with a veneration of ancestors, and perhaps also with a divinization of deceased rulers. That would imply that in contemplating time, the Maya were interested in the past as well as the future. Remains such as the tomb of the ruler Pacal (603–683 A.D.) at the Temple of Inscriptions at the Mayan site of Palenque support this reasoning.

Studying classical Mexican religion, as represented by Teotihuacan and the Maya, we find that religion seems to have permeated all aspects of daily life. Each significant human activity had its patron deity, creating an enormous pantheon (and suggesting the infinity of the divine). At Teotihuacan the people expended great energy and care on temple sites, decorating platforms, many of them pyramids, with numerous temples in different colors. It appears that for Mesoamericans each temple was an axis for the entire world—everything cosmic ran through the temple, and the temple gave the world coherence. What went on below, in the temple and the earthly realm it centered, was a minature of what went on in the cosmos as a whole, directed by the heavens above. How the classical Mesoamericans reconciled the many different temple sites, each considered by those who used it the center of the world, is not clear. Perhaps they grew sophisticated enough, as they traveled and observed, to imagine that the cosmos could be "centered" from numerous different locales.

Finally, it seems clear that government in classical Mesoamerica was a sacred, ritualistic business. Political leaders were as much priests as heads of civic realms. This fusion of the sacred and the secular (as modern western thought might distinguish things) is characteristic of pre-modern peoples. In classical Mesoamerica, the notion that anything significant could stand apart from the influence of ultimate reality, the gods and heavenly forces, would have been rejected out of hand.

The Post-Classical Era and Recent Times

Moving to what some scholars call the post-classical era from about 900 to 1519 A.D., the main interest becomes the Aztec empire, which rose after the mysterious demise of Teotihuacan and the Maya. Certainly the influence of Teotihuacan and Mayan cultural centers remained, but the Toltecs and Aztecs, who dominated after the decline of Teotihuacan and the Maya, introduced a new militarism. Aztec rituals took themes of prior Mesoamerican cult, such as sacrifice and concern with death, to new extremes. Because the Aztecs were the most prominent Mesoamericans whom the invading Europeans encountered, their cult made the greatest impression on sixteenth century Europe. Indeed, it became the archetype of Mesoamerican religion in western eyes, only receding into proper focus in the twentieth century, when archeologists and historians established a more accurate account of Mesoamerican cultural developments.

The Toltecs, who came into power in central Mexico after the fall of Teotihuacan and dominated that area from about 900 to 1200, moved within the general cultural orbit established by the Teotihuacanos (who, we saw, interacted with the Maya). Quetzalcoatl, the feathered serpent, figures prominently in Toltec religious symbolism, and then passes on to the Aztec. Often he is a rattlesnake covered with feathers. From their capital city Tollan (or Tula), north of the basin of central Mexico, the Toltecs established a dynasty in which the human ruler was associated closely enough with the feathered serpent to suggest that he was divine. Apparently this apotheosis of the human ruler of the Toltecs, who was their high priest, shaped the Aztec custom of considering the head of the priesthood the representative of Quetzalcoatl.

The best known Toltec high priest, Topiltzin, added Quetzalcoatl to his name. He is credited (if the word applies) with introducing self-sacrifice into the cult. Lower Toltec priests would immolate themselves. Eventually Topiltzin believed that he was being persecuted by other gods, so he led his followers out of Tollan, to the Gulf coast. There he died, was cremated, and, according to his followers, became the Morning Star. Later dynasties looked back to him for their legitimation. Rulers of the Aztec capital Mexico-Tenochtitlan considered him their ancestor and expected that he would return one day, to reclaim his throne. Clearly, then, the mythology of Quetzalcoatl was a political as well as a ritualistic power in post-classical Mesoamerica. Clearly, one could not separate politics and ritual mythology.

Since the Spanish conquest, Mesoamerican traditions have had to contend with Christian influences. The results have been varied, to say the least. In some cases Christianity has made little profound impact. In most cases the official, apparent religion has been Catholic Christianity, but under the surface pre-Christian elements have remained strong. The more educated that people have been, by western standards, the more likely they have been to consider themselves Christians *simpliciter:* with little need to make distinctions. Inasmuch as wealthy people, or people in the professions, have been most able to offer their children higher education, Christianity (and then secularization) has been strongest among such people.

Peasants have usually considered themselves to be Christians, but their faith (sometimes called "folk" or "popular" religion) has usually mingled Christian beliefs with pre-Christian attitudes. Some Indian tribes, usually those living in remote areas, have kept their native cultures relatively intact, but they have become a smaller and smaller minority. Until very recently, when native American traditions became more respectable, there was considerable pressure to consider native ways backward, primitive, pagan. Thus, when one speaks about the general shape of Mesoamerican religious history during the past four and three-quarters centuries, one tends to stress how Christian ways came to sit atop pre-Christian rituals, beliefs, and instincts.

Guadalupe

Perhaps the simplest way to make this thesis concrete is to take one example, devotion to the Virgin of Guadalupe. In 1531, tradition has it, Mary, the Mother of Christ, appeared in the form of an Indian maiden. This was only twelve years after the conquest by Cortes. She appeared speaking Nahuatl, and the site of her visitation was a hill (Tepeyac, in what is now northeastern Mexico City) consecrated to the Aztec goddess Tonantzin. Tonantzin was the mother of the leading god Huitzilopochtli. She was also one of the main manifestations of the Aztec earth goddess. Aztec myths made her a virgin, despite her motherhood.

As they developed their response to this apparition, the first natives who came to revere the shrine at Guadalupe tended to call the Virgin Tonantzin but to accord her the attributes of the Virgin Mary. In name she was native, Nahuatl, Aztec. In personality she was Chris-

Even when Mesoamericans accepted the Christian faith, they found ways to make it their own. The Virgin of Guadalupe is an example of this.

tian. Still, the Virgin of Guadalupe now looks fully Indian. She is beautiful, dark-haired, and gracious. Her functions include protecting people (her children) from suffering, helping them with their everyday problems, and caring for their health (or curing them when they become ill). In most ways, she fits the stereotype of the Mother Goddess, native American, Asian and Near Eastern alike, but her fertility is more spiritual than physical (as her virginity suggests).

People are supposed to offer the Virgin of Guadalupe homage by praying to her regularly and visiting her shrine. In the measure that their prayers have been answered, they have an obligation to offer her flowers, candles, and other gifts, to adorn her shrines (she is represented in most churches, not just at Guadalupe). Ideally, they will also make a pilgrimage to Guadalupe, and they will amend their lives, dedicating themselves to Christian ethical norms. All of this is quite Christian. Beneath the surface, however, remain aspects of the original Aztec goddess Tonantzin. For example, in the folk strata of this devotion, if people fail to honor the Virgin properly, or if their morals slacken, they can expect her to punish them. The old Tonantzin, like the other Aztec deities, took vengeance on those who did not honor her properly. She would visit sickness or misfortune upon them, in punishment. Indeed, she might even bring about their death. Some of these characteristics have remained in the Indian conception of the Virgin of Guadalupe, however much they are at war with orthodox Catholic mariology.

Many scholars consider devotion to the Virgin of Guadalupe (sometimes called "Guadalupinism") a fine example of how native Mesoamericans strove to keep their distance from their Spanish conquerors. Even when they accepted Christian faith (whether willingly or under duress), they found ways to make it their own, not simply the faith of those who had overpowered them. Matters became more complicated as the two peoples intermarried, but the peasant strata of the population were resolute in developing religious ways that they could consider their own—native, not foreign. The myths and rituals associated with Guadalupe therefore became an important vehicle for native self-understanding. That the Virgin had appeared in native, familiar form, rather than as a European (or biblical) figure, said that God cared for native Mesoamericans on their own terms.

Nature

One way to begin to imagine the sense of nature that pre-classical Mesoamericans enjoyed is to contemplate the Olmec calendar. It seems likely that the astronomical observances on which the Olmec calendar (in which an interesting characteristic of all later Central American cultures crystallized) was based began by 1000 B.C. Monuments at La Venta picture human beings emerging from the cave of a dragon (the mouth of a significant god). The symbolic message seems to be that human beings have been born into a world of temporal rhythms—periods that must be sacred. Related to this apparent reference to time is symbolism that suggests space: patterns of fours (the basic directions, the corners of the earth) and fives (the corners plus a center). Some scholars also find spatial significance in stylized pictures of maize. Early on, then, the basic coordinates of human existence—space and time—appear as worthy of artistic, and so probably religious, contemplation.

A calendar is more important to agricultural peoples than to hunting peoples, because agricultural peoples want to know times for planting and harvesting, while hunting peoples can live more reactively, following the movements of the game. Certainly, hunting peoples delight in anticipating the movements of the game, or the annual run of the salmon, but anticipating nature's shifts is not so precise a factor in their economy. What makes the calendar of more than pragmatic interest, however, is the connection of time with heavenly—solar, lunar, and astral—deities. People realize that the circuits of the sun, the moon, and the stars are the basic determinants of the periods marking off their lives: day to night, full moon to fingernail moon, the annual coming of winter and summer. They are already primed to think that natural forces are the expressions of the ultimate reality on which their world depends, so they study the movements of the heavenly bodies with a religious passion: perhaps they can learn something intimate about the sacred powers that hold their fate.

The more that they reflect on time, the more mysterious it becomes. The sun does not seem to age, but clearly human beings do. The moon goes through regular phases, like women, but it does not age, as women do. So the movement of the heavenly bodies becomes a symbol of immortality, perhaps even of eternal fixity. What is mortal and transient can compare itself to what seems immortal and fixed and lament its fate. It can wonder whether learning about the immortal and fixed will bring it into the (blessed) estate of not having to die and change. Knowledge, after all, is a kind of participation in the being of what is known (one does not have to have an articulate metaphysics of knowledge to intuit this. Men come to participate in the being of women by knowing them, mentally and physically, as women come to participate in the being of men. Shamans can "become" birds or jaguars, through their contemplations.) So native Mesoamericans who studied the sun, the moon, and the stars could find themselves apparently drawn out of human being, into the wonderful, impersonal, divine kind of being that those serene phenomena seemed to exhibit.

Moreover, the manifest effect of the sun—light and heat—on the crops on which people depended could stand for a whole range of influences, most of them unseen, that people preoccupied with the heavenly bodies could suspect determined their lives. That is the point at which astronomy merges with astrology. Granted the tendency of all pre-modern peoples to personify natural forces, it makes sense that so many, the Olmecs apparently among them, began to attribute people's destinies to the time of their birth, the star under which they were born. If this belief became strong, a culture could support a corps of professional astrologers charged with determining heavenly influences. It could pitch civic events, key ceremonies such as the installation of a new king, to times thought (by whatever criteria it had developed to evaluate occasions when stars aligned themselves or came into seeming opposition) to be propitious, and to forbid such events at supposedly unpropitious times. It could correlate people's names (always a key suggestion of a person's fate and inmost identity [and so significance] in pre-modern societies) with the heavenly signs under which they were born. And all of this could serve as a powerful channeling of a religious intuition and hope that something larger than human power (so obviously limited) was running the universe (and thereby providing ultimate meaning and order).

The Symbolism of Teotihuacan

We may gain some sense of the view of nature that prevailed in classical Mesoamerican religion by studying aspects of the construction of Teotihuacan. For example, when the population of this center had swollen, perhaps to as many as 80,000, around 125 A.D., the people erected the impressive Pyramid of the Sun, which stood more than 63 meters high and measured 225 meters on each of its four sides. Following this, they erected a Pyramid of the Moon, and a thoroughfare linking them, the Avenue of the Dead. (These names come from the Aztecs.)

After this, more sacred sites arose, many of them adjacent to the Avenue of the Dead. In addition, the Teotihuacanos painted numerous splendid murals. The sun and the moon were the major divinities honored along the Avenue of the Dead. However, other gods were represented, including the plumed serpent (whom we discuss in detail later). Altars, a house for priests, murals of pumas, plazas, a temple for agriculture, an administrative center, and small temples suggest the variety of interests and activities focused on the Avenue.

Under the Pyramid of the Sun, and constituting the most sacred place in the central complex at Teotihuacan, lay a consecrated cave. Other evidence suggests that throughout ancient Mesoamerica caves were considered holy sites, apparently because they could represent the center of creation, where the first human beings emerged from the womb of Mother Earth. (Recall the kivas of the Pueblo peoples.) At Teotihuacan the sacred cave seems to have determined the site for the most sacred temple, the Pyramid of the Sun. Many scholars speculate that this pyramid and cave became places for pilgrims to visit. (A pilgrimage to a holy site can become an experience of sacred time. The going, coming, and duration of the visit stand out from ordinary time, because of their sacred orientation and purpose.) Perhaps there had been a simpler temple at the cave, and the Pyramid of the Sun merely took a long-standing veneration to a higher level.

Archeologists have found remains of a drainage system, which probably indicates that rituals involving water took place at the Pyramid of the Sun. They have also found evidence of fires—probably sacred flames. Juxtaposing fire and water was basic in classical Mesoamerican religion. One can relate these primeval forces to the sun and the storm, the heavens and the sea. Both can destroy, yet both are necessary for life. Water has some priority, inasmuch as it can extinguish fire. Also, people can live, for short periods or in special circumstances, without fire (and even without seeing the sun), whereas they must always have water.

At any rate, it is not surprising that a great pyramid drawing thousands of Mesoamericans would have been the site of rituals celebrating the basic convictions on which Mesoamerican culture depended. Whether it also housed a powerful priesthood, composed of those who carried out the rituals, and so interpreted Mesoamerican culture, is not certain. The deliberateness of the plan of Teotihuacan's most famous site, the Avenue of the Dead, suggests that powerful religious leaders may well have ruled there. The Avenue of the Dead took its axis from astronomical calculations. Most of the pyramids (there were many, in addition to those for the sun and the moon) faced west, in the direction of the setting sun. (Perhaps those using such temples were being encouraged to contemplate the demise of the current phase of creation, which their mythology said was approaching steadily.) Carved on many floors of ceremonial buildings was a "pecked" cross: a circle cut into four quadrants and made from dots that probably represented quanta of time (by the ritual calendar).

Aztec Cosmology

Aztec thought accepted the classical Mesoamerican cosmology, in that it considered the present state of the cosmos to be the successor of four prior states, each of which had perished. For the Aztecs, the present condition of plants and animals, human beings, and what they required for survival, was an advance on what had existed in prior phases of creation. The first four eras had been ruled by earth, wind, water, and fire. The present, fifth era was ruled by the "sun" of movement. This implied that the present era was unstable. Indeed, the expectation was that it would end by earthquake.

For Aztec cosmologists, the present, final age arose from a divine fire. That fire, located in the darkness of a mythical plane (called Teotihuacan, but different from the famous city of that name), was the medium of the sacrifice that made the present era. In assembly, the gods chose two of their number, Nanahuatzin and Tecuciztecatl, to throw themselves into the fire. The first result of their sacrifice was the appearance of the dawn. However, no sun came forth above the horizon, so there was not full light. The gods faced in different directions, expecting the sun to rise, but only Quetzalcoatl, who faced east, guessed correctly. Creation was not completed when the sun rose from the east, however, because the sun kept wobbling, as though it were not sure of its mission. To stabilize creation, the gods realized that they all had to die (two were not enough). So, one of their number killed all the others, by cutting their throats. Only then did creation stabilize itself.

This story of the rise of the sun and stabilizing of creation became an important influence in Aztec cosmology and ritual practice. The Aztecs believed that the world was intrinsically unstable, and the story of the sun's wobbling at the beginning of the present era undergirded that belief. Equally, the Aztecs thought that only the self-sacrifice of the gods had brought the world into being, and that ongoing sacrifice was necessary to keep the world in being. Thus when they sacrificed human beings, the Aztecs thought that they were imitating the gods and maintaining the power of the sun (and so of the rest of the world).

In the fifth era, the focus of creation shifted from heaven to earth. Agriculture arose upon earth, and it became the great wonder dominating creation. One story of this shift has the plumed serpent Quetzalcoatl bring back maize from "Sustenance Mountain," so that human beings might have a stable source of food. To accomplish this great feat, Quetzacoatl turns himself into a black ant. Accompanied by a red ant, he inches his way to the source of maize. Scholars call this sort of myth "aetiological," because it gives the cause (*aetia* in

Greek) or source of an important cultural feature. His function in myths such as these is the main reason that Quetzalcoatl is a "culture hero" as well as a god. Other gods/culture heroes are credited with giving the Aztecs other important aspects of their culture. For example, the god Mixcoatl created four hundred human beings to fight among themselves. Those who won used those who lost as sacrificial victims. The blood of the losers fed the gods, enabling them to keep the cosmos going. Myths about the origin of cotton, sweet potatoes, and pulque (an intoxicating drink) explain how these other staples of Aztec life had come from the gods, early in the history of the present cosmic eon.

As they thought about the natural world, the Aztecs came to picture it as land surrounded by water. The mythical center, Teotihuacan, was the navel of the earth (which itself was a living being). From this center extended four quadrants—the directions of the wind. The heavens above were associated with the waters surrounding the earth. At the horizon the waters rose up to meet the lowest level of the heavens (which were thirteen layers of celestial waters). The Aztecs were also interested in the under-earth, which had nine levels. The under-earth or under-world was the abode of the dead. The goal of life after death was to reach the lowest of the nine levels. This was called Mictlan, the land of the dead. People buried their dead relatives with charms designed to help them make their way to Mictlan. The eight levels that the dead had to traverse on their way to the depth of the under-world were full of hazards. The charms were necessary to ward off dangers—powers that could keep the dead from reaching their place of rest.

Four quadrants, around a center, became the basic Aztec geometrical symbol. It functioned in religion to organize both space and time. The current eon, of the sun of movement, was at the center of cosmic history, surrounded by the four prior eons. In building their temples, the Aztecs tended to use the same format, surrounding the inner precinct with four outer areas. Even their patterns of economic activity (for instance, how they organized the payment of tribute by peoples under their sway) homed to this paradigm of five: one plus four.

Like the Maya, then, the Aztecs used numbers as more than practical tools. Numbers, reminiscent of particular temporal or spatial arrangements, had a sacred quality. They helped human beings to imitate the patterns of the gods. The gods were the great models who gave the cosmos its order. Clearly, the best thing that human beings could do was to imitate these models.

Recent Attitudes

Native Mesoamerican religious traditions divinized nature, inasmuch as their roster of gods amounted to the foremost natural powers. Christianity secularized nature, inasmuch as its God stood beyond the world, as the world's creator. The meeting and mingling of these two traditions produced what one might expect: a compromise. Officially, where Christian orthodoxy reigned, the world was a reflection of God but was not itself divine. Actually, where native traditions continued to be strong, the sun, the moon, the stars, the waters, and all the other arresting aspects of nature continued to command a religious awe.

This is clearest among tribes that have not pretended to accept Christianity. For many of them the sun is still the most powerful figure, accompanied by the moon, his consort. He organizes the world and oversees its processes. She is the goddess of fertility, water, and earth. Among the Quiche and Yaqui, for example, she is a great mother, the source of all life and growth. Among the southern Tepehua, the moon has joined with Jesus of Nazareth. It is no longer female or a great mother, but it is still the main principle of fertility. Most tribes still venerate the stars, especially the Pleiades and Morning Star. This suggests that they still look to the heavens with considerable awe. For the Tepehua the Morning Star is Mary, so its light carries reminders of the Christian story of salvation.

The agricultural deities that the invading Spanish found native Mesoamericans worshiping have continued to be significant forces down to the present day. The gods that brought rain, that cared for the earth, that nourished the corn, that sent the wind—almost all have remained significant in tribal religion, even in the folk religion of nominal Christians. So, for example, the Chorti say that the rain gods and the gods of the wind sit together at the four corners of the earth, and they give these gods the names of saints. The rain gods and gods of the wind are pre-Christian. The saints come from Christianity. They coexist, because the new has not ousted the old, and the old has not repulsed the new. The saints make sense to native Mesoamericans. They are nearer, more familiar, more approachable than the strictly divine personages. So why not associate them with the forces of rain and wind, on which so much of agricultural existence depends? Why not intuit that their function in the spiritual order is like that of the forces of nature in the material order: to be shapers of prosperity, powers having a lot to say about how life unfolds?

For the Yucatec, the cross symbolizes the rain god, perhaps because he operates in all four directions. Still, the cross also changes the rain god, because with the advent of Christian religious consciousness the cross is bound to connote the suffering through which salvation may have come. So how does the rain god function in salvation? What role might the Yucatec imagine him playing? He spends himself for the nourishment of the crops. His arms stretch out in labor. This is hardly a profound reinterpretation of the Christian cross or a significant Christianization of a pre-Christian symbol. But it is a minor venture in adaptation, appropriation, crossing two systems to stimulate new angles of vision. The Zapotec did a similar kind of work when they associated their god Gusi with Saint Peter. For the Quiche, the winds of destruction are Santiago (Saint James). For the Chorti such winds come from the devil.

The Group

In contrast to the tribal scale that we found among most native North Americans, in Mesoamerica we find large aggregations of people. Whether we should call the Olmecs the founders of a "state" depends on the definition of that term, but it seems likely that they moved in the direction of composing a relatively populous group controlled centrally and organized for many cooperative undertakings. (It is beyond dispute that the Maya and Aztecs ran states.) Olmecs apparently traded quite broadly, for Olmec artifacts have been found far afield. If we postulate that La Venta was the center of early Olmec culture, then the presence of Olmec artifacts at sites such as Monte Alban suggests that Olmec influence was considerable. The easiest way to explain such influence is to assume that the Olmecs were pioneers at the practice of trade (a practice highly developed by their successors in Mesoamerica), as they were pioneers in numerous other things (formation of the calendar, monumental art, developing a military priesthood, and more).

It is also interesting that at sites near the center of Olmec control, such as La Venta, no artifacts have been found that were not in the Olmec style. This suggests that trade was a one-way street (or, at least, that the Olmecs did not import the kinds of goods that could survive for thousands of years). The later pattern in Mesoamerica was for a dominant group to control trade through military power. There was little free trade—economic activity not joined to military power. Indeed, military power is the chief characteristic of Mesoamerican social life in the classical and post-classical periods. The rulers of many later groups combined the roles of high priest and military generals.

The tradition was for traders to travel accompanied by soldiers, and it seems likely that those with military predominance set the terms of the trades. The artifacts that have been found outside of Olmec areas proper tend to be small—things that could be transported easily. Since many of the artifacts found at Olmec sites are large, the pattern may have been to trade only in a fraction of the material expressions of Olmec culture. Whether non-Olmecs traveled to Olmec sites for the inspiration that made them imitate Olmec styles in larger artifacts that they made themselves is difficult to determine. Perhaps Olmec artisans traveled to work at "foreign" sites on occasion. At any rate, the more salient point is that the Olmecs seem to have arisen at a key moment in the transition of Mesoamerican culture from an agriculture that would make people self-sufficient to an economy that dealt in surpluses and luxuries. Such a period of historical change can be very creative. People can see new opportunities, because of increased leisure and wealth. And what they can see is not limited to economic entrepreneurship. The sense of coming into a new era tends to influence art, politics, and religion as well as economics.

Classical Social Life

Because Teotihuacan has been excavated carefully and extensively, we have a fair idea of how it was laid out and functioned, and so of social life in classical Mesoamerica. At its height, it may have housed as many as 250,000 people—a figure that few European or Asian cities of the era reached. The central area covered more than twenty square kilometers. Most of the city apparently was built all at once, though in later eras a few sections experienced more growth. The basic building unit was a one-story, square apartment complex. It measured 50–60 meters on each side. The seemingly more affluent living quarters lay close to the Avenue of the Dead, while poorer quarters lay at a greater distance from that most important thoroughfare.

The more affluent apartments included roofed and open quarters, the latter having low platforms, perhaps for family rituals. A high exterior wall gave the entire apartment considerable privacy and protection. Many walls were painted with murals, the themes usually coming from Mesoamerican mythology. The most famous of these murals, called The Paradise of Tlaloc, seems to represent the afterlife open to those who died blessed deaths (largely associated with water: by drowning, for example). The apartments of poorer folk, perhaps artisans (in contrast to the government officials who lived near the Avenue of the Dead), were smaller, at times almost like warrens. Probably they were cramped and crowded.

One of the main industries at Teotihuacan involved working obsidian (volcanic glass, usually black). Obsidian was the usual material for edged tools, indispensable in many crafts. Archeologists have unearthed hundreds of workshops. Ceramics was another key industry, and artists from Teotihuacan exported many of their ceramic wares to outlying areas. Commentators note the popularity of slab-footed tripod cylinders decorated with mythological figures. Another popular product was a thin orange-ware. It often appears at grave sites of apparently important people, probably as a favorite offering.

Although Teotihuacan depended on an agricultural base outside the city limits, its cultural eminence rested on its trade. In Aztec times the people cultivated ingenious *chinampas:* rectangular plots made by cutting channels into swampy land at the edge of Lake Texcoco (or Tezcoco). These were amazingly fertile and supplied much of the city's food requirements. For the rest, the Teotihuacanos depended on contributions from other areas in the Valley of Mexico. The source of prosperity, however, was trade. Teotihuacan controlled obsidian mines, and it housed the industries that produced the tools that outlying regions needed.

Various other cultural complexes of the classical era—Monte Alban, Veracruz, the Mayan—add variations on themes from Teotihuacan. The Mayan civilization that flourished from about 300 to 900 A.D. is famous for tall temples built of limestone and faced with stucco. It also featured large housing structures, sometimes called "palaces," with rooms spanned by distinctive arches. Mayan cities had sections linked by causeways, and on occasions causeways linked distinct cities. The Maya also constructed ballcourts of masonry, and their burial sites, often in the basements of buildings, could be very elaborate.

Maya of the classical period wrote hieroglyphics on stelae adorning altars, many of the inscriptions apparently related to the elaborate Mayan calendar. Remains vary considerably from site to site, reminding us that "Mayan" is a broad designation. A major distinction separates the developments of the Guatemalan highlands from the developments in low-lying areas. Kaminaljuyu, near the present-day Guatemala City, was an important site during the earliest Mayan period (sometimes called Formative). Because it lay close to both Pacific and Atlantic waters, it was a natural center for trade and cultural exchange. In the period around 400–500 A.D., Kaminaljuyu came to the attention of Teotihuacan, then the dominant power. It was remodeled along the lines of Teotihuacan. A series of elaborate tombs, apparently for representatives of Teotihuacan culture, suggests that Teotihuacanos had actually taken rule away from native Maya.

Both the Teotihuacanos and the Maya developed social structures far beyond the complexity of the tribe. In North America, as we have seen, the typical native American group was relatively small. In the southeast of what is now the United States there could be larger aggregations of people, perhaps not coincidentally in cultural settings that seem to have been influenced by Mesoamerican developments: mounds, platforms, villages large enough to be called small cities. But there was nothing in North America like Teotihuacan, or even like lesser Mexican or Mayan sites. There was nothing that could be called a metropolis or an empire.

Perhaps we should not call the Maya, let alone the Teotihuacanos, builders of an empire, but we have to speak of the later Aztecs (and, in South America, the Incas) in such terms. Still probably we should speak of a Mayan or Teotihuacan civilization. There was sufficient complexity—development of ideology, art, politics, economics, and architecture—to make the major Mayan sites, and Teotihuacan, centers of a sophisticated way of life. The social sense that must have prevailed in such centers was that families (and the other groups into which people naturally formed themselves, under the umbrella of the broader culture) had their particular place in a large structure willed by the gods but carried out by human ingenuity.

Probably priests were the real leaders at both Teotihuacan and the major Mayan sites. The predominance of temples for ritualistic activities, the indications of religious dimensions to most artifacts, the manifest interest in the astronomical calendar and burial practices, all suggest that religion called the tunes. Yet there is also sufficient indication of efficient civil administration and control of trade to suggest that priestly leaders would have depended on civil bureaucrats and, perhaps, military personnel.

Aztec Themes

In a study entitled "The Nature of Aztec Society," Laurette Séjourné has indicated some of the nobler spiritual aspects of Aztec culture. Were it not for these nobler spiritual aspects, we might be able to condemn the Aztecs out of hand as barbarians who thought that their gods craved human blood. We consider Aztec sacrifice of human beings in the next section. Here let us consider some of the reasons for thinking that the Aztecs were capable of significant spiritual refinement.

The main source on Aztec spirituality, a study by the Franciscan missionary priest Bernadino Sahagun, is open to the criticism that Sahagun interpolated Christian sentiments. However, the friar is sensitive to this charge and so declares explicitly that he is translating Aztec sources faithfully. Indeed, he says that were the evidence in the texts not overwhelming, no European could have found in Aztec culture not only religious wisdom but also such sacraments as baptism and confession.

As evidence of religious wisdom and delicacy, Séjourné quotes an Aztec song: "I weep, I grow sad, I am only a singer; if I could only sometimes carry flowers, and adorn myself with them in the Place of the Fleshless! I am saddened. Only as a flower is man honoured upon earth. . . ."[37] He also quotes from speeches to students entering an Aztec college and advice of a father to his sons: "Look that thou be not surfeited with food, be temperate, love and practice abstinence and fasting . . . and also, my son, thou must take good care to understand our lord's books; unite thyself with the wise and clever, and those of good understanding. . . . Take great pains to make yourselves friends of god who is in all parts, and is invisible and impalpable, and it is meet that you give him all your heart and body, and look that you be not proud in your heart, nor yet despair, nor be cowardly in spirit; but that you be humble in your heart and have hope in God."[38]

Much of this advice could come from the book of Proverbs in the Old Testament. The reference to flowers, though, stamps the song as Aztec. The Aztecs loved flowers, and one of the conundrums with which reflective historians have struggled is how and why so militant a culture should have developed such a love. Apparently it was nothing so simple as women loving flowers and counterbalancing the martial spirit of men. Both sexes loved flowers, and both supported the militaristic ethos of the Aztec empire.

Perhaps it was the very vulnerability of flowers that appealed to refined Aztecs. Knowing that human beings could be only food for the gods, only a quick step away from being required to sacrifice themselves, refined Aztecs may have found flowers a good symbol of human existence. Vulnerable, brief, projecting pathos because they are soon to fade, flowers could stand for the spirit of an Aztec citizen saddened by the proximity of death. What would make this sentiment especially acute would be the active promotion of death in Aztec culture. Whereas all people have to die, and so all cultures have mourned human mortality, Aztec culture rooted itself in the need of the gods sustaining the world to be fed by human blood. Thus in Aztec culture mortality was quite active. Priests were urging people to step forward to sacrifice themselves, or requiring the sacrifice of slaves captured in battle. How reluctant such priests were we do not know. Any sensitive citizen might mourn, though, to see victims cut down in the flower of life.

Recent Tendencies

Modern Mesoamericans exhibit most of the social dynamics that one finds in other tribal situations, but perhaps focusing on one situation, that of a Chamula boy growing up among a group of Tzotzil-speaking Indians living in the rural areas of the highlands of San Cristobal de Las Casas, in the southern Mexican state of Chiapas, will make our reflections more vivid. Chamula is a tiny village, where the political and religious authorities live. A boy like Juan (who is a composite created from ethnological research) would probably live outside the village, close to the fields where he and his family worked. Let us plunge into a dramatic part of the narrative created in his name: "Seven months had passed since I ran away from home. A week after I came back my father [broke his promise and] began beating me all over again and shouting what a trouble it had been to find me. I had an uncle who defended me, and he said, 'You shouldn't hit the boy so much.' My father told him, 'It's none of your business! He's my son and I can kill him if I want to!'

"One day my father asked for twelve pesos from one of the men that go around hiring people to work on big farms. When the day came for him to leave, they couldn't find him because he was out getting drunk, and they took me in his place to pay off the money he'd received. My uncle Marcos went with me. It took us four days. There were plantations of cocoa and rubber on the farms. But I didn't work with the others, I just carried water for the foreman. The men were under contract for one month and they were paid twelve pesos. When they completed the month, other groups arrived at the farm to take their place. My uncle and I went back home.

"When I arrived my father asked, 'Did you pay off what they gave me? You didn't leave anything owing?' He asked my uncle the same questions, and my uncle told him that everything was paid off. He added, 'Look, don't hit your son any more. You didn't give him anything out of those twelve pesos. You didn't even buy him huaraches for the trip.' 'But if he doesn't obey me . . .' my father said. A few days later he began to beat me again. He only hit me when he was sober. When he was drunk he never hit me."[39]

Do people tend to express themselves truly or falsely when they are drunk? Is there truth in wine ("in vino veritas"), or in sobriety? We can never know, as a general principle, but surely it is more chilling to find parents beating their children when sober. Surely when they have command of their faculties and still abuse their children we have to worry more about their character. Little Juan is virtually a slave. His mother loves him, does not beat him, and tries to protect him from his father. But his family is so poor that they must always work in the fields, for a pittance, and his parents are tempted to rent him out to the best paymaster. Juan runs away, finding a kind woman who will feed and house him if he will tend her sheep. But even there he is open to exploitation, for the woman is forced to lend him to other work projects, and his fate depends completely on the kindness of the people into whose control he comes. At one point the local authorities hear that he is an orphan, so they come to force his employers to send him to school. When they learn that he is not an orphan, simply a runaway, they haul him back to his parents, and his father begins to beat him again. Clearly traditional social life broke down badly in modern times.

The Self

One of the ways that ancient Mesoamericans retained realism, even sobriety, about the human condition was by contemplating the heavens. The serenity of the movements of the heavenly bodies tended to cool any overheated emotions. Certainly, ancient peoples also used the apparently uncaring ways of the plant and animal worlds to achieve the same end. And, on the whole, they were so much more concerned about the common good (the survival of the group, including its long-held traditions) than about the individual that few individuals had the chance to become self-centered (perhaps chieftains and high priests could be exceptions, but even for them role was usually more important than individual genius). The picture that we usually receive of older (pre-historical) cultures, whether of large or small scale, does not stress the psychological. The individual self, with its concerns for feelings and fulfillment, does not bulk as large as the natural, social, and religious aspects of the typical ancient culture. The likelihood is that this was also the case in ancient Mesoamerica, at the foundations that came to rich cultural expression with the Olmecs.

Second there are many indications that the Olmecs were a creative, energetic people. They dominated their own geographical area, and they impressed people in neighboring areas so much that their cultural style became much imitated. The monumental character of much of their architecture shows that they did not hesitate to engage in projects requiring considerable investments of time, energy, and resources. Their tendency to build ceremonial centers adds a note of cooperation: most likely they enjoyed chances for socializing, celebrating feasts, carrying out rituals in which they could express their deepest beliefs.

Along with the ancient sense of the awesomeness of the heavens and the rest of the natural world, the ancient sense of celebration is another clue to the typical person's sense of himself or herself. We have to struggle to imagine what it meant to be a Hopi kachina dancer (to take an example from the native North Americans whom we have studied). Even more do we have to struggle to imagine what it meant to take part in rituals in an Olmec temple. For example, what did it mean for a typical Olmec citizen to contemplate the dragon that adorns some key sites? How did the dragon factor into the sense of creation, or of destiny, that the typical person used for orientation through the life cycle? The dragon seems to have been based on the caiman, a Mesoamerican member of the alligator/crocodile family. (The dragon is also important in ancient Chinese mythology, of course, but what connections there may have been to the Asian homeland from which we have assumed that the early Mesoamericans, as well as all the other native Americans, ultimately drew their cultural traditions is impossible to determine.) Something in its impressive shape, teeth, slithering on the ground (it was an earth-deity), and dangerous character fascinated the Olmec mind.

Even more fascinating was the jaguar, the largest of the spotted cats, and a figure very important in many different Latin American mythologies. The jaguar had such grace and power, such speed and ability to kill, that it drew the Olmec imagination to it again and again. But the caiman and the jaguar did not remain players in only the individual dramas that Olmec men and women might create in their own minds. They also entered into the public liturgy. There they took on even larger proportions, because the whole group paid attention to them and celebrated their impressiveness.

We have said that it is typical of pre-modern peoples to subordinate the self to the group. That pattern continued in classical Mesoamerica, though the "group" was often quite large. Quite possibly, the subordination of the individual was not so much to the thriving of what was virtually an extended family as to the good functioning of what was nearly an empire. In that case, the subordination would have approached the modern case, where, when individuals have languished, they have felt the largeness of their social context to be depersonalizing. In a Teotihuacan, or a large Mayan city, the individual was confined by elaborate ceremonies, considerable administrative apparatus, and a religious ideology that spotlighted the fatalistic force of the heavens and the significance of death.

On the other hand, trade and art only prosper when individuals have enough freedom, and sense of potential reward, to exert themselves with enthusiasm. Even if trade were under the supervision of the central government, so that much of it amounted to tribute from outlying areas, forced upon them by military strength (as well as economic need), there had to be a place for middlemen, entrepreneurs, suppliers of money (and perhaps credit). Analogous reasoning proposes that the great business in artifacts that excavations of classical Mesoamerican sites suggest opened spaces for people of talent and initiative. Even when they are carving or painting to honor the gods, artists move by an inner sense of satisfaction. They work to make beautiful things, as they understand beauty, and their work sets them free of the cravenness nearly bound to afflict the people whose contributions to larger society are not so much creative as dutiful.

Religion and Individualism

A third potential source of individualism lay in religion. Though most of the remains that we have suggest that classical Mesoamerican religion was formalistic, controlled by priests as a mode of social power as well as a service of the heavens, any significant religious activity puts people in the position of trying to descry the will of the powers that they think are determining their lives. This, in turn, places them close to contemplation: Why are these powers so mysterious, what in fact do they want of us, how can we be sure that we are pleasing them, what fate are they likely to deal out to us, what will happen to us at death?

Questions such as these, which can come in an unpunctuated rush, if people are really trying to please the gods, are bound to individuate those who ask them. Even when such people accept the traditional, stereotyped answers that their religious authorities have prepared, merely by raising serious questions they have stepped apart from the mob. To raise a serious question is to experience, for oneself, that reality is both mysterious and knowable. Implicit in the process of questioning is being carried by hope, indeed confidence, into a wider reality that just has to be intelligible, because otherwise one's ability to seek understanding would make no sense.

Take speculation such as this to provocative artifacts such as masks and portraits found at the tomb of Pacal, at Palenque in the southwestern Mayan lowlands, and the figures gain another dimension. Pacal acceded to the throne in 615, at the age of twelve, and he ruled for sixty-eight years. Buried in a handsome tomb inside the Pyramid of Inscriptions, he has come to serve archeologists and scholars of classical Mesoamerican religion as a handy point of reference. Inscriptions concerned with his lineage, before and after his rule, suggest the interest of the Maya in dynastic justifications. Both descent from a legitimate predecessor and the approbation of the gods were necessary to justify a rule. The differing portraits of Pacal that have been found at his tomb show that the Maya probably wanted their rulers to display a broad range of humanity, perhaps as an indication of the legitimacy of their rule.

For example, a life-sized stucco head, perhaps that of Pacal at age twelve, when he became ruler, presents him with a broad nose, full lips, and large bulging eyes. He has a ceremonial headdress, elongated earlobes (reminiscent of the Buddha), and is not, by current western standards, a handsome young man. He looks somewhat unformed, and the heroic nose is flatter than the aquiline profile that Mayan art seems generally to have favored as handsome. This stucco head does not suggest the full shape of his skull, but a mosaic jade mask found on his tomb does. The flattened forehead implies that Pacal had had his skull pressed between two hard boards as an infant (a Mayan custom) so that the bones hardened to make the forehead and the back of the head flat. The jade mask, which is precisely cut in geometric sections, presents an oval face. The eyes are even larger than on the stucco mask, though the lids seem too full and the pupils too small to be realistic. The nose is not so broad, but it is long. It might be called aquiline, but it droops slightly, marring any likeness to a hawk. There is a suggestion of fleshiness or self-indulgence, despite the hardness of the jade, as though Pacal had lived too well. Religion could be coopted to support self-indulgence.

Aztec Self-Indulgence: Human Sacrifice

In the sixteenth century a sergeant in the army of the Spanish invader Cortes described the sacrifice of some comrades who had been captured by the Aztec enemy. Aztec warriors and priests dragged these victims up the steps of a temple. In the midst of drumming and trumpeting, they dressed the victims in Aztec garb and forced them to dance before the war-god Huitzilopochtli. Then they placed them on their backs on narrow stones, sawed open their chests, and drew out their still beating hearts, which they offered to statues of the gods. When this offering was complete, the Aztec officiants rolled the corpses down the steps of the temple. At the bottom, experts "cut off their arms and feet and flayed the skin off the faces, and prepared it afterwards like glove leather with the beards on, and kept those for the festivals when they celebrated drunken orgies and the flesh they ate in chilimole."[40]

This practice was not reserved for captured Spaniards. It was a standard ritual use of prisoners of war. The Aztecs had come into power in central Mexico by arms, and throughout the hundred years or so of their imperial rule they engaged in regular warfare. From their capital city of Tenochtitlan, which they considered the inner circle of the cosmos, they tried to expand their power in all four directions of the compass. On the whole they were successful, though the Tlaxcala-Pueblo Valley kingdom to the east of Tenochtitlan and the Taracan kingdom to the west resisted and won important battles against them.

The ritualistic sacrifice of prisoners captured in battles with the neighbors they were subjugating served Aztec political as well as religious ends. During periods of peace or truce, the Aztecs would invite leaders of neighboring peoples to witness their human sacrifices, apparently to cow them. Ordinary Aztecs themselves had to witness these sacrifices with some trepidation, because they knew that they could become victims, if they stepped out of line. Indeed, for rituals such as the annual ceremony to pay debts to the rain god Tlaloc, "children (called 'human paper streamers') with two cowlicks in their hair and favorable day signs were dressed in costumes—some set with pearls—of dark green, black striped with chili red, and light blue and were sacrificed in seven different locations. The flowing and falling of tears of the children insured the coming of rain."[41]

We have already alluded to the mythical foundations for Aztec human sacrifice: the self-sacrifice of the gods that made possible the current eon of the sun of motion. Inasmuch as this eon always remained unstable, regular sacrifice was necessary to keep it in being. Even though the Aztecs were convinced that this fifth eon was sure to end (violently, by earthquake), they tried to prolong it by feeding the gods with human blood. Other sacrifices were useful, but human blood was the key. The Aztec imagination seems to have preferred the most vivid symbols possible—for example, the still palpitating heart torn from the victim's chest. Once every fifty-two years a special ceremony commemorated the passing of the Pleiades through the zenith, which completed a calendrical cycle. At this ceremony the Aztecs sacrificed a captive warrior and lighted a fire in his chest cavity, to signal the regeneration of the cosmos for another calendrical cycle.

Most of the Aztec ceremonies that called for human sacrifices had precedents among prior Mesoamerican peoples. The Aztecs greatly expanded the bloodshed, however, just as they had greatly expanded war and militarism. Their empire lived by killing. Politically and ritually, bloodshed was at the core. The cannibalism included in some ceremonies seems to have been less significant than the offering of blood to the gods. Scholars generally regard cannibalism as a means for sacrificers to identify themselves with what they have sacrificed. Taking the flesh of a victim into oneself is a way of letting that victim become one's own substance. The reek of Aztec temples that Sahagun reports came from their resembling slaughter houses. Indeed, there were slave markets where wealthy Aztecs could purchase victims for private banquets.

Recent Attitudes

The Mam Indians of Guatemala offer us a good example of the mixing of old and new religious ways that has developed in Mesoamerica since the arrival of Europeans. The saga of the self obviously begins at birth, so let us first study a report on how the Mam tend to handle birth: "When labour pains commence the midwife is called in. She usually attempts, not always accurately, to foretell the baby's sex. She usually rubs the mother's belly with camphor and vaseline, or some other form of grease. Often she gives the woman herbs to drink which facilitate delivery. If the woman has a difficult time the *chiman* [shaman] is summoned. He calls on his gods or beseeches San Francisco or Santa Lucia to take care of the woman and begs them that death be warded off. He promises that when she is well she will carry a flower to the church. Then he prays that the baby may have a long life and promises that, twenty days after its birth, the new mother will carry a flower to the church for the saints or gods. . . . The father goes to the *chiman* to see what name the child is to bear. Then the *chiman* consults his count of the days (sacred calendar), and ascertains the day of the child in this count. After that he casts the *mixes* [sacred beans] and tells what luck the child will have in its life. A child born during the last five days of the year will have very bad luck."[42]

The first thing that we should note is the easy combination of traditional folk ways and more modern ones. The midwife is a staple of traditional obstetrics. But vaseline is a modern invention. The herbs that the midwife ministers are also traditional. The shaman comes in when the birth becomes difficult—a matter threatening to step outside human skills. His function is to deal with the world of spirits. If he can get them on the mother's side, the birth may still go well. Note that the shaman is equally at home praying to his own, native gods or to such Christian saints as Francis and Lucy, who are considered special helpers for troubles such as difficult childbirth. The promise that the mother will bring a flower to church if she recovers is partly a quid pro quo, but in Guatamala a flower is not an exceptional gift. So the symbolism seems to stress offering a fragile thing of beauty in gratitude to divinity for its having preserved the fragile, beautiful life of child and mother.

The process that the shaman goes through to name the child draws on the ancient Mayan interest in the calendar. The sense of the sacredness of time that we found among the classical Maya seems to have lingered into the present era. The name that the child will bear ought to express its destiny, and its destiny lies in the time when it was born. This astrological view of the human situation obviously conflicts with Christian views of providence, but perhaps not completely. If the shaman were trying to convince a father partial to Christian doctrine, he might say that God uses the stars and planets to mediate divine providence.

Casting the sacred beans is a way of divining the future. The shaman interprets the pattern into which the beans fall and finds a favorable or unfavorable future. One might consider this a harmless exercise, until one reflected on the psychological impact that feeling one had been fated for good luck or bad might make. To learn as a young person that the fates frowned at one's birth might be discouraging. The sense that children born at the end of the year will have very bad luck reflects the notion, common among many traditional peoples, that the world runs down each year, losing power at the end. Usually the New Year's observance is a commemoration of a new cycle and so a new time of vigor. This belief assimilates the year to a human being who, at the end of his or her life, is often weak and merely waiting to die. The notion that a child partakes of the vigor or weakness of the time of year in which it was born is another indication of the symbiotic relationship that traditional peoples posit between the natural and human worlds. When the stars are in "unfavorable" positions a human being can suffer a lack of vital strength.

Ultimate Reality

The Olmec pantheon has attracted much scholarly debate. While the dragon and the were-jaguar have received the most attention, artifacts from Olmec sites represent such other interesting figures as a harpy eagle, a serpent, and a shark. Usually these figures are not distinct but rather mixed forms: human and jaguar, eagle and jaguar, and so forth. Since all of the argument about the significance of these artifacts (of the creatures who appear again and again in ceremonial settings) depends on interpretations of the Olmec iconography (which has no accompanying texts), scholars are free to shift the data this way and that, trying to gain the most pleasing set of relationships. An important methodological question is how much to weigh what is known about deities of later Mesoamerican cultures, such as the Aztec, which seem to resemble the Olmec figures. In other words, is it more reasonable to think that most of what developed after the Olmecs in Mesoamerica elaborated what they had begun, or does arguing from later forms violate canons of parsimony (methodological rules intended to keep people from going beyond the manifest significance of the data directly relevant—the Olmec artifacts alone)?

Pictorial representations of the were-jaguar, crocodile, harpy eagle, and shark show them to have been carved (at least occasionally) with exquisite skill. The Olmecs often worked in jade, and they have gained the reputation of having been the premier Mesoamerican carvers of jade. Two stone representations of the were-jaguar, one from Las Limas and one from San Lorenzo, agree in virtually all details, suggesting that Olmec iconography had its own orthodoxies, which carvers were required to observe. The sculpture from Las Limas is of a small child being carried by a human figure in seated (almost lotus) position. The human figure has eyes that seem absorbed with mysteries, and some interpreters have given the opinion that it represents a royal son coming of age (other Olmec art seems to present clearly royal figures carrying similar infantile deities).

The were-jaguar is a relatively small child, with short arms, and legs that extend helplessly (the figure is described as "floppy"). The impression is that the were-jaguar is in the care of the human figure carrying it—is helpless. The face of the were-jaguar combines human and feline features (human eyes and nose, a mouth distorted into a snarl, like that of a big cat). The were-jaguar also has an elaborate head-wear. Incised into the shoulders and knees of the human figure are four deities: the harpy eagle, the shark god, perhaps the feathered serpent, and a god difficult to place (but apparently found on bowls from the Mexican highlands). Each of these deities has a cleft head. The were-jaguar from San Lorenzo was found at the head of the deeply buried stone drainage system that we described earlier. This suggests that it may have represented the rain god.

Other wonderful carvings show the dragon/caiman, sometimes with the mouth of the jaguar, a human nose, and the crest of the harpy eagle for eyebrows. The dragon appears in quite various settings, and in many different sorts of Olmec art: monuments, small carved jade pieces, household ceramics, and more. One possibility is that, in a composite form like the one we have just described, it served as a summary or shorthand for the Olmec sense of the deity. The harpy eagle was represented as a raptorial creature, with a cruel beak. Often it, too, had the snarling mouth of the were-jaguar, and human features, as well as a characteristic crest. The real harpy eagle attacked monkeys living in the canopy of the tropical forests. Depending on what the monkeys symbolized, the Olmecs might have seen the harpy eagle as a token of the death awaiting everything quick and full of life.

A remarkable stone figure of a shaman, kneeling and being transformed into a jaguar, suggests some of the personal implications that the Olmec deities probably carried. If shamans could become jaguars (or were-jaguars) through their trances, they presumably could have experiences in that form. That is to say, their imaginative identification with the jaguar would lead them to imaginative adventures that called on their combined powers, human and jaguar. In suggesting that the coupling of a jaguar-figure with a human female represented the Olmec sense that they were children of the jaguar, scholars may well imply more than a flat totemism. The Olmecs could have used their religious ceremonies the way that the figure of the kneeling shaman in the process of transformation into a jaguar suggests that shamans used their trances. The objective might have been to feel what it was like to be children of the jaguar—try out the potential.

Mayan Theology

In the classical period, Mayan religion presented a great number of different gods. The majority seem to reflect the agricultural origins of Mayan culture. Indeed, the deities most closely connected with the concerns of cultivators—rain, fertility, sun, the seasons of the agricultural year—continued on after the fall of the Mayan empire, and so of the priestly religion that dominated in the classical period. (Many commentators note that these gods even continue to be influential today, long after the arrival of Christianity in Mesoamerica.) In contrast, a priestly god such as Itzamna, who served as a heavenly prototype for Mayan religious functionaries, seems to have disappeared from contemporary Yucatan.

Much of what the Mayan priests did in developing a more elaborate ritual for a large, sophisticated society amounted to integrating older agricultural deities with the new Mayan interest in chronology and astrology. Scholars also note the tendency of Mayan gods to change their appearance from locale to locale, as though each significant Mayan center insisted on giving the gods a local character. The result could be to endow a given deity with considerable ambiguity. In fact, the Mayan gods do often appear to be dualistic. Even if a given deity has a clear identity and function, often he or she will be accompanied by another deity whose function contradicts what the first deity symbolizes.

Perhaps, as the Mayan priests developed their religious ideology, this contradiction led to a sense that the cosmos as a whole was dualistic: composed of clashing powers. For example, Hultkrantz notes a representation in a Mayan codex of Chac, the rain god, in which he is caring for a young tree (emblematic, no doubt, of vegetation as a whole). Right behind Chac stands another god, Ah Puch, who stands for death. He is breaking the same tree in half. The visual message is that the universe has a will to create, nourish, sustain, but also a will to destroy. When we recall that the Mayan calendar, like other Mesoamerican calendars, assumed cosmic cycles of arising and declining, we sense that a dualism of creation and destruction ran very deep in classical Mesoamerican culture.

Aztec Divinity

The Aztec sense of divinity was that it permeated ordinary life. What was ultimate could appear in anything proximate. The Nahuatl word *teotl* meant a sacred power. Spanish translators have rendered it "god," "saint," or "demon," but probably closer to its intent was naming the force at work in a given phenomenon. For example, *teotl* could apply to a rainstorm, a tree, a mountain, a priest, a warrior, a king, an ancestor. It could appear in anything mysterious or chaotic. The Aztecs were sensitive to the forces in their world. Power impressed them. Indeed, we have seen that the life-force, represented in blood, came to dominate their sacrificial ceremonies. So when we speak of the various Aztec gods, we mean mainly the force represented in the activities with which they were associated. Even when a given god became prominent and acquired some personal characteristics, his or her force remained the key.

Inasmuch as the Aztecs grouped kinds of divine force and gave them faces, we may speak of clusters of gods. There was no Aztec pantheon, organized the way that the Greeks organized the college of gods that lived on Mount Olympus. But there were groups of gods organized around such themes as the birth of the world, fertility, war, and nourishing the sun. True to their instinct that reality is structured by a pattern of a center and four outer aspects, the Aztecs would depict a god of fertility, such as the rain god Tlaloc, as inhabiting the central region of a given heaven (there were nine celestial layers) and having four auxiliary gods (Tlaloques). Each would dispense a different kind of rain and care for a different direction.

The gods were supposed to be invisible to the human eye, but Aztecs claimed to see them in dreams and visions. During religious ceremonies costumed human beings would impersonate given gods, which provided another way to see them. The gods might also be seen in non-human representations: statues of wood or stone, effigies of dough. As in India, the gods had characteristic regalia (masks, weapons, feathers, jewelry) by which the common people could recognize them.

Some Aztec gods served as patrons to human beings, usually groups rather than individual men or women. When such a group traveled a representative would carry along a bundle of mementos of its patron. This representative would report to the group any visions of the patron that he had received (for example, in a dream), and any commands that the patron made. Because of their intimacy with the patron, such representatives were powerful figures, especially during times of migration and other sorts of change. When the group reached its new home, it would erect a shrine to its patronal deity. Until this shrine came into being, the settlement was not founded. In time of war, an important objective was to capture the enemy's foundational shrine, carry away its patronal deity, and so remove its legitimacy.

We have seen some of the characteristic of Quetzalcoatl, the feathered snake, god and culture hero. He became the great symbol of Aztec, indeed all Mesoamerican, culture, because he represented the wisdom, order, intelligence, and finesse on which Mesoamerican culture prided itself. Quetzalcoatl shared the work of creation with Tezcatlipoca. Together they blended intelligence and force, both of which were necessary to form the cosmos and keep it going. Quetzalcoatl had a role in the prior eons of cosmic history, and he was one of the gods who sacrificed themselves so that the present, fifth eon could arise. (Now he is present in Venus, the morning star.) As a culture hero, he was associated with the discovery of fire, maize, and pulque, the intoxicating drink. As the feathered serpent, he suggested the blend of heaven and earth necessary for a vigorous empire. Some depictions show Quetzalcoatl bringing agriculture, the arts, and the calendar. His antagonism to Tezcatlipoca was in part that of day to night, of reason to shamanic dealings with smoky irrational forces.

Recent Trends

Christianity has influenced the majority of Mesoamerican tribes sufficiently to make the Christian view of the godhead prevail in modern times. This has meant the prevalence of God the Father, who is all-powerful and all-knowing, as the Christian catechism teaches. However, few tribes have retained the trinitarian context of the traditional Christian teachings about God the Father. The all-powerful deity has not been the community of Father, Son, and Spirit that orthodox Christianity proposes. It has not had as its essential structure relations of knowing and loving that define it as the perfect achievement of identity-in-difference.

So, for example, when the Tzotzil speak of God the Father as the Holy Savior (*San Salvador*), they neglect the Christian understanding of the relation between the Father and the Son, to whom the Father has given the work of accomplishing salvation. Admittedly, many Christians in other lands have thought about divinity vaguely, without the trinitarian overtones or the theological precision that a conscientious Christian theologian would like. Nonetheless, in Mesoamerica the forces resisting such an orthodox development have clung to stronger pre-Christian components. The Quiche and Tepehua, for example, have identified God the Father with the Sun. Inasmuch as they have credited him with salvation, the overtones inevitably have been of the sun conquering the darkness and the cold.

The Tarascan and Yaqui do not consider God the Father the peak of divinity. They give this honor to Christ. Thus they also run aground on the doctrine of the Trinity, if one analyzes their sense of divinity from a traditional Christian standpoint. For the Yucatec, God the Father has no direct dealings with human beings. Thus they treat him as what comparativists call a "high god," leaving space for intermediary deities, among whom Christ is the most powerful. The Totonac present still another interesting confusion of Christian terminology with traditional pre-Christian instinct. They call God the Father "the most holy sacrament," a term that Christian tradition reserves for the Christ present in the eucharist. The Tzotzil identify Christ with the sun, as do the Chamula and Otomi. For the Chorti Christ is a cultural hero responsible for the coming of maize.

We see, therefore, a great variety of combinations. Different tribes have latched onto different aspects of Christian theology, making the correlations with their pre-Christian beliefs that most appealed to them. The Totonac, looking at the blessed sacrament, probably think of the nourishing qualities of divinity. For them the highest god is the one who gives the people all that they need. So they associate the blessed sacrament with God the Father, in blissful disregard of Christian insistence that it is Christ whom the devout believer receives. What "receives" would mean in a Totonac context is hard to say. Probably the sacramental ritual implies the action of an undifferentiated godhead, rather than something precisely laid out by Christian traditions about the last supper or the sacrifice of Calvary.

Some tribes fuse Christ and the Father. Thus the Tzeltal speak of "Dios Tatik Jesuchristo." Lost is the distinction between Father and Son, as well as the distinction between the Logos who existed before the incarnation and the Christ who is his enfleshment. The Cora merge the Father, God, Jesus Christ, the Sun, and Fire. All are aspects of a single supreme divinity who lives beneath the earth. The Zapotec have several Christs alongside God. Moreover, their Christs are not necessarily benevolent. Indeed, they can be the source of human suffering. The Zapotec reject the Christian view that Christ conquered death and ascended to heaven. For the Nahuatl, Christ is the destroyer of humankind, not a being who loves men and women. The Nahuatl also have several Christs, but none of them fits the orthodox Christian pattern.

In these negative views of the Zapotec and Nahuatl we sense a strong resistance to Christian influence. Where other tribes have accepted much of the Christian view of divinity, or have at least assimilated Christian concepts to the positive content of their pre-Christian senses of God, the Zapotec and Nahuatl make Christ the enemy. Certainly, they have assimilated Christian theology to pre-Christian views of divinity, according to which the godhead shows destructive as well as constructive sides. But by choosing to make their Christs destructive, they have closed the door to a Zapotec or Nahuatl Christianity.The fulfillment of their people cannot come from Christ or Christianity. What makes for growth, health, and happiness will not be found in the religion of the conquerors. So the suggestion is that much antipathy remains. Christian views of God are the enemy.

Spirituality

One of the more intriguing pre-classical remains excavated at La Venta is a circle of humanoid figures, standing upright, in what may be a ceremonial posture. Behind them are celts (knife/axe-head implements) that seem to represent columns (like the standing-stones that one finds in pre-historic Celtic ceremonial contexts). This group of figures had been buried, but with indications that those doing the burying wanted them to be found easily. The faces are mask-like: slitted eyes, mouths stretched wide in what might be either a grin or a grimace, high (bald) foreheads, heads flattened in the back. The heads are disproportionately large, like those of infants. The shoulders are wide and the arms long, but without hands (some figures clearly have been broken, but of others it is hard to say whether they ever had hands). None of the figures seems to be female (all chests are flat). Something ghostly emanates from this group of figures, and perhaps that is deliberate. Perhaps the group represents spirits of the dead, or Olmecs involved in mortuary rites. Something of the power of abstract African masks waves out from the circle. The artists responsible for this group of figures knew how to suggest transpersonal characteristics. Though the figures vary, none of them could be considered a portrait. All seem to express the essence of a human existence centered not on personal idiosyncrasies but on demanding, natural or cosmic, issues of sober contemplation, strong endurance, perhaps fear and the need to keep up one's guard.

Although we have concentrated on Teotihuacan and the Maya, it bears remembering that other Mesoamerican cultural centers, such as Monte Alban, where Zapotec religion flourished during the classical period, also present interesting data. At Monte Alban, for instance, exemplary funerary remains testify to the cult of the dead that was a strong presence throughout classical Mesoamerica. Tombs, probably built during people's lifetimes, received the dead as though receiving gods. The status of the dead seems to have hovered between that of spirits needing to be placated and that of gods whom one would worship. Indeed, at Monte Alban evidence suggests a cult of the dead, a species of ancestor veneration, much like what we associate with traditional China.

Another interesting feature of classical Zapotec religion is a widespread animism. Trees, stars, hills, and other significant features of the natural world were all considered live, spiritual entities. The Zapotecs thought that they themselves would become clouds at death (a belief reminiscent of what we found in southwestern tribes of North America, who probably were influenced by Mesoamerican customs). The Mixtecs, another cultural group we might have studied thoroughly, had it not been for the greater eminence of the Teotihuacanos and the Maya, considered trees to be their main ancestors. Both Zapotec and Mixtec remains exhibit a sensitivity to the ultimate significance of the natural world, suggesting that such a sensitivity probably was present at Teotihuacan and Mayan sites, moving beneath concern with ritual and "higher" gods.

Classical Themes

Mesoamerican spirituality of the classical period strikes the comparativist as discernibly different from the spirituality of the tribes of North America, and even from the spirituality of Mesoamericans in earlier periods. Culture has taken a quantum leap, with the creation of good-sized cities and the elaboration of an imperial sort of religion. Writing, however rudimentary, has become part of the religious scene. The scribe, as we have seen, was an important figure, worthy of being represented in the pantheon (even though by rabbits and monkey-men).

The power of the priests derived from their control of ritual and ideology, which in turn was facilitated by writing. If they could determine what was entered in the different codexes, they could determine how people would be expected to think in the future. Moreover, because the priests could write, they could construct the sacred calendars, on which so much of Mesoamerican politics, as well as ritual, depended. Granted, the writing was hieroglyphic, not abstract as modern writing has become. Nonetheless, it set in stone (sometimes literally) the figures, symbols, calendrical numbers, and other key reference points.

So, something new had entered into Mesoamerican spirituality. Key reference points were now fixed, in ways that they had never been when tradition was completely oral. The correlation between the accession of priests to religious authority (usually by replacing shamans) and writing is not hard and fast, but it is customary. In ancient Egypt, for example, the priests were the (hieroglyphic) writers. Naturally, most of the cultures that one would study, in trying to determine the connections between priests and sacred writing, did not distinguish secular and sacred matters as we moderns do. Priests could use their skill at writing to keep the accounts of the temple that they served. They could be bookkeepers, as well as supposed amanuenses of the gods, taking dictation that became scripture. But in all the writing that bore on religious things, they could capitalize on the wonder of transferring to the written page the flashes of insight that gave rise to religious imagery, myths, and rubrics, seeming to be masters of the Word (which, for most traditional peoples, has had something divine about it).

Thus Mesoamerican spirituality of the classical period shows not only the concerns that we would expect of agricultural peoples—

interest in fertility, sensitivity to the sacred significance of natural objects, interaction with animals, speculation about the unions between human beings and animals, fascination with the heavens—but also concerns peculiar to urban, highly cultured peoples. To become absorbed with time, for example, as the Mayan calendar indicates that large portions of the Mayan population must have, was a new phenomenon in Mesoamerica. We saw that it probably began with the Olmecs, but, if North American patterns offer any valid comparison, prior to such seeds of what became classical Mesoamerican culture, it would not have commanded special attention. Only when the population became dense enough to free a class for speculation about the foundations or leading features of traditional religion did a complicated, sophisticated measurement of time come into being.

It took much time and energy to make the observations and calculations on which the classical Mesoamerican calendars depended. It took a class of people able to convince themselves that working out the patterns of time past, and projecting forward the patterns (the numbers) of time future, was a pressing task. Whatever intellectual delight Mesoamericans took in their calculations, it seems clear that they were motivated more by the need to engage with the ways of the heavenly gods. Those "ways" might be available in calculations of the movement of the heavens. They could submit to being clothed in mathematical formulas, as well as in astrological speculations. When a people takes the step to trust the work of the human mind and associate insight with "divinization" (either learning the will of the gods or entering into the divine substance, which implies ongoing understanding), it moves away from tribal religion.

Aztec Themes

In Latourette Sejourné's interpretation of Mesoamerican spirituality of the post-classical period, everything positive in Aztec culture comes from the Toltec traditions about Quetzalcoatl, while everything debased stems from native Aztec interpretations of the needs of the gods for blood. Quetzalcoatl is responsible for all noble aspects of culture. He made human beings from his own blood, and he discovered maize while seeking a way to nourish them. Similarly, he discovered precious stones and taught human beings how to polish them. Weaving, dyeing, making mosaics (using quetzal feathers), mathematics, astronomy, and religious ceremonies all were his gifts. As king, Topilitzin Quetzalcoatl performed all ceremonies exactly, developed religous doctrine, purified the priesthood (making virtue rather than heredity the criterion for advancement).

In contrast, the native Aztec god of war Huitzilopochtli was the focus of a power-hungry people content to live by strife and blood. Sejourné calls the Aztec empire a betrayal of Quetzalcoatl. While this god's spirit lingered on in the refinements that we have mentioned (including the notion that the priests were to be kind, and punctilious about the rituals), the body of Quetalcoatl's influence had vanished from political and ceremonial life. There power and blood-lust ruled. There spirituality took the form of perversion: sophistication about ways to sacrifice human beings, ingenuity about flaying the body and working its skin.

Sejourné's interpretation may be tendentious, but it reminds us that the Aztec fusion of refinement and perversion begs a cultural explanation. It also reminds us that many religious traditions have gone through periods of decline, when the relatively noble, pure ideals at their origins degenerated into supports for all too human lusts for power, wealth, and pleasure.

Recent Trends

In the mid-1940s, the North American anthropologist Oscar Lewis studied the culture of Tepoztlan, a town just south of Mexico City. Central to this culture was the Catholicism that had evolved there. Consider the following descriptions of a small aspect of Tepoztlan Catholicism: "Tepoztelans do not like to confess; the majority do so only once a year. Not giving much importance to sin, Tepoztelans do not regard confession as necessary. Most men consider confession important only when one is about to die but 'with the pangs of death, who's going to remember to confess properly?' Women, particularly married women, are less reluctant to confess, and about fifty women are known to take communion and confess quite often. Through the Accion Catolica the number of young people of both sexes who do this has increased. Perhaps the most important deterrent to confession, especially among the old people, is that the priest may exact from the confessor [*sic*] the recitation of certain prayers which most people cannot say accurately. Fearing a scolding from the priest, they prefer to avoid the situation. There is no such difficulty with communion. 'We would all take communion more often if we didn't have to confess; that we always avoid.' "[43]

While we may question how fully Lewis has understood Tepoztlan Catholicism, since certain usages seem unusual, we can suppose that he has reported the average person's sense of confession accurately enough to permit some speculation. Why is it that Tepoztelans do not give much importance to sin? That seems a strange attitude for Christians. Inasmuch as sin summarizes the painful aspects of the human condition, without a strong sense of sin people are not likely to appreciate or celebrate redemption. The strong influence of the apostle Paul on mainstream Christianity has guaranteed that sin would be important in all orthodox faith, liturgy, and ethical analysis. Certainly many people who are only nominal Christians never think deeply about sin. Perhaps the Tepoztelans are little different from people in Detroit or Phoenix or Paris who go to church now and then but don't think deeply about their faith. On the other hand, perhaps something from native, pre-Christian Tepoztlan culture also shapes this attitude. Perhaps Tepoztelans have found it difficult to appreciate the precisely personal character of the Christian God.

Traditional Mesoamerican religion, as we have seen, deals with deities that are largely personifications of natural forces. However full the mythology of a particular god, he or she does not become personal the way that Jesuchristo can. Many Mesoamericans accept the full personalism of Jesus and become ardent disciples. But popular Mesoamerican religion may resist such a development, in part because dealing with a fully human, truly personal deity goes against traditional, pre-Christian instincts. Thus, long-standing pagan attitudes remain strong, even when Christianity seems dominant.

Chapter 8

TRADITIONS OF SOUTH AMERICA

Background

We begin with traditions of the Andes, a chain of mountains running north-south through the length of South America, dividing the western, Pacific coast from the interior regions. The culmination of pre-European Andean religion was the magnificent Inca religious culture, but much history preceded the Inca. Human beings have inhabited the Andean area for perhaps ten thousand years. Paleontologists sometimes assume that these early settlers were descendants of the Asiatic peoples who came to North America across what is now the Bering Strait. In that scenario, they would have slowly migrated southward, through Mesoamerica, eventually reaching not only the southern Andes but even Tierra del Fuego, the southernmost part of South America.

The earliest Andeans were hunters and agriculturalists of the Neolithic period. By the period 3000–2000 B.C. more complex cultures had developed. For example, the Aldas of the north coast of Peru built huge temples (perhaps influenced by Mesoamerican forebears). During the next two millennia peoples such as the Valdiva and Chavin advanced Andean culture. The glory of the recent two thousand years has been the Inca empire, which at the time of contact with Europeans, early in the sixteenth century, covered more than four thousand miles. The northern boundary lay at what is now southern Columbia, while the southern boundary lay at what is now south-central Chile. The Inca ruled over much of present-day Ecuador, Peru, Bolivia, and Chile. Between the Chavin culture of about 800 B.C. and the Inca empire lay such intermediary peoples as the Nazca and Moche, the Tiahuanaco, the Huari, and the Chimu. Thus, the Inca did not spring from nothingness. They built on the achievements

176

The Cat God. The dominant design of the Chavin culture (1200—400 B.C.)

of a long line of Andean predecessors, even though they greatly expanded the territory that these predecessors had dominated.

The physical setting of the Andean region includes a variety of ecological systems. There are deserts along the coast, intersected by valleys with fertile lands. The highlands can be farmed to as high as 12,000 feet. Rain forests of the Amazon cover areas that Andean peoples controlled, while in areas that geologists call montane, moist, cool upland slopes were covered with evergreen trees. This variety of ecological systems provided several valuable sources of subsistence. People could hunt, fish, gather roots and berries, plant crops, and herd such animals as llamas, alpacas, and guanacos. They could build with wood or stone, clothe themselves with skins, fleeces, or wools. The abundance of natural resources provided the larger cultures, including the Incan civilization, a solid economic base.

None of the Andean cultures developed a written language, but *quipus* (knotted strings) filled some of the functions of hieroglyphs. The Inca kept records through a system of such strings. Local officials would send information and the "keeper of the strings" would organize it in terms of knots. Both economic and military information was stored in this way. While such a use of strings was practical, in the background lay the notion that the universe, though unruly, could be managed (tied down) somewhat through the *quipus*. Time, fate, even guilt come under human control, if a people finds a symbolism to bind or loosen them.[44]

The Andes divide into northern, central, and southern regions. In the northern Andes Caribbean and southern Mesoamerican influences were significant. The central Andes were the zone of greatest cultural development in all of pre-Columbian South America. Archeologists divide the central Andes into such cultural sub-areas as the northern highlands, the north coast, the central highlands, the central coast, the southern highlands, and the south coast. The coastal areas were rich in fish, while the valleys were watered by rivers. On the eastern side of the Andes lay tropical forests. The earliest cultural remains suggest that nomadic peoples created stable villages because they wanted centers at which to hold their ceremonies. Before 1500 B.C. or so agriculture was fitful, while making pottery and weaving textiles were just getting under way.

By 500 B.C. building had progressed considerably. The Chavin style of art and architecture developed in this period, coming to dominate what is now northern and central Peru. A great ruin, Chavin de Huantar in the northern highlands, represents this style, but archeologists debate whether this site was where the Chavin style originated.

This beaded collar, strung with shell and stone beads on cotton cords is an example of the Chimu style, Peru. The Chimu people were predecessors of the Incas.

Among the ruins there lie remains of a massive complex of temples made from dressed stone blocks, rectangular in shape. These temples had interior galleries with bas-relief carvings on pillars and lintels. Among the motifs of the carvings are figures of animals (cats, crocodiles, serpents), and also figures of human beings. Sometimes all of these figures are mixed together to make complex, fantastic images. The Chavin culture seems to have flourished because agriculture had progressed sufficiently to undergird a sedentary way of life. Such a way of life allowed the development of weaving, making pottery, and carving stone.

The Tropical Forest

For most commentators the great culture of South America was that which arose in the Andes and culminated with the Inca. This culture dominated until the Spanish conquest. At first it was centered along the coastal regions of the central Andes, after which it moved to the highlands. To the north, small chiefdoms were the rule. To the east, moving into the great tropical forest, much less impressive tribal structures prevailed. In east-central South America, farming only came after 500 A.D., being introduced from the Amazon basin into the Brazilian forest and savannah. The northern tribes had cultivated manioc (cassava), a plant raised in the tropics for its starch. In the savannah of the Chaco, in the south-central portion of the continent, and on the steppes of the eastern portion of the south, hunting continued to be the way of life even after 500 A.D.

The area denoted by "the tropical forest" is vast, but we must also note developments that occurred in tribes that ranged outside the rain forest, such as the Ge of northern Brazil. On the whole, most tribes employed cultivation, hunting, gathering, and fishing, though the precise plants and animals on which they depended, in concert with the particular mythologies that they developed, led to significant differences in their religious cultures. Although a tribe of ten thousand is large nowadays, prior to the European conquest that began in the sixteenth century perhaps as many as ten million natives inhabited this vast area. In fact, the overall population of natives today may be only five percent of what it was at the first contact with whites.

The main centers of population traditionally were coastal regions and along rivers. Villages could number over one thousand inhabitants (in contrast to today's native settlements, which tend to be much smaller). This change in size is bound to reflect significant cultural changes, but we do not know the political arrangements, economics, or full ritual life that prevailed in pre-Christian times. Still, today's natives bear enough religious similarity to the people described in accounts by early missionaries to let us suspect that some continuity has occurred in religious matters. (We might expect this, because religion tends to be a conservative aspect of culture, probably because it frequently calls into question and play a people's deepest sense of itself.) For example, accounts from the mid-eighteenth century of the religious practices of Carib peoples of the coast of Guiana describe beliefs and rituals still held today.

When we speak of the lands dominated by the Amazon, the area in question is huge: more than 2.6 million square kilometers. The Amazon is a great receptacle, receiving water from over a thousand tributaries. Most of these tributaries are relatively small, but seventeen are over 1,000 miles long. Indeed, while the Amazon itself is the world's largest river (in terms of volume and area drained), two of its tributaries rank third and fourth. In places the Amazon is over ten miles wide. It receives waters rushing down from the Andes, but other sources, in the lowlands, run slowly, in leisurely curves. The Amazon forest has produced a great variety of trees and plants. In the western lowlands people have long raised maize, but to the east manioc is the traditional staple. One hypothesis is that farming manioc began in what is now eastern Venezuela and moved south and east. In the lowlands related to the Amazon and the Orinoco rivers it continues to be the main crop, people practicing the slash-and-burn farming that has prevailed for centuries. The yearly deposits of silt from the rivers guarantees fertile farmland. Away from the rivers, however, farmers using slash-and-burn techniques have to move their crops every few years.

Eastern Colombia, Ecuador, Peru, Bolivia, Brazil, and eastern Venezuela all depend on the Amazon or its tributaries. The Amazonian rain forest can be extremely dense, and at points the canopy over it, created by its tallest trees, can reach more than one hundred feet. Innumerable species of both plants and animals are native to the rain forest. From its trees natives have derived rope, rubber, barkcloth, and thatch for their huts. It is difficult to hunt in the denser parts of the forest, which inclined most tribes to settle along the edge of rivers. Farming was also easier there. Archeologists estimate that the rivers of the Amazonian system have been inhabited for at least seven thousand years. The great variety of languages spoken in this area proves that many different peoples filtered in and out. For example, there are tribes speaking Arawak, a language now found in the Antilles. This suggests a scenario in which tribes migrated downriver, and then spread out to the upper Amazon and the region of the Orinoco River, eventually reaching the east coast, whence they moved on to Trinidad and the Antilles. In the same vein, the presence of Carib speakers in the Amazon basin suggests considerable movement in and out of this area, since the distance to the Caribbean is considerable.

To travel, Amazonian peoples apparently favored dugout canoes and explored the system of rivers. At the time of contact with Europeans, many Amazonians were living in houses constructed from planks of cedar. They slept in hammocks, employed mats made of large palm leaves, and wore garments woven from cotton, which they usually painted. Some favored cloaks made of feathers. Musical instruments were much in favor, including drums, rattles, and flutes. For hunting, and fighting, they developed spearthrowers and shields. Their burial rites, somewhat like those of Andeans, included deforming the skulls of the deceased and burying them with numerous goods. They also developed impressive skill as potters.

Simply listing these features of traditional life in the Amazonian basin suggests that traditional South American peoples had considerable contact among themselves. Which people first developed the practice of deforming skulls, or first created artistic pottery, may be hard to determine, but it seems clear that, once a given practice had arisen, it tended to migrate to other areas. In the course of such migration, it usually changed. Thus tribes tended to develop their own patterns in pottery and weaving, sometimes so distinctively that these patterns became like signatures.

What scholars know about the social arrangements in the areas dominated by the Amazon and its tributaries suggests that rule by chiefs was the normal pattern. In some areas villages were organized into larger structures, which in turn were ruled by superchiefs. One of the most important functions of the chief was to direct the schedule of planting and harvesting. This depended on knowing the ways of the rivers, their rising and lowering. Such knowledge was not purely scientific, however, because local belief held that the gods were responsible for how the rivers behaved. So the chief was a religious functionary, as well as a natural scientist. He had to consult the gods, if he were to learn the best schedule. Associated with the gods was the tribute offered to them at such moments as death. In the Amazon the funerary practices included shrinking heads and cannibalism, apparently as ways to honor the spirits of the departed and absorb some of their power.

Tribes of the tropical forest tended to supplement their diet of manioc with such meat as that of turtles and manatees. They would gather turtles and keep them in pens, not only because turtles were a

Men and women plowing the fields. The men use a footplow; the women break up the clods of earth.

Men and women sowing the land. Note the difference in dress. The plowing above was festival: here men and women wear common work dress.

source of food but also because turtle shells could make cutting tools. Much fishing was actually a form of hunting, since the people used spears. For hunting animals they tended to use not only spears but also bows and blowguns. Both arrows and the darts projected in blowguns could be dipped in curare, a poison. Other sources of food were mounds of insects and the honey of wild bees. In the upper Amazon other roots supplemented manioc. Sweet potato, yam, and arrowroot thrived. The peanut probably developed in this area, and also tobacco. People farmed chili peppers, pineapple, and beans, and they cultivated fruit trees. Cotton and gourds were also important.

The Gran Chaco

The last geographical area that we treat in this chapter features the Gran Chaco, but it includes the far south of the continent as well, running to the end of Tierra del Fuego. The Gran Chaco derives its name from a Quechua word meaning "hunting area." It is a huge alluvial plain dominating the interior of south-central South America. Population is sparse, and most of the area is arid, marked by low forests and savannas. To the west the Andes are the barrier to the Pacific. To the east the Paraguay and Parana rivers mark a boundary. The northern border, imprecise, comes from the high plains and swamps of southern Bolivia. The Rio Salado of Argentina serves as a southern boundary.

The area within these four rough boundaries is approximately 280,000 square miles. More than half now lies in Argentina, about a third now lies in Paraguay, and the rest lies in Bolivia. Traversing the Chaco are two great rivers, the Pilcomayo and the Bermejo. They are the major sources of water. Some geographers divide the Gran Chaco into northern, central, and southern regions, using these rivers as dividers. The northern region lies above the Pilcomayo. The central region lies between the Pilcomayo and the Bermejo. The southern region lies below the Bermejo. In such a division, the southern area is by far the largest, and the central area is by far the smallest.

Physically, the Gran Chaco is composed of sandy sediments as much as 10,000 feet deep. It is virtually without stone. West bank tributaries of the Paraguay and Parana rivers drain all but the northwest of the area. The Bermejo and Pilcomayo are typical Chaco waterways, in that their tributaries lose most of their waters before reaching the parent streams. Yet it is typical of the Chaco to suffer extreme flooding, because of poor drainage, and in times of strong rains as much as fifteen percent of the area can lie under water.

The feature most significant to native South Americans was the abundance of animal life, which made the Gran Chaco a prime hunting area. The jaguar, ocelot, puma, tapir, giant armadillo, and spiny anteater have been the predominant larger animals. Foxes, small wild cats, agouti (large rodents), capybara, deer, peccaries, and guanaco have also been important. Among its many birds is the rhea, a South American ostrich. The streams have carried more than four hundred different species of fish, including a version of salmon and the fearsome pirhana. Insects and snakes abound, including pit vipers and constrictors. There are also poisonous tree toads.

Because of this wealth of animal life, many native tribes hunted in the Gran Chaco. They also fished and gathered. Because their life tended to be nomadic, their groups tended to be small. Because fresh water was in short supply, the majority of the native tribes settled along streams. Anthropologists consider the Guaycuru, Lengua, Mataco, Vilela, Zamuco, and Tupi native to Gran Chaco. Their material cultures traditionally depended on wood and bones, since few stones were available. The pineapple-like ground cover called *carraguatas* was the usual source of fiber. Though the Chaco forest was harsh, it contained many food sources: edible pods, fruits, berries, and tubers. In fact, the forest was the best area for gathering foods. Natives have tended to hunt by trapping, netting, clubbing and spearing game, which they have attacked cooperatively, driving them toward traps or nets.

The natives who have retained traditional cultures continue to live by hunting, gathering, and fishing, though many now have domesticated animals and metal tools. Jesuit missionaries were the only successful European occupiers of the Chaco, prior to the middle of the nineteenth century. Their agricultural communes (*reducciones*) have drawn much study, and perhaps equal measures of praise and blame. Natives were extremely hostile to European presence, and the land was forbidding, so incentives to foreign settlers were small. Since World War II the governments of Argentina and Paraguay have encouraged settlement and development. Mennonites from Canada and the Soviet Union settled during the 1920s and 1930s. Other refugees from the Soviet Union arrived after World War II, and the total population from these colonies now numbers more than 30,000. The Bolivian Chaco has been used successfully for ranging cattle, and proximity to oil and gas supplies, along with hydroelectric power from fast-flowing streams, suggests that this area may be developed extensively in the future.

South of the Gran Chaco is the immense (260,000 square mile) desert of southern Argentina known as Patagonia. This is a tableland extending from the Andes in the west to the Atlantic ocean in the east.

On the whole it is a vast, treeless steppe. The land rises, east to west, from about 300 feet at the Atlantic coast to 3,000 feet at the base of the Andes. The table land region stands as much as 5,000 feet above sea level. Plant, animal, and fish life is considerably poorer than that of the Gran Chaco. The native inhabitants seem to have moved north from Tierra del Fuego, perhaps as much as 5,000 years ago. They stand out for their height and robust constitution. The Puelche-Guennakin have predominated in the north and the Chonik (Tehuelche) in the south. At the time of Spanish invasion the native tribes were nomadic hunters who followed the guanaco and nandu (ostrich). Spanish towns date from 1778, and during the nineteenth century various immigrants (for example, Welsh) came in search of religious or political freedom. Recently many Chileans have come as temporary laborers.

Nature

The gods traditional in Andean religion represented the forces of nature that the people thought most significant. As we have seen, virtually all other native American peoples have thought this way. In the case of Inca cosmology, we find the belief that the Inca gods commanded the development of the capital city, Cuzco, and that the imposition of order on surrounding peoples was an act of benevolence. In other words, the Inca gods represented the harmonious order of the universe, which they mediated to the people who reverenced them. The central temple of Cuzco was dedicated to the sun. There occurred the sacrifices and other ceremonies on which the health of the Inca depended. One of the tributes that conquered people had to pay was material for such sacrifices. This could include young people, the flower of the conquered tribe, whose vitality would help the gods keep the vitality of the Inca strong.

The Inca divided their empire into four quadrants (perhaps continuing the cosmological symbolism that we saw in Mesoamerica). A system of imaginary lines radiating from the center of the capital established the axes for ancillary shrines. At the time of the Spanish conquest such shrines numbered 428. Clearly, the Inca thought it useful to consecrate the lines that organized their realm, so that what we might call its web or skeleton was protected at all significant points. When it came time to build ceremonial centers in outlying parts of the empire, the Inca followed the pattern established in Cuzco.

Another feature of Inca cosmological thought was a dualism that distinguished villages, and even whole territories, into a superior and an inferior half. This dualism, somewhat reminiscent of the Chinese *yin* and *yang,* created a half considered high, superior, right, and masculine, and a half considered the opposite: low, inferior, left, and feminine. The notion was that the cosmos itself was organized in this dualistic way, so that the human realm merely reflected reality as a whole. The two halves did not carry completely opposite values, as the descriptions of them might suggest. Both were necessary for the healthy functioning of the cosmos and the human realm. Only when they were in harmony could one expect full health and prosperity. Still, the associations of the "upper" half were more positive than those of the "lower" half, so this dualism was a basis for discrimination or lower evaluation. For example, women did not command the respect accorded to men.

The Mapuche, who currently number about 250,000 and reside mainly in Chile, show that Inca patterns have continued to prevail in areas that the Inca once controlled. The Mapuche have retained much of their traditional religion, despite intense attention from Christian missionaries. Their worldview divides the cosmos into the part that is bright or belongs to the day and the part that is dark or belongs to the night. Dawn and midnight are the two poles of this system. A symbolism of color expresses the chromatic aspects of Mapuche thought. Blue is the color prevailing when light is in the ascendant. White-yellow shows the decline of the cosmos, as the light and the day run down. The worst colors are black and red, which suggest the presence and work of the *wekuft,* the evil spirits who rule the night. The Mapuche use this dualistic system, which of course is much more complicated, to interpret dreams, predict the future, and, in general, orient themselves in the world. The patterns of the cosmos determine human fate, so the more that people (especially shamans) can grasp the ramifications of cosmic dualism, the better able they are to cope with human fortunes.[45]

The Andean god Illapa, who rules thunder, lightning, and the weather, expresses another aspect of traditional Andean attitudes toward nature. Illapa takes many different forms, and goes by many different names throughout the Andean region, but the consistency of his appearance and supposed deeds suggests that there is only one god in question. The great symbol of Illapa is the hawk, who flies proudly through the sky (surveying the weather). This symbol is also associated with the sun god Inti, so some analysts speak of a fusion of

Illapa and Inti, weather (or storm) and sun. Both are divinities of the sky. Both influence the weather that has so significant a say in human experience and prosperity. Indeed, Illapa controls not only the storm, but also the rainbow. He is lord of peace as well as trouble. Inasmuch as the rain comes down from the sky, and the clouds contain the rain, both rain and clouds come under his dominion. The gift of rain puts a benevolent shade on the figure of Illapa. The destructive power of the storm puts a malevolent shade. So we find that Illapa himself is a dualistic figure, from several points of view. At the least, Andean peoples have grappled with the ambiguity of nature by making their major gods ambivalent figures.

The Tropical Forest
The impact of nature on peoples of the rain forest appears in the description of life among natives of that area that the anthropologist Florinda Donner experienced in the 1970s. Her tribe, the Yanomama, lived along the border of Venezuela and Brazil. Their travels took them through the rain forest, but also to sites from which one could see over the forest. On one journey the beauty of the Yanomama habitat nearly overwhelmed her: "We reached the top of a plateau eroded by winds and rains, a relic from another age. Below, the forest was still asleep under a blanket of fog. A mysterious, pathless world whose vastness one could never guess from the outside. We sat on the ground and silently waited for the sun to rise.

"An overwhelming sense of awe brought me to my feet as the sky in the east flowed red and purple along the horizon. The clouds, obedient to the wind, opened to let the rising disk through. Pink mist rolled over the treetops, touching up shadows with deep blue, spreading green and yellow all over the sky until it changed into a transparent blue.

"I turned to look behind me, to the west, where clouds were changing shape, giving way to the expanding light. To the south, the sky was tinted with fiery streaks and luminous clouds piled up, pushed up by the wind.

"'Over there is our *shabono* [settlement],' Etewa said, pointing into the distance. He grasped my arm and turned me around, into a northerly direction. 'And over there is the great river [the Orinoco], where the white man passes by.'

"The sun had lifted the blanket of fog. The river shone like a golden snake cutting through the greenness until it lost itself in an immensity of space that seemed to be part of another world.

"I wanted to cry out loud, but I had no words with which to

express my emotions. Looking at Ritimi and Etewa, I knew they understood how deeply I felt. I held out my arms as if to embrace this marvelous border of forest and sky. I felt I was at the edge of time and space. I could hear the vibrations of the light, the whispering of trees, the cries of distant birds carried by the wind."[46]

The Ge of Brazil have attracted the attention of scholars because of their mythology. Its main interest is the interactions among human beings and animals, including imaginative monsters. As though to mediate the contact beween the human and natural worlds, many stories feature creatures half-human and half-animal. Another suggestion that the main Ge interest is the interface between humans and animals comes from the fact that the focus of many stories is the edge of the village, where the forest approaches. (Other myths deal with the sky or the underearth.) The Ge seem fascinated by the transformations that occur at the border between the human and natural worlds. They are also interested in relationships (for example, with in-laws), more than in individuals (the exploits of heroes). Only the myths about the sun and the moon violate this general rule.

The Ge story about the origin of fire illustrates this people's interest in both transformations and relationships. A man and his brother-in-law go into the forest to find young macaws, whom they plan to raise to adulthood for their feathers. When they reach a nest, the man places a pole against a rock and the boy climbs up to look into the nest. The man asks the boy what the birds look like, and the boy replies, "your wife's pubic hair." Insulted, the man throws down the pole and leaves the boy isolated. The boy grows thin and covered with bird-droppings. A jaguar comes by, and the boy tells it of his plight. The jaguar tells him to throw down the young birds. The boy does so. The jaguar eats them, and then replaces the pole. The boy is terrified that the jaguar will eat him too, but he climbs down and follows the jaguar to its house. There the boy sees fire for the first time. (Previously his tribe had only warmed their meat in the sun.) The jaguar gives the boy roasted meat.

The boy returns home and describes the jaguar's fire. His tribe decides to take it away. Disguised as animals, the men reach the jaguar's house and find its family sleeping. They pour hot beeswax on the animals' eyes and paws, sending them screaming into the jungle. The men take the log of fire back to their village. They carry the log in relays. When it comes time for the man disguised as a frog to carry it, the log is so hot that the frog drops it in water. Following the log have been various birds, who have been swallowing the live coals dropped on the way. (That is why their neck feathers are bright red.) They vomit forth these coals and the fire starts up again. The tapir picks up the rekindled log and races with it to the village. There the men return to human form and divide the fire among all the houses. Ever since the tribe has had roasted meat.[47]

This Ge myth is a traditional source of entertainment. Acting it out provides many comic moments. It is interesting that the boy and the man do not get along, and that the disrespectful boy becomes the source of the tribe's greatest blessing. The jaguar is the most striking cat of the forest, and here it does the tribe (in the person of the boy) a great favor. For this good deed it receives only pain, which leaves the question of relations between human beings and animals hanging. Perhaps the story means to underscore the cruelty of human beings to animals. The transformation of the men who steal the fire into animals suggests the kinship of human beings and other species. They cannot be far apart, if such transformations occur easily. The help of the birds in rekindling the fire is another suggestion that animals do human beings many good deeds. The note that the fire-throated birds had been picking up live coals is an intriguing aside, designed to answer the question of where such birds got their brilliance.

The story as a whole seems designed to explain the origin of the tribe's possession of fire, but as it unfolds, many other aspects of tribal life pass review. Still, central to the entire myth is the interaction between human beings and the natural world, especially that of animals and birds. The jaguar, representing the animal kingdom, is wiser and better than the human beings he helps. The natural world is more powerful, beautiful, and mysterious than the world of the village. And yet human beings triumph over the natural world, by trickery and perseverance. The great strength of human beings is their cunning.

The Gran Chaco

As we might expect, nature figures prominently in the mythologies of tribes of the Gran Chaco and southern South America. For example, the Chiriguano speak of twins, Yanderu Tumpa and Ana Tumpa, who are connected with stories about the moon. Yanderu Tumpa is responsible for the cosmos. He gave the Chiriguano the goods of the earth, and so is their great benefactor. He also instructed them in what are now their main cultural practices. For his own purposes, he created Ana Tumpa, a likeness of himself, but this twin revolted, out of envy, becoming a dark deity. The mission of Ana Tumpa is to undermine the good works of Yanderu Tumpa. Thus the Chiriguano live in a dualistic cosmos. A principle of goodness is responsible for all that they enjoy, all that gives them sustenance and delight. But a principle of evil causes malfunctions and illnesses. Because Yanderu Trumpa was generous, Ana Tumpa has considerable power. Witches share in his power, helping to fulfill his wicked purposes.

The minions of Ana Trumpa, known as *anas,* are now great influences in the Chiriguano world. Their worst works are those that bring death, the summary of the pain now afflicting human beings. Students of Chiriguano language and thought debate the meaning of the term "tumpa." Apparently it refers to the state or condition of a given being. One conjecture, then, is that Yanderu is the being of extraordinary state or nature who is the source of positive things, while Ana is the being of extraordinary state or nature who is the source of negative things. All things—beings, effects—get their "state" from one of these two primary sources. Shamans tend to derive their power from Ana Tumpa, which suggests that they focus mainly on wickedness—either to do harm, or to ward off harm. For shamans, the anas may be either helpful or hurtful. (Perhaps shamans are those human beings strong enough to negate the negativity of the anas and so bring about positive effects through power given by the anas.) The kind of career that a shaman will have can be determined during his initiation. If he does not gain a good result from contacting the anas, he may be condemned to work only evil.

It is not clear how this basic dualism relates to the moon, except that the moon is the heavenly being that changes most dramatically. More than the sun, the moon varies in intensity and size. The contrast between sun and moon stimulates many peoples to think about the world in dipolar ways. Certainly, other dualisms, especially that of males and females, are further stimuli, but when traditional peoples look to the heavens (the main source of their archetypes, and the place where, it seems instinctively, many peoples seek guidance), they find the contrast between the sun and the moon especially provocative. It is not clear that the Chiriguano think of the two primary deities as sun and moon, but they do seem to associate Ana Tumpa with the moon. Quite like the Chiriguano worldview is that of such other tribes of the Tupi-Guarani family as the Tapui and the Guasurangwe.

In Paraguay the Lengua-Mascoy family of tribes, which includes the Agnaite, the Lengua, the Kaskiha, and the Sanapana, shows signs of having developed a syncretistic mythology. Many influences seem to have shaped the stories that one finds in this language group. Basic to their general worldview is the three-storey world that we have found in other geographical areas: the heavenly realm above, the earthly zone in the middle, and the underworld beneath human beings. In each of these levels of reality, supernatural beings are at work. Their attitude toward human beings is ambivalent: both good and evil occur on all three levels.

Prominent among the deities one finds among these tribes is Moksohanak, who rules the dead. He stalks those who grow sick, and his delight is to carry them off to the west, where lies the land of the dead. Probably the west is the land of the dead because that is where the sun disappears at the end of each day. "Deadness" is most powerful under the earth, but it can afflict the heavens as well (as the "death" of the sun at night, and on occasion the moon, suggests). The earth is the land of the living, as are the skies above it where the birds fly, and the first sections of the underworld, where plants and animals can dwell. But creatures of the earth have to fear Moksohanak. He is strongest at night, so even if one is not sick, one should be careful in the dark, lest Moksohanak draw near and cause mischief.

Natives of Tierra del Fuego apparently show little interest in cults of the dead. In their conception of the cosmos, the afterlife is not a passionate concern. As anthropological observers construct it to date, the typical worldview in the southernmost portions of South America places more emphasis on initiating young men and women into the various societies that will structure their adult lives. A marked separation of men and women occurs in Tierra del Fuego, and in some initiation ceremonies men, made up as demonic spirits, try to frighten women. The men wear masks, paint their bodies such colors as black, white, and pink, and impersonate spirits thought to control the forest or the sea. They also represent the spirits of significant animals.

The Group

The Paracas Peninsula on the south coast of Peru is adjacent to rich fishing grounds, which apparently attracted a settlement before the Christian era. Archeological finds there at a site known as Cerro Colorado have revealed the presence of three cemeteries, the oldest materials in which may date to as early as 600–400 B.C. One of the names for the style of this burial site is Carvernas, because its tombs, dug in shafts, resemble caverns or bottles. The custom was to bury thirty to forty people in such a tomb, along with their goods. Many of the skulls found in the Cavernas burial sites had been trepanned (had

had holes bored into them), and almost all were distorted. The bored skulls tended to have rectangular pieces removed.

Bundles of remains of some bodies were adorned with cotton masks. These represented a head, or a whole human figure, painted red, dark brown, purple, or gray. The style was that of Chavin-like textiles. The high quality cotton and wool garments in which the typical bundle was housed suggest that this site was for wealthy people. The garments were often embroidered carefully. Archeologists found such bundles buried in the walls or foundations of nearby houses, apparently to protect them against looters. The typical bundle was cone-shaped and could stand as high as four and a half feet. The large bundles contained many more artifacts than the small ones. Because each bundle was distinctive (decorated in unique patterns), it appears that considerable care went into burial procedures.

The trepanning probably was part of a process of mummification. Scholars dispute whether internal organs and brains were removed. It also seems possible that the inhabitants of this area dried or smoked their corpses. Typically, the dead person was tied into the fetal position (often a sign of hope for rebirth). Sometimes the person was left in a loincloth or other covering, but more often it was naked. Investigators have found gold sheets at the back of the mouths of many corpses. Between the chest and the legs would usually be a gourd bowl. Some bodies also had gold jewelry nearby: earrings, nose rings, and adornments for the brow. The entire combination—corpse plus gifts—was wrapped in a coarse cotton cloth, which then went into a basket or onto a mat. More artifacts went into spaces left in the basket, to make the compact "bundle." The hallmark of the Paracas culture is the large embroidered mantle that usually covered the entire bundle. This could be as much as eight feet long.

Thirty years after the European conquest a messianic movement swept into the Andean regions. Called Taqui Oncoy, this movement sought to drive the whites away and reinstate the Inca past. The defeat of the Inca forces by the whites had caused the sun god to lose respect. A new form of religion, not focused on the sun, replaced the solar cult and formed the basis of popular understanding of this messianism. People sought to purify the land and invigorate the *huacas*, beings taking over the center of divine power. Although Taqui Oncoy declined after ten years or so, it continued to intrigue native intellectuals. To this day, some scholars claim, intellectuals in Peru and Bolivia contemplate a return to a pre-Christian, Inca past. Whether they would desire the full Inca ritual, or merely see the Inca past as a symbol of autonomy lost to European influences, is hard to say.

The Tropical Forest

The Mehinaku of Brazil provide ample illustration that many forest tribes have developed dramatic ways for their members to interact. In the 1970s the anthropologist Thomas Gregor studied this tribe through the lens of the theory of how human beings are regularly, perhaps constitutionally, dramatic. One pointed example comes from his observation of children's games: What is to me the most stirring of the games of role playing is 'Women's Sons.' . . . Held at a good distance from the village where the children cannot be seen either by their parents or their other siblings, 'Women's Sons,' quite unlike most plaza games, is played by boys and girls together. The age of the players runs from about five to twelve years.

"The game begins as the children pair off as married couples. The husband and wife sculpt a child from a clump of earth, carving arms, legs, features, and even genitals. They cradle the baby in their arms and talk to it. The mother holds the child on her hip and dances with it as she has seen her own mother do with younger siblings. After the parents have played with their child for a while, it sickens and dies. The parents weep and dig a grave for the infant and bury it. All the mothers then form a circle on their knees in traditional fashion and, with their heads down and their arms over each other's shoulders, they keen and wail for the lost offspring.

"On the occasions that I have seen . . . ['Women's Sons'] played, the children were enormously amused by the entire enactment. When the time came to bury the 'babies,' the boys smashed them into pieces and the girls interrupted their ritual crying with bursts of giggling and shrieks of laughter. Nevertheless, 'Women's Sons' provides a tragic commentary on Mehinaku life—death in infancy and early childhood is all too common in the village. The game helps the children prepare for the time when they may lose a sibling and, later on, an offspring of their own."[48]

Other games that Mehinaku children play illustrate further aspects of their culture. For example, in playing at marriage, groups of children act out the ritual of placing the groom's hammock above that of the bride. They also organize themselves in the relations that govern Mehinaku marriage, where avoiding close incest is crucial but marriage between cousins is desirable. The children play out the sexual roles of husbands and wives, the boys going off on fishing trips and the girls cooking the catch on palm leaves. They may also pair off for sexual exploration (Mehinaku culture allows this) or even intercourse. In further variation, the children will act out the beating that a jealous husband would give his wife, were he to find her with a lover.

The core of the Mehinaku religion that undergirds tribal life is a belief in spirits. Living beings, including large animals, have an insubstantial form, their spirit. These move like the wind, and the Mehinaku consider such phenomena as whirlwinds, eerie sounds, or showers of meteors to demonstrate their presence. The sick, the dying, and the shamans who attend them are all likely to see spirits. People can also see spirits in dreams. Usually the spirits are frightening, having huge heads, long teeth, eyes that glow in the dark, and deep, terrible voices.

The Mehinaku classify the spirits into those that deal with foods, such as manioc and corn, those that deal with the festivals that dot the calendar, demons that haunt areas of the forest or lakes, and those that have a human appearance (once one zips off their skin, which is a disguise) but are immune to disease or defect. These latter spirits can steal away a normal person's soul. The time when people are most vulnerable to such theft is when they are depressed or lonely. Shamans can regain the lost soul, however, and much of the shaman's business is concerned with either restoring souls or curing illness (which is somewhat cognate: the person is in danger of losing his or her vital spirit). Special ceremonies also deal with paying gifts to the spirits, to ensure their good will or overcome their potential harm.

Far South and the Gran Chaco

The masks that the men of Tierra del Fuego wear apparently are one of several features derived from natives of the forests. This reminds us that South American tribes, like North American tribes and peoples of Mesoamerica, interacted significantly. Even when they did not develop formal systems for trade, they observed one another's behavior and often borrowed shamelessly what they admired or thought effective. In the present case, we find that masks are a feature of initiation ceremonies throughout central South America. To dance while masked has been a primary way of escaping from normal reality and entering the world of the spirits that the initiations celebrate.

"Initiation" can be either a critical event, when a person changes state, or a part of an ongoing, lifelong maturation. As a critical event, it represents a transition that may be unrepeatable. For example, a young woman comes to maturity slowly, but the menarche marks a decisive, critical moment, after which there is no going back from physical maturity to childhood. Interested in their bodies, full of wonder at fertility, native South Americans instinctively tended to ritualize this dramatic time of somatic change. By analogy, they developed similar rituals for young men at the time of puberty.

Birth and death were other, even more dramatic, critical events, from which there was no going back. Some ceremonies might act out rebirth, but the difference between being in the womb, or not even conceived, and being out in the world as a human being, however small a baby, was unalterable. The same with passing from life to death. Any "coming back" that ghosts might accomplish was attenuated—nothing like a full return to ordinary, healthy, embodied existence. Some peoples have also likened marriage to a change of state, while others have barely ritualized it. When marriage is celebrated as a rite of passage, the theme is often that the spouses are advancing a fuller measure into adulthood. Spouses bear responsibility for bringing forth children and raising them. They have to work out a shared life, which can be a significant change from single living (even in societies where the sexes bond more closely, males with males and females with females, than occurs in contemporary mainstream North American culture).

Masks help to underscore the newness of the states that people are entering upon, when the initiation is concerned with critical changes. They also help to release people from their normal identities, and so their normal inhibitions, which can be useful when an "initiation" is ongoing. For example, South American tribes, like African tribes, can sponsor men's and women's societies that underwrite dances and other rituals designed for both bonding and advancing wisdom. When elders oversee such rituals, the ceremonies tend to become exercises in penetrating further into tribal lore. We might see them as "continuing education" or "graduate work." Inasmuch as what men or women are learning is how the world of spirits impinges on the tribe's life, whatever helps them to free their imaginations and loosen their feelings can stimulate their learning. As we have observed previously, the goal of traditional people's "educational" efforts is more than the conveyance of information. The fully mature traditional person feels in specific ways, sets his or her heart on specific values. Affectivity is as important as intellectual clarity. Being able to sing and dance the traditional stories with enthusiasm and grace is as significant as knowing the music or the steps.

Thus when forest people like the Chamacoco celebrate their feast called the Anaposo, which deals with spirits of the forest, they want to emerge with good feelings about the forest. People of the Gran Chaco who take over aspects of this forest festival have the same motivation. Even as they adapt the notion of the spirits of the forest to fit their own milieu, they accept the idea that wearing masks and dancing ecstatically will help them achieve a new, or renewed, integration with the spirits important in their own locale. The adapted forest festival is a time when those representing forest spirits adorn themselves with feathers, no doubt paying homage to the birds of the forest, who can symbolize the quick-moving spirits. The men dancing in this festival may hide their identities because, like the kachina-dancers among the Pueblo, who hide their identities from children, they want to maintain the conceit that it is not human beings who are dancing. The dancers "become" the spirits whom they make present. The women go along with this conceit, because they too want to live in a ceremonial time and space. Suspending ordinary judgments is a small toll to pay for so useful a journey. The ceremonial time and space constitute the tribe's truer, sacral home. The masks and suspension of disbelief are necessary if the women and men alike are to enter into what they consider a more real, better condition, however temporarily. The implication is that though ordinary space and time are fine, they cannot fulfill the human spirit.

The Lengua of the Gran Chaco traditionally held dances that dramatized the malign potential in changes of state. For example, during the female puberty rites single young men would dance in masks, representing the bad spirits that could come with menstruation. The young women supposedly took the masked dancers to be real presences of such spirits, so it was a relief when older women chased the dancers away.

The Lengua have grounded their sense of tribal identity in the creation of the world, and the first ancestors, by the great Beetle. This deity also fashioned the giant supernatural beings important in the early ages of creation. The Beetle used mud as his building materials. He made human forms from mud, and then he placed them to dry on the bank of a lake. However, because he placed them too close together, they stuck to one another. They had to be separated (which perhaps explains the tension between desires for union with other people and desires for independence). Even separated and mobile, however, they were no match for the giant supernatural beings, who troubled them. The Beetle took their side, depriving the giants of their bodies. Only the spirits of the giants remained, and now they long to regain their old bodies. Their sufferings make them hate human beings, so when human beings are afflicted by pain, it is probably the *kilikhama* (giants' souls) who are responsible.

The Self

When the Inca had consolidated their power, their religion became rigid. It defended the Inca system of government against foreign influences that might have challenged it. Indeed, the Inca supported missionary activities designed to bring surrounding peoples into the fold of Inca religion. As they conquered outlying territories, the Inca would build temples to their sun god, teach people about their other gods, and preach the glories of the Inca religio-political culture. By way of accommodation, they would also incorporate the local deities of defeated peoples into their own pantheon, giving them a significant but secondary status. The official, state religion of the Inca was the expressed reason for conquest, though most scholars consider this a veneer. At the top of the Inca empire, however, the old gods held pride of place, and extending knowledge and service of them to outlying tribes justified imperial expansion. Only rarely (for example, in the case of the Peruvian god Pachacamac) did a local deity enter the first tier of the Inca pantheon. Apparently the influence of Pachacamac was so great in the region south of present-day Lima that the Inca had to place him alongside their own sun god and encourage worship of him. Pachacamac was considered the creator of the earth, so his role did not conflict directly with that of the Inca solar deities. The tendency of the Inca themselves was to assimilate Pachacamac to their own Viracocha, thereby lessening any potential dissonance. Accepting Pachacamac also allowed the Inca to take over his great temple near Lima and enrich themselves with its proceeds.

What impact did movements such as this tend to have on individual Andeans? We can be confident that, inasmuch as they were aware that one conquering people (for example, the Inca) took over the ways of its predecessors (or of peoples newly conquered) and incorporated them into its own religious culture, individual Andeans became casual if not cynical about the claims for particular deities. The goals of syncretism are plain: to remove possible conflicts between deities, thereby reconciling the underlying cultures in question. This need not be fully planned and manipulative. In general, however, religious amalgamation has served the political interests of new rulers. The common people may not have been aware of the fusion of religious and political interests, but any astute individual would have been. So, seeing such manipulation of religious symbols and doctrines, the astute citizen of a regime such as the Incan would have relativized the claims of a given god or priesthood. How could their claims be truly divine, if they could change to serve temporary political interests?

Andean shamans have always operated on the margins of official religion. That has made them good candidates for the critical role that we have assigned to a creative minority. Inasmuch as their personal skills made their shamanic performances credible, and their practices stood in tension with the priestly religion practiced in the temples approved by the state, such shamans were nearly bound to cast a skeptical, "show me" eye on pronouncements of the priests. The shamanic tradition in the Andes has included the use of hallucinogenic substances to facilitate shamans' travel into states of trance, where they might encounter the spirits on whom their work depended. If they were to heal or gain visions of the future, they had to gain the support of such spirits. But hallucinogenic experiences are not fully subject to human control. For shamans that makes using them an act of faith: one disposes oneself to the uses that the gods have in mind.

We have mentioned the burial practices of the Paracas peninsula. Even into the present, death is a powerful occasion for Andeans to express their religious emotions. Mourning has traditionally involved much sobbing, along with praise for the virtues of the deceased. After mummification, corpses would be taken on stretchers to their final resting place. In the mountains, that tended to be in mausoleums created from nearly inaccessible outcroppings of rock. In addition to arranging the deceased in a fetal position and providing them with many gifts, some Andean tribes would leave the mouth open, probably to suggest terror at the sacrifices that the gods could require (and perhaps terror of death itself). Another interpretation that some analysts make is supplication of the gods, in pursuit of such continued benefits as fertility of the crops. In this latter interpretation, the deceased remained concerned about the welfare of the tribe.

Another religious occasion that has shaped how most Andeans have felt about their lives is the pilgrimage. Since Chavin times it has been customary to visit sacred sites. Such sites could be artificial, in the sense of otherwise nondescript locales dedicated to a god such as Pachacamac. Or they could be spectacular settings, such as mountain peaks, that seemed to radiate holiness by their beauty or singularity. To the present day pilgrimages such as the Collur Riti festival, which coincides with the observance of the Christian feast of Corpus Christi, draw crowds who climb to mountain sites nearly 15,000 feet high. Some of the pilgrims dress in animal skins, apparently mediating between the sacred forces (as understood according to pre-Christian mythology) and the rest of the crowd. The ancient focus of this festival was to honor the god of water, and so ensure plentiful supplies in the coming year. People would bring home pieces of ice carved from glaciers found high in the mountains. They might well fast, abstain from sexual relations, drink no beer, and accept other disciplines, to prepare themselves for a profitable pilgrimage. Such traditions have been a strong source of the asceticism that Andeans can manifest.

The Tropical Forest

In 1960–61 Michael Harner, an anthropologist from Columbia University, participated in the shamanic rituals of the Conibo, a tribe of the Peruvian Amazon. Taking the hallucinogenic drink that the Conibo shamans took, he experienced amazing visions. One of them suggests how the Conibo conception of the world was translated into Harner's American consciousness: "I could only very dimly perceive the givers of these thoughts: giant reptilian creatures reposing sluggishly at the lowermost depths of the back of my brain, where it met the top of the spinal column. I could only vaguely see them in what seemed to be gloomy, dark depths. Then they projected a visual scene in front of me. First they showed me the planet Earth as it was eons ago, before there was any life on it. I saw an ocean, barren land, and a bright blue sky. Then black specks dropped from the sky by the hundreds and landed in front of me on the barren landscape. I could see that the 'specks' were actually large, shiny, black creatures with stubby pterodactyl-like wings and huge whale-like bodies. Their heads were not visible to me. They flopped down, utterly exhausted from their trip, resting for eons. They explained to me in a kind of thought language that they were fleeing from something out in space. They had come to the planet Earth to escape their enemy.

"The creatures then showed me how they had created life on the planet in order to hide within the multitudinous forms and thus disguise their presence. Before me, the magnificence of plant and animal creation and speciation—hundreds of millions of years of activity— took place on a scale and with a vividness impossible to describe. I learned that the dragon-like creatures were thus inside of all forms of life, including man. They were the true masters of humanity and the entire planet, they told me. We humans were but the receptacles and servants of these creatures. For this reason they could speak to me from within myself."[49]

Hallucinogens apparently reorganize our perceptions, arranging memories of things we have sensed or felt into nearly kaleidoscopic patterns. Here Harner may be re-experiencing pictures of prehistoric birds that he saw as a child, pictures from astronomy books, visions he had when first contemplating the sweep of evolution, thoughts he had when pondering the question of inner inspiration, even speculations he had made about the presence of divine, creative power in human beings. No one can know for certain where the components of his vision came from or why they combined in the patterns that they did. For our purposes, though, the experience that

Harner had at the hands of Conibo tutors is instructive apart from such issues. If we think about the analogous effects of his hallucinogen on the Conibo themselves, we can speculate that many tribal myths have been overwhelmingly vivid.

The Gran Chaco

In the central Chaco the tribes that speak Mataco-Makka languages predominate. The Mataco are most concerned with power. Their religious worldview centers on the belief that the supernatural beings responsible for the world are the repositories of power. These beings can be demonic or human. Many are simply natural (representations of the sun, moon, storm, or stars). They are significant in the measure that they have the power to effect change, or to impose their will, or to make human beings reckon with them.

The human being combines material and spiritual power. While living, the Mataco man or woman manages to command the body in virtue of the power of the spirit. At death, however, the spirit alone remains significant, and the power of the ghostly spirit tends to be negative. The shades of the departed are usually malevolent, wanting to do human beings harm. They resent their departure from the life they once knew, so they envy those who still possess that life.

For the Mataco, a deity named Tokhwah imposed cosmic order in the beginning of the present phase of history. (So, genuine Mataco shamans could assure their people that nothing in the world was wholly irrational—everything had to make sense, if only to Tokhwah.) Even though Tokhwah presented many demonic aspects, as well as the ambivalence of a classical trickster, the people could look to him for confidence that something more powerful than human understanding or force had formed the world. Indeed, it is interesting that the Mataco encouraged people to picture Tokhwah as sad, even suffering. He was aware of the imperfections of the world that he had created. He sympathized with human beings in their sufferings, for his own lot was not perfectly happy.

Out of such sympathy, one could think, Tokhwah provided ways to tame the potential chaos of human affairs. He set forth laws to govern trade, developed tools to make life easier, instituted the stable relationship of men and women in marriage, and taught human beings how to get drunk (to ease their burdens). Fighting and warfare are part of his dispensation: he realized that people need an outlet for their anger. He even tamed women, so that they would be less fearsome to men. When women originally descended from the sky, their vaginas were rimmed with teeth. Men feared to enter, and few children were born. So Tokhwah removed those teeth, facilitating both procreation and pleasure.

The Mataco shaman was the main defense against illness. When people felt sick, they looked to the shaman as their hope. The shaman had to follow Tokhwah's teaching about how to cure. The Mataco conviction was that all wisdom of this sort had been established in the beginning. To gain access to not only the knowledge that Tokhwah imparted but also the power to heal, the shaman needed the help of demonic spirits. They could take away the sick person's soul, causing death, but they could also return it. Often the shaman had to travel in search of the departed soul. To accomplish this, he had in effect to become a demonic spirit. (Whether interpreters are fully justified in calling the Mataco spirits "demonic" is doubtful. They are capable of inflicting harm, but they are also the shaman's resource for doing good.) To accomplish such a transformation, the shaman used techniques such as smoking the dust of sumac leaves.

The Mataco self is therefore ecstatic, in the sense that it needs to go out of the body to deal with the powers that shape its destiny. The usual anthropology consequent on this conviction is dualistic: the self is both body and spirit, but the spirit is more significant and lasting than the body. The problem, then, is to join body and spirit, material needs and spiritual hopes, so that people can function gracefully. The major impediment to such a graceful functioning in the Mataco world seems to have been fear. Inasmuch as the powers having the greatest say about a person's destiny were "demonic," there was much to fear.

Ultimate Reality

The Inca gods afford us a good indication of how traditional peoples of the Andes tended to think about ultimate reality. The center of the Inca realm was the temple of the Sun (Coricancha) in the capital city of Cuzco. The kings who ruled the empire from this capital were considered sons of the Sun. Behind the sun, as the ultimate creator, was Viracocha, who carried attributes of the sea as well as of the sky. The temple of the sun was richly decorated. Golden pumas guarded its precincts, while on its walls lay plaques of silver and gold. In the halls stood statues of gods, as well as mummies of earlier rulers, both kings and queens. A favorite representation of the sun depicted him as a trinity: a father accompanied by two sons. The father stood for the solar disc itself. The two sons represented the light and warmth that it generated. Other statuary included a man sitting between two pumas. He had serpents at his waist and from his shoulders came rays (apparently of power). Within this statue was a reliquary filled with the powdered entrails of prior kings. The head of the empire, the "Inca," kept a close relative in the office of chief priest. Also at the Coricancha were women, known as "virgins of the sun," who dedicated their lives to making cloth and corn beer for the cult. They also served the sexual needs of the "Inca," who represented the sun, and were available to dignitaries visiting the "Inca."

Balancing the influence of the sun god in the heavens was the influence of the creative god Pachacamac under the earth. Active in the creation of human beings, he and his wife Pachamama ruled the waters of the deep underworld. His daughters and he also ruled the seas. His temple was by the sea, and his representative animal was the golden fox. He could also be worshiped in the form of a wooden pillar located in a dark room of an adobe pyramid. The feminine forces accompanying Pachacamac witness to both his polar relation to the sun, who had sons, and to his associations with the earth, the waters, and all the nether forms of generativity.

Illapa, whom we have already met, controlled the weather, including the rain, thunder, storms, lightning, snow, and frost. The center of his cult lay in the highlands, perhaps because people could witness the weather beginning there. Illapa was also a triad: father, brother, and son. Many tribes traced their descent from further sons of Illapa, known as *huacas*. The myths told of Illapa throwing these sons off his mountaintop. Human beings raised them in the mountains. The *huacas* dominated life in the mountains, ruling the animals and crops that lived there. The mythology suggests some ambivalence toward Illapa and the weather. On the one hand, this god was the source of fertilizing rain. On the other hand, his storms caused much trouble. Inasmuch as they identified with the *huacas*, many mountain tribes could feel that Illapa was their father, but difficult to please. Also associated with Illapa was worship of mountains themselves. Some Andeans grouped the mountains, gave them names, and ranked them all under the lordship of Illapa. (Mountains are usually reverenced for their closeness to the heavens.)

One of the major deities of special interest to women was the Moon goddess Quilla. She was both the wife and the sister of the Sun. The consort of the "Inca" was considered to be the daughter of the Moon. Inasmuch as the "Inca" was the son of the Sun, the earthly couple represented the heavenly, divine pair. Quilla was represented in statues made of silver, while the Sun was represented in statues made of gold. She ruled over a lunar calendar, though the Inca also used a solar calendar. Among her other associations were ties to the earth and to the dead (whom the earth received). She was special to women because of their menstrual rhythms, and through her associations with the fertility of the earth. Common opinion had it that Quilla disliked thieves and would pursue them into the underworld after their deaths. Each year one month was dedicated to Quilla. Men worshiped her in Cuzco. The temple of Nusta, located on an island in Lake Titicaca, was her special shrine.

Most important among the Inca gods, though, was Viracocha. We have noted his development from being one of the many personified deities associated with the creation of the cosmos to a certain primacy. Inasmuch as his mythology dealt with both rain and sun, he was the ideal being in whom to locate the ultimate sources of fertility. Eventually he was considered the creator of the sun, and all the other heavenly beings. He also became the father of many Andean tribes, including the Inca. His was the credit for separating night and day, and from him came the cycle, and so the calendar, that the movement of the sun created. His sons became culture heroes, teaching the Andeans about the plants and animals of their habitats.

The Tropical Forest

Although some of the Europeans who first encountered peoples of the Amazonian forest thought that they were monotheists, the consensus has grown that most tribes have not worshiped a single divine being. At the most, a few tribes refer to a figure who brought them the rudiments of their culture but now dwells apart, in splendid isolation. So, for example, the Tucanoans of the northwest Amazon speak of the Sun as a father who created the universe and then withdrew. He is not the same as the physical sun that rules the skies today, but originally he was the great source of creation. Since his withdrawal, a host of other spiritual beings have become the focus of Tucanoan ritualistic life.

Natives living along the Orinoco River confused missionaries of the eighteenth century. The missionaries could not be sure whether the supreme native deity was the creator of the world or the first ancestor of the tribe. Clearly, therefore, the natives did not confess that a single overwhelming divinity possessed the fullness of everything venerable. Since the advent of Christian missionaries, it has been difficult to separate pre-Christian ideas from natives' appropriations of Christian theology. For example, the Acawai of Guyana and Venezuela speak of a supreme being, but this seems to be due to Christian influence. Originally, it appears, the most that native views stipulated was a primordial brightness associated with the sun. This brightness is at the heart of what the Acawai revere: light, understanding, life, and the soul or spirit.

A safer postulate than monotheism is the thesis that the vast majority of native Amazonian tribes have been preoccupied with spirits. Virtually universally throughout this region, natives think of the world as having three layers. Above is the sky, at the center is the earth, and below is a watery underground. Each layer contains different beings, real (in the sense of perceptible by ordinary human senses) or fantastic. For example, under the earth dwell the anaconda and the caiman, on the earth dwell human beings and the familiar forest animals, and in the sky dwell the birds, paramount among which is the harpy eagle or the king vulture. With these creatures, however, dwell various spirits, and human beings have to reckon with these spirits, if they are to defend themselves against disaster. Only shamans have the ability to pass from the middle zone, the earth, to the heavens or the underearth. Still, the basic symbolism of the human house in the Amazon refers to both above and below, suggesting that wherever human beings live is a kind of microcosm.

The invisible world is the place where unusual powers dwell. If one wants to do great things, or to experience the more dramatic aspects of ultimate reality, one has to travel there. Yet the power that one approaches when making such travels is ambiguous. It can bring evil as well as good. The shaman is a hero inasmuch as he braves the dangers of evil powers in order to bring the power of good to his or her tribe. The shaman takes on burdens that ordinary tribal members tend to shun, because the general suspicion throughout the Amazon is that it is bad luck to see a spiritual being. Thus only a strong person, well versed and well protected, should set out to bargain or battle with spirits deliberately.

A tribe living along the border of Venezuela and Brazil, the Sanema, is representative in listing as many as eight different kinds of *hekula* or spiritual beings. The Yanomama with whom Florinda Donner lived have a simular sense of ultimate reality, directing their shamans to mobilize spiritual beings to bring good to their own tribe and afflict their enemies. The Yanomama ingest a hallucinogenic snuff, which often brings them arresting visions of their spiritual beings, and they are renowned for the fierceness with which they attack their enemies, under the conviction that their spiritual helpers are with them.

The Tucano-Desana who live in the northwest Amazon represent numerous tribes who think that the animals have spirits and are controlled by a master. For this tribe, one such master controls the land animals while another controls the fish. The conceit is that the land animals and fish both live in houses, much like human beings, under the guidance of their masters (chiefs). The master controls whether the animals come out, and so are available to hunters. The main criterion that the master uses is whether human beings have given sufficient souls to replenish the supply of animals or fish. The idea seems to be that land animals, humans, and fish are part of a circular (spiritual) ecosystem. Whether human beings give souls in ways other than by dying is not clear. Perhaps when they reverence the master of the animals or make sacrifices (set aside gifts) they are nourishing the source of what they hunt and fish. But it seems likely, once again, that native South Americans are expressing their profound intuition that hunters and animals are linked soul-to-soul. If there are to be fish and game, there has to be a human contribution to the pool of living things, either by the natural return of human beings at death or by spiritual equivalents (self-sacrifice through devotions).

Many tribes assume that the masters of the animals have fantastic appearances that tend to frighten ordinary tribal members (though not shamans). The guardians of the animals are usually described in anthropomorphic terms, though as giants or dwarfs. They are hairy or black, and thoroughly frightening. It is dangerous to go about the forest at night, because that is when they are most likely to roam. They are not as dangerous as witches, however, because witches take on monstrous forms solely to kill other human beings or bring them under malevolent control.

Finally, we must note a powerful belief in ancestral spirits. Amazonians, like many East Asian peoples, believe that the founders of the tribe continue to be present, and that they require devotion. The Tucano-Barasana of the northwest Amazon are representative in associating the ancestral spirits with an important aspect of tribal culture, in their case the sacred flutes and trumpets. The term *He* refers to both the ancestral spirits and these musical instruments, and the inference is that when one is playing such instruments, or listening to them, one is involved with the ancestors. Some scholars have likened these *He* to the mythical ancestors that aboriginal Australians find in the "dream time." There are *He* animals as well as people, and the idea seems to be that in the rituals where the *He* control the people's sensibility one moves back into the primordial era, when the foundations of the world were laid.

Some tribes pass the same names along, generation after generation, to give the ancestral spirits a body and so mitigate any grievances or regrets that might incline them to afflict the current generation. In the tropical forest area (and, to a lesser extent, in the lowlands), what we might call an "economy" of soul-matter operates. The "stuff" of the spirits circulates—through the generations, in the experiences that the *He* stimulate. The people come to grips with "history," inasmuch as the instruments call them to contemplate times that preceded the present era.

The Gran Chaco

A significant family of languages in the Gran Chaco embraces the tribes who speak Guiacuru-Caduveo. They tend to live in the northern part of this area, as well as in what is now Brazil. One of these tribes, the Pilaga, exhibits cycles of myths that focus on Dapici, a celestial god. He inverted the cosmic planes and transferred some of the animals that had been on lower planes into the skies. Because he had so much to say about the foundations of the current world order, people pray to him when they want help with any of a great variety of problems.

Another god whom the Pilaga revere is Wayakalciyi, who is responsible for death. Prayers to him come from considerable fear. Originally there was no death. Wayakalciyi changed this happy state of affairs, introducing hunting. Now hunters inflict death on animals, because human beings need food. Human beings in turn die, becoming food for the earth. The myths clustered around death, hunting, and the "fall" of creation from its original state show the Pilaga struggling with a sense that death is unnatural. Why should any beings have to die? There is no good answer to this question, though any serious examination of how nature works reveals that mutual death-dealing is at the heart of nature's economy. Still, death is repugnant, because it requires the dissolution of body and spirit. Body and spirit belong together. Human beings do not know how to understand their dissolution. So human beings approach Wayakalciyi with fear and trembling, wishing that he were not so powerful an overlord.

A third cycle of Pilaga myths focuses on Nesoge, a powerful female deity. She is the patroness of witches, and she feeds on human flesh. Most analyses of human cannibalism speculate that the eaters want to appropriate the powers of the eaten. Apart from the cases in which people are starving and seek any food, cannibalism seems to represent a horribly elementary effort to take in the substance of another human being and so be revitalized or enriched. Tribes that eat only the heart or the brain of a victim reinforce this analysis. Those are organs associated with the higher attributes of the victim (courage, intelligence). Cannibalism in such cases may not be radically different from ceremonies in which tribes eat the brain or heart of a totemic animal—for example, a bear. The Pilaga myths dealing with Nesoge raise the question of whether the gods are cannibals, living off human substance. Minimally, the gods that support witches (who can be imagined carrying out any enormity) seem open to such a charge. Still, repulsive as such gods may be, peoples like the Pilaga have to reckon with them. Once a tribe accepts the idea that evil or demonism exists in the divine sphere, it cannot escape reckoning with perverse gods.

When the Pilaga speculate about the nature of the gods, they use a notion called *payak*. Scholars interpret this notion as a description of the non-human. The gods are not human, and not human as well are the shamans who take on attributes of the gods. Animals, plants, and many inanimate objects are also *payak*. Behind this notion lies a division of reality into two principal spheres. What falls within the human sphere is familiar. What falls into the non-human sphere runs a gamut. If both a striking natural setting and a god are *payak*, the non-human includes most of reality.

Balancing this distancing of human beings from the rest of reality, however, is the tendency of the Pilaga to personify beings of the non-human realm. This tendency is common, perhaps even constitutive, in the mythologies of small-scale societies. The animals who appear in stories of how human beings gained fire or how hunting came about have minds and wills. They make plans and express emotions. Human beings seem bound to personify nature, and also the gods. Even when we deny that animals think as we do, we approach their behavior as though they think. The same with our instinctive theology. Even when we deny that divinity works as we do, we approach divinity as though it were humanity at a higher level.

The Pilaga try to acquire *payaks* (beings belonging to the non-human realm, especially divine spirits) as helpers. When human beings are not able to acquire *payaks,* they are in danger of falling ill, even dying. All bad fortune—death of animals, failure of crops— comes from *payaks* bent on doing human beings harm. The *payaks* are organized into a hierarchy of non-human powers, and the Pilaga work diligently to classify them. No doubt the hope is that if they can get to the head of a given bureau, the head *payak* may be able to control lesser powers and prevent harm to the crops, the animals, or even the children.

The myths of the Mocovi, a tribe akin to the Pilaga, include a story of how the earth was separated from heaven. In the beginning, a great tree reached from the earth to the sky, which was a land populated with lakes and rivers. People could climb the branches of this tree and avail themselves of heaven's bounty. But one day an old woman, angry at many things, cut the tree down. Ever since, human beings have been separated from heaven.

This story probably operates on several different levels. The Mocovi have wondered about the relations between above and below, suspecting that connections ought to be closer. The sky has struck many peoples as a projection of the ocean or other bodies of water, and so as filled with good things. Inasmuch as the sky is the home of the creative spirits, it also symbolizes the powers that human beings wish were closer, more involved in human affairs, doing more to ease human existence. (Demonic spirits can live in the sky, but more often their home is under the earth.) So the story of how the disgruntled old lady chopped down the cosmic tree (the pillar that shamans climb to reach heaven) fits a type. It is another version of the story of the fall of human beings from the intimacy with holiness that they enjoyed in the beginning.

Since "in the beginning" can stand for "when human nature was functioning as it ought to function," the time of the story is irrelevant. Many peoples imagine a golden age, usually at the origins of the race, when the powers of creation were stronger. Since that golden age, the state of the world has declined. Some peoples imagine a restoration of that golden age, at the end of time, but others think that creation is fated to undergo many cycles of arising and declining.

Why the old woman was so angry is not clear in the sources available to us. Whether the story is misogynistic or prejudiced against old age is also not clear. Men tend to blame women for the fall. Universally, old age is pictured as a time of both wisdom and malevolence. The main point is that an ancestor unhappy with her situation "cursed heaven." She thought that things were so bad that she would be better off without god. In a traditional worldview, that is a counsel of despair (not the bold, Promethean gesture that some modern Europeans celebrated). Truly mature human beings in traditional societies did not curse the gods. They had learned how to live with the gods. Their wisdom allowed them to accommodate to the way that things were, which was governed by the gods.

Spirituality

If we accept the proposition that much in Andean religion was a response to difficult conditions, so that the people's basic attitude toward the gods was one of petition, even desperate appeal, how are we likely to view Andean spirituality? Probably quite sympathetically. If the physical conditions of a given people make their survival difficult, that people's spirituality is bound to reflect such difficulty. If much of what happens to them is negative, full of pain and suffering, they are likely to think of their gods as demanding, even cruel. The wonder, in fact, is that the majority of religions are so positive about the cosmos and the powers responsible for it. The wonder is that beauty, love, honor, and other positive experiences or virtues so frequently predominate over ugliness, hatred, and dishonor. The cult of the Inca certainly displayed fear, a need to placate the high gods. More decisively, however, it displayed awe, the desire to honor the sun and the moon, the divinity of the storm, Viracocha and Pachacamac. In part this was a response to the dazzling quality of the natural phenomena associated with the sun, the moon, the storm, the division of day into night, the fertility of the earth and the sea.

In at least equal part, however, it was a response to the *idea* of a fullness of light and warmth, cool beauty, fertilizing wetness and power, order in the heavens, fecundity in the nether worlds. Human beings love to contemplate the ideal side of what gives their lives hope, what raises their spirits by being beautiful or consoling. Their rituals and spiritualities derive as much from what they hope is the case as from anything that they can deduce from physical phenomena or even their own experience.

For traditional peoples of the Andes, these motivations appear in the concern to give the gods worthy shrines. Especially strong in Andean spirituality, however, has been fear that the good possibilities, the things that the human spirit would contemplate hopefully, might prove less powerful than the destructive possibilities. So it is noteworthy that many Andean rituals involved assuming a craven attitude. For example, though in worshiping Inti, the sun, Andeans found reasons to praise his light and warmth, and to make these prominent, in the mythic cycle associated with Pachacamac, the creator of the earth, solar phenomena also suggested the possibility that the entire cosmos could wind down. (Perhaps Mesoamerican beliefs also shaped this possibility. Recall, for example, the Mesoamerican cycles of creation and destruction—the succession of various "suns" and the expectation that the present sun-age would end by earthquake.) Insofar as the sun was a solar fire, it might burn out, like earthly fires. Insofar as it disappeared (under the earth) at the end of each day, it might not come back. There was no certainty that light would keep overcoming darkness. The sun might lose his power, which would cause the destruction of humankind.

Thus the cult of Inti featured expressions of anxiety. To show that this anxiety was not limited to human beings, people would whip their domestic animals, to make their howls enter into the chorus of lamentation. Another Andean way of trying to ward off anxiety was to "tie" the sun at a stone altar, as though to make sure that it would not go away. The gold featured in the cult of the sun expressed the people's sense that this was the god's appropriate metal. By adorning his shrine generously, they might make it a place where he would be happy to dwell. Shamans would wear headdresses with metal discs, to represent the sun's radiance. The Moon was treated similarly, though in silver. In many ways, then, traditional Andeans acted out a deep fear that their gods would not stay with them and be protective.

The spirituality of Andean women seems to have been shaped by the cult of Pachamama, the divine Mother. She is more passive than the male deities with whom she interacts and on whom she depends for her fertility. In her relations with them, she is modest and submissive—traits that some commentators find in Andean peasant women to the present. In contrast to the mother goddesses of other peoples, Pachamama is nearly asexual. She seldom appears pregnant or with pronounced breasts or hips. Exceptions to this rule occur, for example in artifacts from Northern Peru, but on the whole female sexuality is muted. Pachamama rules the world of grains and corn, but more as a general source of fertility than as a powerful female.

We have mentioned the *huacas,* gods or holy beings associated in mountain regions with the origins of human tribes. The word *huaca* could apply to anything considered holy or sacred. Comparativists have noted that rocks and beautiful places, animals and human beings, aspects of the weather, clothing worn by shamans, and virtually any other aspect of either human culture or the natural world can be considered sacred, inasmuch as divine power can rest upon it or draw near through it. Thus in the Andes the "Inca," the human ruler, was *huaca,* as were the mummies, the statues, and the other aspects of the imperial cult. To deal with the *huacas,* Andeans would perform acts of reverence (*muchay*). Typically they would remove their sandals, blow in the direction of what they were revering, and bow low. The intent was to convey their desire to please the holy being, and so to placate it. Thus *muchay* became a shield, a way to ward off the displeasure of the powers that might damage human existence.

From Chavin times people could visit oracles to learn the intentions of the *huacas* in their regard. Priests or shamans attending oracle sites would interpret the message. The Inca empire, no doubt following practices of prior ruling peoples, required tribute for its shrines. A voluntary offering was a good deed, but the Inca found it desirable to make sure that their shrines were well supported. Two typical offerings were a powder (*mullo*) concocted from ground sea shells and a paste made from coca. The practice was to throw wads of such paste in the direction of the deity being venerated. People might also make offerings to the dead, in which case fruits or grains would be presented in special jars. More formal sacrifices, of animals or even children, came into play when the dead person was august or it was necessary to placate a deity (for example, in time of great need). The Inca thought that by treating the dead well the dead would become intercessors for them with the gods.

The Tropical Forest

It should be clear that the peoples of the tropical forest have lived in small-scale groups, unlike the larger federations developed in the Andes. Relatedly they have been dominated by shamans rather than priests. The imperial organization of the Inca, which earlier developments in the central Andes anticipated, has had no counterpart in the Amazonian regions. On the whole, hunting and gathering have continued to play important roles, and the result seems to have been a concern with animals and spirits that only shamans could satisfy. For many tribes, becoming a shaman required a solid apprenticeship. People could aspire to be shamans, or they could come from a family that had long produced shamans, or they could have dramatic experiences (be cured of a serious illness, receive a powerful revelation in a dream) that convinced them that they ought to work as shamans. The next step would be to gain a teacher—usually a living shaman, but occasionally the spirit of a dead shaman.

Depending on the lore of the given tribe, the apprentice shaman would have to master a greater or smaller collection of traditional myths. Virtually all of the Amazonian shamans' duties have involved singing chants and performing dances. The principal apparatus that the shaman now employs is the rattle, whose pebbles are taken to represent helping spirits (or to be spiritual weapons to hurl at enemies). Generally a shaman requires the help of a tutelary spirit. To cure or guide the souls of the dead, he or she must call on the power of something more than human. Since the majority of the Amazonian tribes use drugs in shamanic séances, the shaman also has to learn to operate while hallucinating. What shamans experience depends on the worldview with which they operate. Since the typical Amazonian worldview sketches the three-leveled universe that we have described, the travels of the shaman tend to be either up to the heavens or down to the underearth. The apprentice shaman becomes adept at seeing realities that are invisible to ordinary people. Some shamanic traditions require considerable asceticism (for example, sexual abstinence), and the usual rule is that the shaman must do whatever is necessary to acquire and maintain contact with his or her spiritual helpers.

Shamans gain considerable status, but their standing always depends on their effectiveness. Their tribe tends to be quite pragmatic: if cures occur, the shaman enjoys prestige; if cures fail, the shaman can be in trouble. Part of "curing" is dealing with the disorders or disharmonies that afflict the tribe. Sickness is more than a physical dysfunction of the sick individual, more even than a psychosomatic dysfunction. It is also a social dysfunction: the community has fallen out of harmony with the invisible, spiritual world. This may be due to evil influences of its enemies, who have attacked it (through the offices of their shamans). Or it may be due to the community's own failures: breaches of taboo, injustices. Typically, shamanic séances occur quite publicly, inviting the entire community to observe. This affords the tribe considerable entertainment, but also the chance to become involved in the curing process. It affords the shaman the chance to charge members who have broken taboos or otherwise contributed to the disorder that the sickness manifests—to chastise them and bring social pressure to bear so that they reform their ways.

In addition to performing cures, shamans are responsible for what we might call prophetic functions. If the tribe needs to determine what is likely to happen in the future, or what the weather will be, or what an omen means, it goes to its shaman. These are all matters that involve the invisible world, the domain of the spirits, and the shaman is the specialist in that domain. For many hunters, the shaman is responsible for good relations with the master of the animals, so that game will be plentiful. Tapirape shamans try to fulfill this function by having sexual relations with wild sows. Shamans are also major figures in larger-scale tribal ceremonies, such as times when the tribe rehearses its mythology, to remind itself of how the world arose.

The Warao of the Orinoco delta have been studied quite thoroughly, and many of their traditional ways, which seem to preserve features of a hunting and gathering culture more than seven thousand years old, illustrate South American shamanic beliefs. The traditional mythology says that originally the Warao lived in the sky. One day a hunter shot his arrow wide and in searching for it found a hole in the sky. He descended by a rope to what proved to be earth. Since he found an abundance of food there, he returned and made an enthusiastic report to the other members of his tribe. A pregnant woman who got stuck in the hole became the morning star, and because she blocked the exit some of the Warao had to remain in heaven. On earth they found out that they would have to suffer. Thus they entered a new epoch, in which childbirth would entail pain, people would have to work, and there would be death. A wise chief tried to outwit death, telling the people that if they would resist sleep and answer not the first call out of the dark, which would be that of death, but the second call, which would come from a good spirit, they would be fine. But a young man fell asleep, awoke at the first call, and answered. Ever since, death has been the rule.

In Warao cosmology, the earth is a disk floating on water. The main waterways of the Orinoco delta run through cracks in this disk. "The Warao universe is divided into various realms. The celestial realm is a smaller disk that parallels the terrestial one. The maximum height of the solsticial suns determines the bell-shaped cosmic vault, which rests on the world's axis. Located to the northeast of the zenith is an ovoid house that is two storied; the lower level is inhabited by a plumed serpent and the upper level by the Creator Bird, the ancestral shaman and his wife, and four pairs of insects. In the central space of the upper floor, the male residents assemble to play a game that perpetuates humanity on earth. At the end of each game the plumed serpent emerges from below to produce a luminous ball. Ropes of tobacco smoke connect the house with the zenith and with the world's axis."[50]

The Gran Chaco

Two tribes of the Gran Chaco, the Chulupi and the Toba, provide further suggestions about the existential religion—the spirituality—that traditionally obtained in this area. The Chulupi have long repeated a cycle of myths concerned with the deities who fashioned the world in primordial times. Having created, these deities removed themselves from the daily operations of the world, becoming otiose. This removal is a regular feature of the creative deities in many parts of the traditional world. The instinct seems to be that if the original creators were present, human beings would be able to sense their operations. Since human beings do not sense the presence of all-powerful creators, these deities must have removed themselves. Typically, in their place stand lesser deities or demons, who are the forces to be reckoned with, when it is a matter of practical needs. In extreme circumstances, however, people may turn to the creative powers. If the goodness of the world order itself seems called into question, perhaps human beings can interest the original makers of the world in making things right.

Among the supernatural beings to whom the Chulupi pay special attention, Fitsok Exits stands out. This god was involved in making the spots on the moon, in establishing the rules for the initiation of women, in bringing women into existence, in creating honey, and in the expulsion from the universe of the creator who first set it moving. Perhaps Chulupi shamans, having long lived within the cycle of myths, intuit connections among these different aspects of Chulupi culture, but to the outsider the list seems haphazard. Often the logic that connects stories is one of accidental similarities or differences. For example, the spots on the moon may remind people of the lunar cycles, and that in turn may remind them of women's cycles.

The Chulupi also believe that the primordial age of the creative deities came crashing down, and that a lesser deity, Kufial, had to step in to restore order. Many stories deal with the deeds of Kufial, explaining how important features of the current world order arose. Nothing is without its possible meaning. In a traditional, mythological culture, the world became as we now find it to be through specific actions. Even when a people describes these actions as flawed (to account for the flaws in creation), nothing is left to chance. The myths themselves express the equivalent of what more differentiated cultures struggle to understand metaphysically.

For example, the flaws of the gods, the limitations on their powers, suggest the questions that metaphysicians group under the headings of contingency and finitude. Implicitly, many such myths say that unless ultimate reality is different from the order created by imperfect divine crafters, nothing will ever make complete sense. Occasionally myths make this explicit: Who knows how everything fits together, or why fire arose in precisely this way? More frequently, myths let this perception remain implicit. If they thought about the effect of their stories, those who first told the myths probably wanted their hearers to come away dissatisfied. From such dissatisfaction might follow efforts to experience a more ultimate reality face to face, and so gain a better explanation.

The Chulupi speak of an ultimate power (*sic'ee*) that determines a great many aspects of their world. This ultimate power is strange, even weird. It presents human beings with experiences that they cannot understand. Such power may express itself in strange, eerie sounds or unusual sights. A whirlwind, or a haunting call in the forest, can represent it. The shaman has to contend with this power. It visits him, sometimes in the guise of an old man. If the shaman gains the help of spiritual "familiars," it is due to the dispensation of *sic'ee*. Certainly the shaman has to prepare himself: fast, endure solitude, take mind-altering drinks. But what he gains is still the gift of the ultimate power, which no human being can control completely. The shaman must be brave, because he can receive terrifying visions. He finally learns, though, that what will be will be, and that facing his enemies down is better than trying to flee them.

The Toba are especially interested in celestial phenomena. Their myths include stories about the stars. They have rich lore dealing with the destructions through which the cosmos has passed. Their list of divine beings includes tricksters, lawgivers (culture heroes), and monsters that cannot be seen without grave harm, even death. Many of the Toba divinities possess forms midway between the human and the animal. Apparently this expresses the intuition that we have found important in other tribes: the different kinds of beings are more alike than different.

Eric Voegelin has spoken of "the cosmological myth," which emphasizes the sameness of all creatures. A single "stuff" offers the "material" from which all creatures come. Thus a human being and a tree are not wholly alien. The cosmos is a living entity, a living unity. There is nothing outside the cosmos. It is co-extensive with reality. Indeed, the world is the "body" of divinity, and divinity is the soul of the world. Consequently it makes sense to depict beings with both human and animal features. It makes sense to stress the significance of the non-human, in order to combat anthropocentrism. Even what seems most different from human beings, most distant and least understandable, is part of the single cosmos. No divinity transcending the cosmos, existing independently of the cosmos because beholden only to itself, measures the cosmos or suggests how human beings can be free of the world, as well as indebted toward it.

This cosmological mythology generalizes what analysts have found in dozens of different traditional tribes, raising their assumptions to a level of clarity that they might not recognize, but also suggesting both the immense gains and the dangers of revelations of a transcendent divinity. On the one hand, such a divinity offers an escape from imprisonment in a reality so intrinsically limited that it can never provide full sense. On the other hand, a transcendent divinity can seem to alienate people from the world, destroying their capacity to feel at home in nature.[51]

The Toba speak of *Nowet*, a supernatural being who structures the world. He is expressed in the beings who control the animals and run the different spheres of the universe. Shamans gain access to *Nowet*, through their initiations, and he grants them a share in the power that structures the world. They can use this power for good or for ill. When they heal, they use it for good. When they turn to witchcraft, trying to harm other people, they use it for ill. This same power works in skillful hunters, dancers, fishermen, weavers, potters. Although it is personified in *Nowet*, it is so different from ordinary human personality that we may consider it impersonal: the force of ultimate reality itself. Ordinary human beings can receive illuminations about *Nowet* and the organization of the cosmos in dreams. Shamans use their familiar spirits. We may say, then, that Toba spirituality encourages people to strive for ecstatic experiences. When they can step out of ordinary consciousness, they have a better chance to sense how the ultimate power running the world operates.

Chapter 9

CONCLUSION

We have considered major aspects of the traditional religious lives of native peoples in all parts of the Americas. To conclude our study, let us review the data on the native Americans as a whole, asking what summary estimates we can make of traditional attitudes toward such key matters as human origins, the natural world, family life, lesser spirits and the Great Spirit, ethical taboos and requirements, and death.

Human Origins

For native Americans on both continents, human beings have neither made themselves nor come about casually, as a sport of blind forces of evolution. The first human beings were the result of deliberate acts by supernatural powers. Tribes seldom claimed to understand why such supernatural powers should have decided to make the human race, but they had no doubt that the gods or spirits had acted purposefully.

Moreover, the tendency was to associate the origins of human beings with the origins of the natural world as a whole. Human beings were far from the whole of creation, perhaps were not even its most important part. But they could not be separated from the division of the land from the waters that originally made the earth, or from the creation of the various animal species with whom they presently interacted. Even though human beings stood apart from the other animals by their kind of thought, they did not live in a radically different world. The cultures that human beings produced were no match for the power of the natural world to shape human existence. Unlike

218

citizens of the industrialized nations of the present day, traditional native Americans had no technology to dominate nature. They were no great ecological threat. Nature was vast and indominable. Human beings were small, and even their cleverest inventions could bother nature little more than a fly could bother a buffalo.

Consequently, human affairs tended to seem like a small world set within the much larger world of the cosmos. This explains symbolism such as that of the Delaware bighouses, which were constructed to mimic the different levels of the cosmos. Recall that in these long-houses the ceiling stood for heaven, the floor for earth, the eastern wall for the rising of the sun, and the western wall for the sun's setting. The implication was that the dances, speeches, feasts, business meetings, and other activities that took place in the bighouses tran-spired in a cosmic setting. They did not compose a world unto them-selves. Human beings could not wisely segregate themselves from the larger context of the heavens and the earth. The symbolism of the bighouse reminded the Delaware that all their activities lay open to the powers that had made the world. Indeed, all their activities would be as fruitful or barren as the degree to which they integrated the people with the larger patterns of nature or alienated them.

The Cherokee attributed the origins of the natural world to an earth-diver, a water-beetle that brought up a bit of mud from under the primal waters. The mud was fashioned into the ball of the earth. In fact, the earth is still only an island, floating on the primal waters. Only cords hanging from heaven keep it from sinking under the waters. If it does sink under, human beings and the other animals will lose their home and the present phase of cosmic history will end. Originally human beings and the other animals lived crowded to-gether in heaven. The earth was fashioned to relieve this overcrowd-ing, but there is no guarantee the earth will continue to provide a haven.

Another influential view of human origins in North America pic-tures the first human beings as living in darkness under the earth. Until a hero comes to liberate them, they cannot emerge into the world they now inhabit. Sometimes tribal myths and rituals re-enact the arduous journey that the hero (who may be accompanied by a god) has to make to locate the proto-human beings and lead them up into the light. Other times the myths tell of the numerous attempts of benevolent beings to break through the surface of the earth and make a passageway for the first humans. When the first people journey to the surface, they may ascend a rope, climb a vine, or follow a moun-tain route. The order in which they emerge can determine the social organization that the tribe follows on earth: those who emerge first (either classes of people, such as chiefs and shamans, or now-eminent families) will tend to rule. If a group violates any of the taboos that the hero or god can impose for the duration of the journey, it can be condemned to stay forever under the earth, consigned to darkness.

The interesting feature of this symbolism is the strong motif of ascent. Just as human beings had to make their way up from the depths of animality toward the light of reason, so they had to journey from the dark underearth to life under the sun. Other myths speak of the descent of the first human beings from the heavens, introducing a different cluster of psychological overtones. Whereas the journey upward toward the light amounts to a story of progress, evolutionary development, the descent from the heavens suggests a fall from an original grace to a present state of limitation, division, and suffering.

Probably this latter intuition comes from the human capacity to realize that many things in human existence are not as they "should" be. With reflective reason comes the ability to distinguish between what is real and what is ideal. (In fact, ideals have a certain kind of reality. We may dismiss it as "only mental" or "imaginary," yet it can influence human affairs powerfully. Indeed, what are most reform movements but attempts to bring daily affairs, commonsensical "reality," more closely in tune with the ideals that poets and political visionaries have glimpsed in moments of inspiration?)

So both groups of symbols, those of ascent and those of descent, depend on human intuitions of an orientation toward the light, an innate human capacity for living better than one's group presently is. The myths of origin from under the earth pay tribute to the leaden, recalcitrant aspects of human nature (our spark is always enclosed in an earthen clod), even as they celebrate progress from primal dimness to current illumination. The myths of fall from heaven report that things "must" have been better in the beginning, when human beings were newly made, closer to the gods, uncontaminated by earthly chores. Either way, native American reflections on human origins testify that human beings are not simple. Rather, we are a composite of the heavenly and the earthly, the ideal and the fallen. The way we came to be must explain this compositeness. The answer to the tensions in our makeup must lie in how the creative powers laid out our passage to our current situation in the world.

The Complexity of Human Nature

Another variation in the efforts of native Americans to deal with the complexity of human nature and the human condition appears in stories of a dual creation. Perhaps the clearest version of these stories postulates two creative spirits, one good and the other bad. They may be twins, in conflict from their origin in the womb. Or they may be older brother and younger, at enmity for some obscure reason. The good creative power is responsible for the noble aspects of human nature. The Iroquois, for instance, credit the good brother with fashioning a world delightful for human beings. However, an evil brother set out to spoil this work, introducing elements that would frustrate human beings and make their lives difficult. From this second creator came disease, pestilence, unfriendly animals, and the like. The manifest effort of the storytellers is to assure their listeners that both sides of human experience, the delightful and the painful, go back to original times, when the world was made. For the Iroquois the final contest between the two brothers ends with the triumph of the good brother. He moves easily the great mountain that both brothers are challenged to displace, while the evil brother can barely budge it. An interesting twist in the Iroquois' myth is that the good brother spares the life of the evil one on the condition that he sponsor a healing society. The message seems to be that great healers will be those who have had intimate dealings with the painful, wicked side of human existence and so know how to overcome evil (the source of human pains).

Less than creative gods but still crucial to the origins of human culture as tribes now know it are the heroes who originally brought the first human beings such indispensable gifts as fire, the ability to hunt, and skill in planting. Sometimes the culture heroes bestow these gifts against the prohibitions of greater deities and so suffer for their generosity. One motif is that the hero discovers, by great guile, where the superior powers (gods or giants) have hidden precious entities such as fire. The hero then steals the fire or other gift and brings it to human beings. If the hero tries to return to heaven and resume a normal life there, he is likely to meet with rejection and punishment. This punishment can ripple down to earth, limiting the goodness of the hero's gifts and explaining why they have not secured human beings an ideal life or provided them full access to heaven.

More complicated are the roles that trickster figures tend to play in the formation of the earth that human beings now know. Such figures regularly spotlight the ambiguity of central human needs and capacities, such as sexuality, eating, elimination, knowledge, and social relations. The trickster can bring these powers to human beings, but his own exploits tend to display the gross potential they carry. Especially concerning sex, food, and elimination, the stories about how the trickster established these realities often portray him as lewd, gluttonous, and crude.

Psychologically, the trickster seems to provide tribes a figure at whom they can poke fun and so come to grips with aspects of bodily life that can be embarrassing or induce shyness. Eating, eliminating, and having sexual relations pertain directly to human animality, but nothing human is merely animal. So people have to search for ways to elevate their animal needs and urges. They have to find in their inventories of images about how they came into being suggestions of how love is more than sex, cuisine is more than food, elimination can take place apart from the house or hut or teepee where more refined living might flourish. Tricksters have been good negative lessons. In them people could see how not to disport their animality, how the lower potential latent in their creation threatened to reduce their status, unless they subjugated it to discipline and refinement.

The Natural World

Aztec culture, which represents a culmination of long-standing Mesoamerican patterns, can remind us how concerned with the structures of the natural world traditional Americans of both continents have been. Aztec psychology distrusted the world, in the sense that it considered the natural order unstable. Whether from experience of natural catastrophes—earthquakes, volcanic eruptions, floods, fires— or projections of human volatility onto the gods, Aztec culture feared that the world would spin out of control and crash into a destructive chaos. We have noted the theory that the Aztecs thought that bloody sacrifices were necessary to appease the gods and keep the natural world stable.

As they speculated about the build of the universe, Aztec thinkers constructed a world history in five parts. Earth, wind, water, and fire had been the forces presiding over the first four ages. The sun, the dominant power in the collection of forces responsible for the earth's constant movement, presided over the fifth, the current and final age. This current age arose from a divine fire. Two gods sacrificed themselves, by leaping into the divine fire (in the process justifying human sacrifices). From their sacrifice eventually came the appearance of the sun. Quetzalcoatl was the hero in this process. However, the appearance of the sun was not sufficient, because the sun was wobbly (like a newborn colt), not yet stable. To make the sun stable, more sacrifices were necessary—a complete corps of gods who submitted their throats to the knife. Once again, the inference is obvious: if the divine beings were willing to give up their lives to stabilize the world, human beings certainly should be willing.

Quetzalcoatl himself synthesizes much Mesoamerican thought about the natural world. He is the feathered serpent, born of both heaven and earth. As a great eagle, he can fly to the heights above—not just the physical heights, but also the farther reaches of human thought and spiritual aspiration. As a formidable snake, he knows the dirt of earth, the irremovable foundations of human animality. He is both a creative deity, in some myths, and in others a culture hero, responsible for some of the noblest institutions of Mesoamerican life. He is wise as a serpent and pure as a dove.

Venerating him, traditional Mesoamericans were bound to sense the unity of their existence as human beings. They were the species that, like Quetzalcoatl, had ties to both heaven and earth. They were a similar compound of the most lofty and the most lowly. In a word, they were "synthetic" beings, beings "put together" from earthly needs like food and sex and heavenly possibilities like love and honor. They lived within the orbit of nature, as full citizens of the physical cosmos, yet they also escaped from this orbit, possessed a certain liberty that gave them powers over and against the animals, the stars, even the gods who guided the physical cosmos. Because they could think, creating schemes like the five-phased plan of creation, they were not the craven slaves of the cosmos. Because they could map the movements of the stars and calculate their periods, human beings had some purchase against total domination by stellar fate. The future might be determined by the courses the stars and planets would run, but human beings could imagine that future and so defend themselves, gather their psychic powers to resist the horrors of a universe unrolling impersonally, carelessly, perhaps even brutally.

This latter point reminds us that native Americans by and large have not been sentimental about nature. Perhaps tribes like the Inuit living in harsh physical conditions exhibit a special detachment and realism, but virtually all peoples have accepted the vagaries of nature as simply the way things were. Certainly women cried when sickness swept in to take away their children or an ice floe cracked and threw their husbands into a cold grave. But the nearness of these possibilities, the constant precariousness of human existence, bred stoicism into native American bones. Those who lived by the hunter's spear might easily perish by it. It could miss the buffalo at which it was aimed, opening the one who threw it to being trampled. It could come whistling back from the arm of an enemy.

Hunting was not the only violence endemic to native American life; warfare was also regular. Analogously, women became pregnant at their peril. Any birth might cause them to lose their lives. Moreover, when warfare struck, women and children were fair game for capture. To the victors went the spoils, and the victors did not have to be gentle. If one adds to these human occasions of suffering the ever-present possibility of harsh weather or natural disasters, one sees that traditional life in the Americas was perilous, often lived at the edge of human alertness. The only way not to snap was to abandon oneself to fate. What would be would be. The mysterious ways of Sila ran the arctic north, just as the mysterious ways of the prime Aztec gods ran the Mesoamerican middle.

The geometric symbols that many Mesoamerican tribes used to locate their capitals at the center of the cosmos remind us of another regular feature of higher native American cultures. Not only did the Maya and Inca develop intricate astronomical and astrological charts, they nourished a passion for diagramming the quadrants of the natural world. In keeping with such cosmological convictions, the Aztecs would build their cities in four quadrants ranged around a center. The center represented the fifth and present cosmic age. The four quadrants ranged outside represented the prior cosmic ages. When it came to building temples, the same concern with the number five prevailed. The temples would have four outer precincts and an inner sanctum.

In Search of Harmony

Behind many native peoples' attitudes toward the natural world was the instinct that in making the natural world, the physical cosmos, the gods had given human beings the template according to which human affairs ought to be organized. The above of heaven was the model for the below of earth. The below of earth made contact with the above of heaven through the head of the human community. The king or high priest (for example, the Inca) mediated the flow of power from heaven to earth on which the functioning of the natural world depended. Without the regular infusion of power from above, earthly affairs would decline, sicken, fall into chaos. The best explanation for the taboos that so many native American peoples imposed is that these peoples hoped to ensure the regular flow of heavenly power (favor, help). To fall out of harmony with heaven, through behavior considered repugnant to the gods or creative powers, put the entire earthly enterprise in peril.

This explains why human sickness was so daunting a concern. If disharmony had so seized an individual that he or she sickened, it might easily extend its grip to the entire tribe. Human sickness represented a hole in the connection between heaven and earth. So did flood or famine, lack of game or the occurrence of earthquake. Bad things happened to good people often enough to prevent human beings from taking the favor of heaven for granted. Indeed, sometimes the problem was mustering faith that heaven continued to care about earthly affairs. At such times the traditional myths were a great comfort. By reciting the long-held stories, dancing the long-standing rituals, human beings could remind themselves that their ancestors had managed to survive and find the world good. They could recharge their conviction that the creative powers were benevolent enough to have placed them in a wonderful world that usually satisfied their basic needs.

These recurrent patterns of traditional native American thought about nature make it plain that few if any tribes distinguished clearly between the gods and the natural forces. "Divinity" seldom appeared as a reality, a zone of being, completely separate from the world inhabited by animals and human beings, plants and sea creatures. The mysteries of life and death, fertility and destruction, that played so beguilingly yet painfully in the natural world were the sharpest presence of the divinities that most tribes venerated. Even when a given individual intuited that the real force behind the world had to be a reality of a markedly different order, a reality that transcended everything that human beings could imagine or think, his or her tribe tended to focus on the corn or buffalo or rain that dictated whether human life would prosper or suffer in the months ahead.

This is not to say that native Americans had no inkling that the natural world is limited, cannot be divinity pure and simple. The bare fact that many tribes had myths explaining the origin of the natural world, or the future end, suggests that nature was not considered eternal or self-sufficient. Still, nature was so powerful and vast, so influential when it came to questions of survival, that speculative philosophy or theology did not flourish in the Americas. With the possible exception of the academies that arose in the classical Mesoamerican empires, no schools sponsored faculties or think-tanks focused on what ultimate reality is in itself, how the really-real differs from the changing, limited realities that make up the natural world.

Certainly the guilds of shamans passed down esoteric lore, some of which was theoretical. Even if we admit that shamans were more interested in practical techniques for gaining ecstasy and healing, study of their traditions makes it clear that they had to elaborate a worldview, a theoretical framework, in which such techniques made sense. For example, they had to explain why the human makeup was such that the shaman could both lie on the ground, present to the tribe in body, and travel spiritually to the heavens or the underearth. Similarly, they had to explain why the natural world, the sum of the game and plants, so came under the rule of good and evil spirits that the intercession of shamans was necessary. Nonetheless, few shamans pictured human spirituality or divine power as transcending the natural world. Most located the "higher" mysteries of existence within the single realm of nature that included everything that lived, moved, or had being.

Family Life

An obvious tie between traditional native American views of the natural world and the understanding of family life that ruled in most tribes occurs in the notion of totems. Inasmuch as they organized their tribes into groups identified with different animals, native Americans affirmed their deep immersion in the mysteries of the natural world. To claim a special kinship with the wolf or eagle, the bear or crow, was to think of one's group as drawing much of its identity from the animal powers of one's habitat.

The totem did not mean that the group sought to imitate the wolf or eagle slavishly. It did not mean that only the wolf or eagle was important to either individuals or the entire group. It simply meant that certain features of the totemic animal bore a spiritual significance for the group whom it singled out. The intelligence of the wolf, or the glory of the high-flying eagle, or the homely reliability of the muskrat was a virtue to take to heart. The relations among the different totemic animals was mysterious. Who could say with any precision what comparisons between wolves and eagles were best? The point was not to argue for the superiority of one's own totem. The point was to use the spiritual significance of one's totem as an entry to the wonderful world of intimacy with all the animals of creation.

First, then, we must underscore the intimacy with animals and plants that native American peoples treasured. Second, we may use this sense of being inserted into a complicated network of animal relations, an intricate system of dependencies that dictated how life unfolded in the woodlands or deserts, to approach the question of tribal lineages. Within most tribes extended families were the rule, to the point where quite distant relations—third cousins or great-great-aunts—still counted as significant kin. Frequently intermarriage with anyone who fell into one's extended family was forbidden. Exactly why this was so and how such a practice originally arose is not clear. Whether native peoples nourished a deep-seated instinct that a healthy tribe required infusions of new blood on a regular basis also is not clear. By the time that we come upon records of native American "sociology," rules for marriage, taboos against incest, and ways of counting kinship are well-established, not much questioned.

Some Mesoamerican peoples stepped outside this general practice, encouraging intermarriage among close relatives of noble families—sisters and brothers, on occasion. But they are the exception. Usually tribes were serious about forbidding marriage among even distant relatives who shared the same totemic line. Occasionally one gathers that views of undesirable relations between, for instance, wolves and eagles might have been a factor. On the whole, however, the connection between the totemic bases of a family's identity and the rules about marriage remain mysterious. Traditionally kinship was very important, but how it was counted and why it tabooed relations with certain other blood lines seldom became clear to European investigators.

Third, while most native American tribes have been patriarchal, giving rule or leadship to men, tribes that made such rule hereditary could determine it along the maternal line. As well, among tribes like the Iroquois, women might wield greater informal authority, and so have more say about decisions made for the entire group, than the men who had the formal authority. In some ways this meant that women controlled affairs from behind the scenes, while men held forth "out front." But inasmuch as everyone knew how authority functioned and decisions were made, the status of the women who had the decisive say possessed a public, objective quality. For example, if men's decision to go to war had to be ratified by women, everyone knew that whether or not there would be fighting depended on the judgment of the sex that had given birth to the warriors and would have to bury them if they died in battle.

This is not to say that the authority of women seems to prevail over that of men, when one looks at the overall picture of native American religion. Such is not the case. In many tribes, chiefs ruled with little need to consult women or fit decisions to their wishes. It is simply to say that sometimes women's contribution to decisions affecting the welfare of the entire group was not just covert. Sometimes there were overt ways, channels, through which women made their wishes known and had a crucial say.

In religious matters, a certain equality between the sexes obtained in the majority of tribes. Men and women possessed different powers, but each was essential to the flourishing of the entire group. Moreover, the power of each sex derived from heavenly archetypes and fitted into a natural world in which sexuality and procreation were a great law. On the whole, men were the hunters and women the gatherers. If the people subsisted by farming, women usually shared work on the crops, and sometimes they did the bulk of the cultivation. Women were the cooks and homemakers, men the warriors and builders. Each sex was brought up to learn the arts, crafts, and skills necessary if it was to make its proper contribution.

Boys worked, hunted, fought, prayed, danced alongside their fathers. Girls learned the tasks and graces expected of women by working alongside their mothers. Since few tribes broke down into nuclear families, uncles, elder cousins, aunts, grandparents, and other adults often substituted for fathers and mothers. Young people were raised to revere their elders, who could be expected to offer them good advice and example. Elders had a large say in whom young people married, though the wishes of the young people carried significant weight. The religious practices special to men or women often occurred in semi-secret societies. The seclusion that women practiced at times of menstruation and childbirth regularly served as the occasion to instruct girls in the mysteries of sexuality, the arts of marriage and child-rearing, and so forth.

More young men than women were encouraged to secure a vision by which to orient their lives. Whereas girls became mature naturally, through the onset of menstruation, boys often had to pass through an ordeal. The assumption was that boys would need courage to acquit themselves well as men, and that the help of a familiar animal was a great benefit in hunting and warfare. The quest for a vision could incorporate both these aspects of traditional native American assumptions about masculinity. The young man seeking a vision might fast or even sacrifice a finger, as a way of purifying himself and beginning to prove his seriousness and courage.

When the vision came, he usually learned what animal would be his special helper and incorporated tokens of that animal—a feather, a claw—into his medicine bundle. Often the visionary helper taught the young man the song and dance that would be his unique spiritual signature. Like the tokens in the medicine bundle, his dance and song would remind him of the orientation given him from heaven during the peak experience that formed his character. Some girls were encouraged to seek visions, but the relations between women and helping animal spirits do not stand out as clearly as those that structured men's lives.

Difference and Community

In many tribes the sexes lived apart, somewhat segregated during their years of fertility. As children boys and girls might intermingle, and elderly men and women could enjoy an easy familiarity. But during the years when their sexual powers were strong, men and women tended to stay apart. This segregation was relaxed between husband and wife, but the extended nature of traditional native American family life meant that even spouses often found themselves in groups where behavior was rather formal. Women did women's things and men did men's things. The fertility that the tribe needed was thought to depend on a sharp contrast between the sexes' roles and natures.

In practice this contrast could break down, because women could hunt and men could cook or cure. (Interestingly, non-typical people like shamans could have more fluid sexual identities.) Nonetheless, the overall mentality that one finds in the native Americas is that the sexes prized their distinctiveness. Each tended to deprecate the other, often with wicked humor. Each also tended to support the ways of the other, to leave the other alone to bear children or hunt game as it found best.

Common to both sexes, and all ages, however, was the realization that tribal life centered in the annual festivals and religious ceremonies. These were the occasions when the people redefined who they were, what they needed from the spiritual beings running the world, what their ancestors had bequeathed to them as wisdom about the construction of the world, the best ordering of the tribe, the origins and destiny of human beings. For traditional native Americans, the best moments in life were ceremonial and contemplative. One did not live to work. One worked to live, and the fullness of living was worship. Certainly many festivals had a strong social component, for the people would eat and drink together on most ceremonial occasions. But the songs and dances provided the opportunity for individuals to lose themselves in the mysteries that the traditions named as the primary realities of the human condition. The mysteries came alive, because song and dance carried them into nerves and sinews. They could never be merely arid propositions, if one had danced them to the point of exhaustion.

Going out of themselves in celebration, native Americans regularly extended their consciousness of the wonders of creation and tradition. What the shaman did more dramatically the common people experienced through the common rituals. The limits of the traditional native American world were the limits of the people's traditional imagination. Usually that imagination was fertile and nourishing. Even though some peoples feared the spiritual world, thinking it populated with evil forces, the majority loved to deal with it, because dealing with it seemed to settle their souls, bring them a greater vitality, reconvince all participants that it was good to exist as an Algonquin or Hopi, an Inca or Maya.

Related to this staple native American tendency to make traditional wisdom fully embodied was the general presupposition that the richest life occurred in community, not apart from family life and tribal connections. Some tribes allowed shamans a measure of idiosyncrasy, and some shamans extolled the virtues of solitude. But this was the exception that proved the rule, the alternative option that reminded the majority that their own way was safer, healthier, more normal. However much they wanted men and women to retain sharp edges of difference, traditional native Americans also wanted them to interact.

Clearly, such interaction was necessary for procreation and the future survival of the tribe. But it was also necessary for full maturity as a woman or man. One could not be realistic and wise without having contended with love, lust, intimacy, hurt, parenthood, shared responsibility for a household, mutual respect for the roles carried out by women and men. One had to appropriate the humbling yet also consoling truth that human beings were like the animals in being born and having to die, coming into being through carnal intercourse and having to cooperate for survival.

Yes, human beings were also different, reflective and creative in ways that animals were not, but native peoples tended to grant animals greater intelligence than modern Europeans have, so the distinctions they held between how animals thought and how human beings reasoned were not hard and fast and did not always exalt human beings over animals. It was right and good, then, for human beings to share food and sex with an animal forthrightness and gusto. It was part of the simple reality of tribal life that staying close to animal vitality seemed to keep the tribe vigorous.

The Spiritual World

It is no anomaly in native American cultures to credit the animals so important to a given tribe's way of life with spiritual significance.

Indeed, for people like the Sioux, plants such as corn could pack a great spiritual power. "Spiritual" tended to mean "significant, inviting reflection, possessing power." Even if it were axiomatic that such power came in material forms, it remained a gift or burden from the gods. The gods were the unseen sources of spiritual power. They were responsible for the movements of the animals, the growth of the corn or beans. They might be as numerous as the different significant aspects of local culture, but they shared a participation in the unitary power that ran throughout creation. If grandfather sky and grandmother earth epitomized this unitary creative power for many tribes, they did not oust the spirit of the corn or the ongoing influence of trickster or the daily wonder of sunrise and sunset.

The traditional mentality in both Americas refused to choose between many local forms of ultimately divine power and a single transcendent source. The many could remain in tension with the one. Few tribes felt intellectually embarrassed by the juxtaposition of polytheism and monotheism. The important reality was that spirits were at work everywhere. Whether and how they ran together into some overarching Great Spirit was secondary. They might or they might not. More pressing was the business of getting local spirits on the tribe's side.

The potlatch ceremony celebrated in the northwest was especially clear about this. The spirits most important to the northwestern tribes gained effective presence in the foods presented at the potlatch feast. They needed human beings' need of them. A contract or covenant was in force, such that each side, the human and the divine, profited from the potlatch feasting. Northwestern Indians knew that until the spirits became concrete, near, forces impinging on their families and economies, the spirits were of no special account. Such Indians wanted the spirits to be of special account, because they sensed that impotent spirits raised the question whether creation as a whole made any sense, had any significance.

The message of the potlatch that wealth was to be given away and a fair-sharing of goods was the best road to tribal prosperity depended on the use of the foods of the feasts by the gods. The generosity of those who gave the ceremonial feasts came into clearest focus when the people realized that human wealth was being sacrificed to the desire of the gods to become fully real for their human partners in the covenant the two had struck.

The spirits therefore are seldom selfless or completely pure. The tendency in native American religious thought is for the spirits to be as ambivalent as human beings. Until the spirits find a benefit in drawing near, they will stay away, leaving human beings to their own devices. By giving the spirits offerings, foods, prayers, praises, human beings make it worth their while to draw near and do good. This is not a calculated cynicism. It is simply the extension to the spiritual world of a shrewd analysis of the human world that finds most people not good enough to act disinterestedly. Most human beings need to feel that their good deeds are bringing them some useful return. Why should the spirits be very different?

It was different with the Great Spirit. The tribes who fashioned a notion of an overseeing deity, a first among the many members of the family of spirits who might qualify as gods, tended to grant that primary deity a more disinterested goodness. Grandfather sky looked down upon earth benevolently because of his own goodness. Grandmother earth gave forth fruits, animals, and flowers in due season because it was her nature to be generous and fertile. These primary deities did not need human sacrifices or praise. They did not act generously because they had needs of their own to fulfill. They simply were creative, beautiful, generous, so they could not act otherwise. In imagining them, native American tribes probably reached the peak of their intuitions about the nature of holiness and ultimacy.

One of the important obstacles to native Americans' developing a clearly monotheistic spirituality was their keen awareness that they themselves were spiritual, perhaps even divine in important ways. It was hard to be awed by spirits of the river or the mountain when one knew that one's own spirit could travel in dreams or religious transports, that one's own spirit could take a step back and survey a string of experiences to extract their possible meaning. The source of the vitality of the buffalo or the prodigal profusion of the cod might be a spirit that human beings could not comprehend. The sources of life and death might remain simpler, more elemental, that what human minds and hearts could fathom. But even those sources were amenable to rational manipulation. Even life and death could be tamed by being brooded about, meditated upon, made familiar by daily reflection.

Alertness and Meanings

To live in a world of motile spirits was to receive many invitations to stay alert, walk lively, not take anything for granted, look on the world as always on the verge of offering new wonders of beauty or possibility. The Eskimos who thought that the great problem in human existence was the omnipresence of souls that one might offend carried this characteristic to an extreme, but many other peoples partook of the Eskimo fear, in lesser measure. If each plant that one cut down, each fish that one caught, each animal that one trapped had a spirit worthy of respect and appeasement, then gathering, fishing, and hunting were fully spiritual enterprises.

Indeed, there were few if any flat, two-dimensional, merely factitious enterprises and no unspiritual regions of human awareness. Food and sex, plowing and planting, burying the dead and smoking the peace pipe all invited people into a third dimension, one of spiritual significance. Sometimes tribes associated this third dimension with a given spirit. For instance, the sun could easily become more than the physical orb shining in the eastern sky in the morning and blazing in the western sky at evening. Contemplation could make it the great spiritual force responsible for human survival and understanding. In turn, greeting the sun in the morning and bidding it farewell in the evening could become a major human responsibility and privilege. If the sun depended in any way on human appreciation, then the circuit of the sun through the heavens gave human prayer an inestimable value. Perhaps the sun would not run its route if human beings did not applaud it. Then the light would go out of the heavens and all life on earth would go dark.

The same, in lesser intensity, for appreciations of the moon, or the winds that came from the four directions, or the regular provision of new generations of animals. The spring that turned the grasses green and made the trees bud was a spiritual force, a wholesome and lovely mystery. What would any healthy, grateful people do but welcome it, thank it, applaud its quickening of the earth? Even the cold that swept in with the shortening days of late autumn begged appreciation. There could be no full circle of the seasons without the death, the rest, the fallow time that late fall and winter brought.

It follows, then, that when we see the word "spirit" in native American cultures we may usually substitute the word "meaning" or "significance." Certainly, many native South Americans imagined vivid spirits of flood or mountain, sickness or death, birth or springtime. Nonetheless, underlying this vivid imagination may well have been a cooler, more rational intuition. What we call "spirits" or "gods" is often simply the mysterious significance of things too rich for our complete comprehension. Even when we know that children arise from the physical intercourse of men and women, or even that ovum and sperm are the precise factors in human fertility, a wonder attends this process. Whether or not the human couple have come together in tender love, the mere fact that their union can produce new life is amazing. If this remains true today, at least for those with eyes to see and souls not gone to seed, imagine how powerful it must have been for traditional native Americans, who had no textbooks on sexual fertilization, no pills or condoms or vasectomies threatening to reduce human fertility to a technical matter easily controlled.

Surely one of the main reasons that native Americans so often turned silent and contemplative was their experience that the world became richer when they did so. Mysteries are always richer than merely technical problems. Useful as technical advances may be, they cannot substitute for the basal mysteries of creation and destruction with which human beings need to grapple. What may appear to be merely procedural matters, for instance how to control the effects of male intrusiveness into female receptivity, can become windows onto more primary mysteries, if people are inclined to treat them contemplatively.

Whatever deficiencies native Americans suffered by not having a modern western biology or physics or medicine probably were compensated for by their having a rich contemplative life affording them regular access to the primary mysteries the human spirit longs to appreciate. Probably the profusion of spirits in most native American cultures witnesses to this deep human longing. Probably the reason why every tree and pool had its guardian spirit was a keen desire to find all aspects of the physical and cultural environments meaningful, even beautiful.

Taboos and Behavior

Many traditional native American conceptions of virtue and vice differed little from those of whites. To be honest, trustworthy, loyal, intelligent, and kind were the hallmarks of the good person. To lie, steal, delight in hurting others, be unreliable, boastful, not in control of one's passions or appetites was to fail the moral ideals that most tribes promoted. Both sexes took pride in being skillful at their assigned tasks: tracking, hunting, fishing, defending the tribe; cooking, sewing, raising the children, keeping house. Neither sex could praise people who were self-centered, put themselves ahead of the tribe's general welfare, did not carry their load, caused uneasiness, fear, or resentment through their backbiting, laziness, or unhappiness.

Tribal ethics probably were less personalist, more concerned with the common good, than what we find in the modern west. Individuals existed less for themselves, had greater debts to their extended families and local community. Life required greater cooperation than is necessary in modern suburban life. Hunters and warriors had to work together; women did best when they shared such tasks as minding the children, gathering roots and berries, making clothing, working the fields. Thus the social virtues of generosity, helpfulness, sensitivity to the needs of others, and the like were highly prized.

So were wit, talent for story-telling, and the other traits that gave people pleasure at evening gatherings. Practical skills such as healing could single people out as especially valuable members of the tribe. The shamans' skill in this regard, along with their guardianship of tribal traditions, tended to give them high status. But often the most beloved members of the tribe were the elderly whom life had cleansed so that they listened well, gave solid advice, encouraged the young, and provided a dependable fund of affection.

Different from modern western approaches to virtue and vice, praiseworthy behavior and blameworthy, however, was the traditional native American concern with taboos. Taboos were injunctions not to do such and such, because it would violate the order necessary for good relations with the spirits, or the game, or the plants on whom the tribe depended. Sometimes the taboos were relatively straightforward: stay away from blood and the dead. Other times they came from an old tradition no longer fully understood: do not eat the bladder of the seal, do not approach a certain cave.

Blood and death were nearly universal taboos. Inasmuch as blood was the coin of life, dealing with it brought one into contact with something so important and awesome that it was polluting. "Polluting" does not necessarily imply immorality. Many taboos operated quite physically, with little suggestion that the person had freely chosen to defy the gods or tribal traditions. To become smeared with blood accidentally could be as polluting as to kill someone in a rage and have his or her blood on one's hands.

Blood operated like electricity or magnetism. It was an impersonal force. The worst possible combination was to come into contact with blood and death. Death compounded the impact of blood. Being exposed to the force of death, the agents who brought death about, placed one in great peril. All tribes who held strong taboos had ceremonies for purifying the polluted person, but these did not remove the deep shudder that contact with something tabooed could cause. Usually the purificatory ceremonies involved several physical washings, prayers for spiritual cleansing, and removal from the community into isolation for a while, so that one did not transmit one's pollution to others.

Two regular examples of people who required purification because they had come in contact with blood were warriors who had killed in battle and women who had just given birth. Both usually had to seclude themselves for significant periods (at least a week). No doubt there was psychological wisdom as well as deep-rooted fear behind this practice. No doubt it was good for warriors to contemplate what they had had to do in battle, good for mothers to contemplate the bloody origins of new life and never forget its links with sex and death.

Even when we grant that many traditional native Americans had to be more realistic about death than modern westerners are because hunting, warfare, caring for the sick, and burying the dead were commonplace activities, not things carried out by specialists on the margins of mainstream culture, the fact remains that blood and death are primitively powerful aspects of the human condition. The psyche recoils from their blunt message, even as it cannot rid itself of a morbid fascination with them. On the road to maturity people have to come to terms with blood and death, suffering and mortality. But this common necessity does not remove the assault these powerful realities make on our sensibilities.

Animal Taboos and Obedience to the Gods

The taboos surrounding game were less direct than those surrounding blood and death, but somewhat related. Even in hunting cultures, killing animals need not become a commonplace activity. Hunters can wonder about the strange, brutal economy in which they have been placed, asking themselves why the spirits should have arranged things so that life feeds on life. The requirement that a hunter apologize to his kill, or a gatherer offer a prayer of thanks to the plant she has taken, inclined many tribal peoples to stay in close psychic contact with the fellow creatures on whom their lives depended. Meat did not come from a butcher's shop or a specialty section of a supermarket. The hunter saw the deer or rabbit he had to kill. The fisherman saw the salmon or cod. The interaction was immediate, and so was the impact on the hunter's psyche.

In apologizing or offering thanks, the traditional native American expressed sorrow for the necessity of killing, as well as gratitude for the gift that animals made of themselves for human beings' sake. If a given tribe required that hunters save the bladders or hearts or brains of particular animals, either to give them back to the sea or earth to generate more seals or deer, or to allow a later reverence of the part thought to enclose the most significant reality of the animal, keeping this requirement, honoring the taboo against eating or destroying the part in question, was at most a minor hardship. The taboos aimed at ensuring good relations with both the animals and the spirits who enjoined the taboos. Such good relations were much more important than any temporary gratification that avoiding the tabooed action might have afforded.

Itemized taboos, such as not hunting given animals during certain seasons, or not speaking while dragging the animal back to camp, were also intended to honor the importance of this fellow-creature's role in the tribe's welfare. Even when the prohibition on hunting during certain lunar months was practical—intended, for example, to keep hunters from destroying pregnant animals carring the next generation of prey—keeping it honored both the animal in question and the spirits who had imposed the taboo.

The latter point suggests the final rationale that most tribes offered for their taboos. The gods or spirits had imposed them. Usually the wisdom of this imposition was plain, but even when it was not, the gods had spoken. From time out of mind the tribe had survived by honoring what the spirits had required. The part of wisdom was to continue to honor it. Who could know all the purposes that the spirits had in mind? Who would dare to question their right to impose taboos? Modern interpreters may feel that the spirits often were dragged in to justify quite human creations, but traditional native Americans seldom thought that way. Tribal culture tended to be seamless, little inclined to tear away what human beings had thought up from what the spirits had commanded. Obedience was more important than understanding. The more strongly they believed that survival depended on obedience to the spirits, on good relations with them, the more strongly a given tribe tended to require a strict observance of its traditional taboos.

This is not to say, however, that all such obedience took place with clenched jaws and gritted teeth. Traditional native Americans could grow so familiar with their taboos that they obeyed them fairly easily, even gracefully. Such, for instance, was usually the case with the seclusion of women during menstruation and childbirth. This was regular enough, ordinary enough, to require little comment or sense of sacrifice. Both sexes could enjoy the respite it offered from ordinary business, the brief patch of vacation. Women's associations with blood might frighten men, or ring alarms deep in the male psyche, but since half the race had the experience of bleeding regularly the alarms were muted. It remained important to keep the life-giving power of women separate from the death-dealing power of men. It remained potentially disastrous for these two primal forces to interact wrongly. But familiarity bred an ease with this taboo that keep it from seeming daunting. Blood became domesticated somewhat, its frightfulness diminished. Analogously, the blood that men shed in battle or hunting, though less regular than that of women, was familiar enough to become acceptable. Being a man meant finding oneself in dangerous situations where one's own blood might easily be shed.

The deliberate bloodshed created during ceremonies such as the Sioux sun dance played off the general taboo against contact with blood, but it also drew on the regular association of virile men with danger, self-sacrifice, and blood. When the dancers pierced their breasts they deliberately offered an awesome reality for the sake of the tribe. Their blood became a miniature of themselves, their entire existences. In shedding it they pledged to give their lives for the welfare of the tribe, accepting all necessary pain and sacrifice.

The shaman's braving of taboos against contact with the dead was part of his or, less frequently, her special status. In dealing with the seriously ill, and then guiding the souls of the dead to the land of rest (often imagined to entail a perilous journey), the shaman entered a no-man's land between ordinary, unthreatened existence and the terrible realm of the holy or wicked spirits. His value to the tribe depended not only on his skill in curing but also on his courage in braving this no-man's land. He had to be strong enough, psychically, to face down the fears bred through generations of taboos against contact with death and disease. Often his initiation was stern, even cruel, so as to prepare him for this dauting task.

Eskimo shamans could be plunged into icy waters, or forced to contemplate a skull for weeks in harsh isolation. South American shamans could be forced to hazard hair-raising hallucinogenic journeys. The more demanding the physical conditions their people had to overcome, the more powerful the shaman's spiritual resources had to be, for the shaman had to journey to the spirits responsible for those physical conditions, the spirits in some ways revealed through those harsh conditions. Thus shamans knew instinctively how to take the energy packed into taboos and redirect it to physical or psychic healing. They knew how to challenge the gods, and the moral order attributed to the gods, without losing reverence. In learning such things and acting on their tribe's behalf, they became guardians of their people's hope. If the shaman could bring about healing, and knew the way to the land of rest, then the potentially fearsome field of tabooed realities might not be overwhelming, could be survived, even conquered.

Death and Afterlife

Though death was tabooed as a powerful force, contact with which could upset affairs among the living, inevitably death entered deeply into native Americans' religions. Some tribes espoused theories of reincarnation, such that the deceased person might return to earth in a different form. That form could be animal, which offered a further rationale for treating animals well. It could also be human. Some tribes would name newly born children in honor of a deceased grandparent or other ancestor, partly to ensure the continuing memory of the person who first bore the name but also under the expectation that the soul of the deceased ancestor might find rest and a new existence in the life of the newly born child.

The three-decker view of the universe that tended to prevail in the Americas universally depicted the middle zone as the realm of human beings, plants, and animals. It was the present reality that human beings walked through and considered normal existence. The heavens above could be the realm of the departed human spirits, as well as the realm of the major forces responsible for the shaping of the world, but so could the underearth below. Roughly, the more optimistic a tribe was about the happiness available after death, the more likely it was to place the afterlife, the realm of the dead, in the heavens. There, in light, the departed might enjoy a happy life. Food and drink would be plentiful. Labors would be few. People could rest content and enjoy an understanding of how the world functioned not available to them on earth.

The tribes that were pessimistic about the nature of the afterlife tended to place the departed under the earth in realms of darkness. For them death was a special tragedy, because it meant the end of a better fate and the beginning of a worse one. Under the earth the departed did not necessarily suffer torment, but their lives lacked the warmth and satisfactions available on earth, to say nothing of the greater measures of satisfaction that tribes who placed the afterlife in the heavens tended to imagine.

Most tribes believed in ghosts and allowed for an interim period, between death and the settling of the deceased person's spirit in its final resting place, during which the spirit of the deceased might haunt the places special to it during life. Ceremonies to appease the "shade" of the dead person, to assure it that the living remembered it and thought well of it, could go on for several years. Almost always, the first year after the person's death was considered a time when his or her influence could still be felt.

Something eerie might attach to this expectation that the deceased could be prowling in the night, but it also had a common-sensical side. For it represented the psychological reality that death is often a painful loss for the living and brings a period of grieving, during which the living have to come to grips with the changes in their lives that the loss of the dead person has created. By picturing the shade of the dead person (what we might call the memories vividly attached to him or her, including how he or she looked, walked, talked, and the like) as still present on occasion in the midst of the tribe, native Americans probably eased the period of grief.

Not only was it legitimate to talk to the deceased as though they retained a significant reality, it was nearly commonplace to experience visits from them in dreams. Indeed, a favorite uncle or aunt, grand-parent or parent, might be a regular channel for important messages about what an individual ought to do, how an important decision ought to go, what troubles lay ahead for the tribe, or the individual dreamer, or his or her children. Where a modern psychologist might say that such appearances in dreams were simply ways of expressing subconscious intuitions, native American peoples tended to think that the dead really did continue to be interested in the affairs of the living, especially the living whom they had deeply loved. It made complete sense, then, to find that a beloved ancestor was cautioning one to avoid such and such or do this or that, because that was the way they would have spoken while alive.

For the majority of tribes, death also occasioned a rendering of justice. Good people would receive a blessing for their good lives while the wicked would be punished. This notion was not clear, on the whole, but it was influential. Death and judgment loomed as a caution against wickedness, an encouragement to goodness. The story of the Buffalo Woman who on coming to the ancient Sioux to give them such gifts as the sacred pipe had to destroy a man who looked on her with lust is one of numerous myths indicating a desire to have the gods render a justice that human beings could not guarantee. Unless the heavenly powers stood on the side of truth and opposed evil, the world would make no moral sense. Death was the primary occasion when people could expect to have their lives summarized and weighed in the balance.

In the measure that personified deities like the Buffalo Lady figured in a given people's religious imagination, judgment and the assignment of reward and punishment tended to be explicit, even vivid. On the other hand, tribes, such as many small-scale groups of South America, whose sense of the gods did not give them vivid per-sonalities, tended to leave both the rectification of earthly wrongs and reward for earthly goodness quite vague. Somehow the general economy of forces in which spirits, humans, animals, and plants were involved would sift things out and render a rough justice.

Mortality and Mystery

To be mortal, sure to die, impressed all native Americans as a defining feature of the human condition. In cases such as the Aztec, death became a morbid fascination, as though by fixations with death people might heighten their sense of living, breathing, having outwitted the forces of destruction so far. On the other hand, the Aztec love of flowers seems to have stemmed from the metaphoric character of floral beauty. Picked and cut, flowers could remain beautiful, able to give great pleasure, for only a brief time. The life of human beings seemed much the same. As soon as awareness picked one out of animal oblivion, cut one off from the unawareness of creatures not able to worry about their approaching deaths, one became fragile, terribly vulnerable, full of pathos. The more accomplished or beautiful one's life, the greater the pathos in one's certain death.

This rather refined approach to death expresses both the achievements of the higher Mesoamerican cultures and their tendency to degenerate. Only a step separated the Aztec aesthetic appreciation of the ties between beauty and death from a sadistic desire to witness the process of death's destruction of human beauty. The slaughter of living human beings that Aztec ritualism required at its height was atypical, if one considers native American cultures as a whole. Rarely did other tribes sacrifice human beings to their gods. But the mortality at the center of human existence influenced most tribes greatly. People brought forth their children, hunted, and went to war with a vivid awareness that this day might be their last and so they ought to live it fully and nobly.

STUDY QUESTIONS

Chapter 1: Introduction

1. What is the scope of this study of native American religions?

2. What preoccupations range across all geographical areas?

3. In what sense were all traditional groups religious?

4. What factors ensured that disparate groups would develop different cultures?

5. What attitudes ought one to bring to the study of traditional native American religion?

6. How ought the mysteriousness of all human lives to impinge on the study of any people's religion?

7. Describe "appreciation" so that it does not seem insipid but rather becomes a robust, fruitful cast of mind.

Chapter 2: Traditions of the Eastern Woodlands

1. What were the salient geographical features of the areas that the eastern woodlands tribes inhabited?

2. What do representative myths from this area suggest about eastern woodlands views of nature?

3. Explain the significance of the Delaware longhouse's being constructed as a miniature of the cosmic directions.

4. How does death force people to express their deepest convictions about their situation and way of life?

5. Give several examples of how native American groups defined themselves through their relations with specific animals.

6. How might membership in healing societies have helped eastern woodlands people clarify their sense of self (personal identity)?

7. Describe the major roles distributed by sex.

8. What is meant by "dualism" in the eastern woodlands tribes' views of ultimate reality?

9. How would most traditional eastern woodlands groups have thought of "divinity"?

10. What role did "medicine" play in traditional understandings of spiritual growth and flourishing?

Chapter 3: Traditions of the Far North

1. Explain the likely cultural background of recent peoples of the far north—for example, their debts to Asian forebears.

2. What ecological features have had greatest influence in the far north?

3. How does hunting tend to shape a people's attitude toward nature in general and animals in particular?

4. What characteristics have peoples of the far north recently inculcated in their children?

5. Describe the traditional Inuit shaman as a model of individuality and personal development.

6. Explain the myth of the sea goddess, Sedna.

7. How does traditional Inuit culture focus the relation between suffering and evil?

Chapter 4: Traditions of the Plains

1. Locate the centrality of the buffalo to traditional plains life in the context of the ecology of the prairies.

2. How did plains Indians tend to regard other, non-human creatures?

3. What does the Sioux sun dance tell us about the social thought
that dominated traditional life on the plains?

4. Explain the symbolism of the Buffalo Woman and the sacred pipe
that she bequeathed to the Lakota.

5. How would a traditional native American of the plains have
thought of holiness?

6. What is the significance of the trickster?

7. Why have visions played a central role in traditional plains spirituality?

Chapter 5: Traditions of the Southwest

1. Sketch the diversity of traditional economies in the southwest.

2. Characterize some of the traditional southwestern songs.

3. What have been the major functions of the traditional Hopi secret
societies?

4. Explain the role of the kachinas in Hopi culture.

5. What do traditional beliefs about witchcraft suggest about the
Navaho self?

6. Describe the goals of some of the major Zuni dances.

7. How have the Pueblo peoples tended to think about the lifecycle?

8. What has been the traditional relation between the Hopi and their
land?

Chapter 6: Traditions of the Far West

1. Why was warfare important in the northwest?

2. Relate the Kwakiutl *sisiutl* to the sea.

3. What place did the acquisition of power hold among California
and intermountain tribes?

4. How did Pacific tribes tend to think of the relations between human beings and animals?

5. What does the potlatch suggest about social relations in the northwest?

6. Why did tribes of the plateau tend to correlate puberty rites with the acquisition of a spiritual helper?

7. Explain the place of ghosts in Kwakiutl views of human destiny.

8. What were the main themes in the mythology of Raven?

9. Describe the Maidu high god.

10. How did traditional northwestern ceremonies focus interactions between the spirits and human beings?

Chapter 7: Traditions of Mesoamerica

1. What were the main achievements of the Olmecs?

2. How did traditional Mesoamerican high cultures think about the calendar and time?

3. What were the major elements of the Aztec cosmology?

4. What did the urbanization of the leading Mesoamerican peoples do to their religious rituals?

5. What does the were-jaguar suggest about traditional Mesoamerican conceptions of the self?

6. Write a religious defense of Aztec human sacrifice. Write a religious condemnation.

7. Sketch the traditional Mayan sense of divinity.

8. How does Mesoamerican spirituality of the classical period differ from the spiritualities of most North American peoples?

Chapter 8: Traditions of South America

1. Explain the role of the Andean region in the development of traditional South American culture.

2. What was the usual social organization among peoples of the Amazon and the Gran Chaco?

3. Write a brief personal response to Florinda Donner's experience of dawn with the Yanomama.

4. What do the games of Mehinaku children suggest about the social organization of that people?

5. How did the empire of the Inca structure life for the individual citizen?

6. Explain the significance of the shaman in Mataco culture.

7. Describe the main gods of the Inca.

8. How have traditional peoples of the Amazon been absorbed with spirits?

9. What was the role of fear in traditional Andean spirituality?

10. Sketch the traditional shamanic spirituality of the Amazonian tribes.

11. What were the main motifs of traditional spirituality in the Gran Chaco?

Chapter 9: Conclusion

1. How have most native American tribes linked human origins with those of the cosmos?

2. How does Quetzalcoatl summarize much traditional native American thought about the natural world?

3. Why did few tribes distinguish sharply between natural forces and divine forces?

4. What have been the major patterns of social organization among native American tribes?

5. How have the sexes tended to interact in traditional tribes?

6. Characterize the spirits with whom the majority of native Americans have interacted.

7. What is the usefulness of taboos?

8. How do taboos tend to relate to convictions about animal life?

9. How have traditional native Americans tended to think about death?

NOTES

1. Elisabeth Tooker, ed., *Native American Spirituality of the Eastern Woodlands* (New York: Paulist Press, 1979), pp. 7–8.

2. Hartley Burr Alexander, *North American Mythology* (Cambridge: Archeological Institute of America, 1936), p. 60.

3. See Donald P. St. John, "Iroquois Religion," in *The Encyclopedia of Religion,* ed. Mircea Eliade (New York: Macmillan, 1987), vol. 7, pp. 285–286.

4. Ibid., p. 286.

5. Cottie Burland, *North American Indian Mythology* (London: Paul Hamlyn, 1975), pp. 55–59.

6. Åke Hultkrantz, *The Religions of the American Indians* (Berkeley: University of California Press, 1979), p. 57.

7. Åke Hultkrantz, "Arctic Religions: An Overview," in *The Encyclopedia of Religion,* vol. 1, p. 399.

8. Mircea Eliade, *A History of Religious Ideas,* vol. 1 (Chicago: University of Chicago Press, 1978), pp. 7–8.

9. Barry Lopez, *Arctic Dreams* (New York: Charles Scribner's Sons, 1986), pp. 201–202.

10. Ibid., pp. 273–274.

11. Robert Coles, *Children of Crisis,* vol. iv (Boston: Little Brown, 1977), pp. 220–221.

12. Joan Halifax, *Shamanic Voices* (New York: E.P. Dutton, 1979), p. 69.

13. See Inge Klevian, "Inuit Religion," in *The Encyclopedia of Religion*, vol. 7, pp. 270–273; also Werner Muller, "North American Indians: Indians of the Far North," in ibid., vol. 10, pp. 469–476.

14. See W. Raymond Wood and Margot Liberty, eds., *Anthropology on the Great Plains* (Lincoln: University of Nebraska Press, 1980).

15. Reported in Melvin R. Gilmore, *Prairie Smoke* (New York: Columbia University Press, 1929), p. 36; quoted in Joseph Epes Brown, *The Spiritual Legacy of the American Indian* (New York: Crossroad, 1982), p. 40.

16. Joseph Epes Brown, ed., *The Sacred Pipe* (Baltimore: Penguin, 1973), pp. 3–4, 5–7.

17. On the entire Oglala sacramental system, see ibid.

18. See William K. Powers, *Indians of the Northern Plains* and *Indians of the Southern Plains* (New York: Doubleday, 1969, 1971).

19. See Peter M. Whitely, "North American Indians: Indians of the Southwest," in *The Encyclopedia of Religion*, vol. 10, pp. 513–525.

20. Adapted from Ruth Murray Underhill, *Singing for Power* (Berkeley: University of California Press, 1976), pp. 44–47.

21. Frank Waters, *Book of the Hopi* (New York: Penguin, 1977), p. 135.

22. Sam D. Gill, *Native American Traditions* (Belmont: Wadsworth, 1983), p. 28.

23. Whitely, art. cit., pp. 519–521.

24. Bertha P. Dutton, *American Indians of the Southwest* (Albuquerque: University of New Mexico Press, 1983), p. 76.

25. Clyde Kluckhohn, *Navaho Witchcraft* (Boston: Beacon Press, 1967), pp. 133–134.

26. Ibid., pp. 77–78.

27. Coles, op. cit., pp. 469–470.

28. See Cottie Burland et al., *Mythology of the Americas* (New York: Hamlyn, 1970), pp. 30–38.

29. Stanley Walens, "Potlatch," in *The Encyclopedia of Religion,* vol. 11, p. 465.

30. John Bierhorst, ed., *The Red Swan* (New York: Farrar, Straus and Giroux, 1976), pp. 233–235.

31. See Burland et al., op. cit., pp. 38–39.

32. See ibid., p. 39.

33. Hultkrantz, op. cit., p. 20.

34. Wayne Elzey, "Religions of Mesoamerica," in *The Encyclopedia of Religion,* vol. 1, p. 119.

35. George Stuart, ed., *Peoples and Places of the Past* (Washington, DC: National Geographic, 1983), p. 359.

36. Ibid.

37. Laurette Séjourné, *Burning Water* (Berkeley: Shambala, 1976), pp. 7–8.

38. Ibid., p. 8.

39. Richard Pozas, *Juan the Chamula* (Berkeley: University of California Press, 1962), pp. 16–17.

40. David Carrasco, "Human Sacrifice: Aztec Rites," in *The Encyclopedia of Religion,* vol. 6, p. 518.

41. Ibid., pp. 522–523.

42. Maud Oakes, *The Two Crosses of Todos Santos* (Princeton: Princeton University Press/Bollingen, 1951), pp. 41–42.

43. Oscar Lewis, *Life in a Mexican Village* (Urbana: University of Illinois Press, 1951), p. 274; quoted in H. McKennie Goodpasture, *Cross and Sword* (Maryknoll: Orbis Books, 1989), p. 207.

44. See Giulia Piccaluga, "Knots," in *The Encyclopedia of Religion,* vol. 8, pp. 340–342.

45. See Miguel Angel Olivera, "Mapuche Religion," in ibid., vol. 9, pp. 185–186.

46. Florinda Donner, *Shabono* (New York: Delacorte, 1982), pp. 162–163.

47. See Anthony Seeger, "Ge Mythology," in *The Encyclopedia of Religion,* vol. 5, pp. 492–493.

48. Thomas Gregor, *Mehinaku* (Chicago: University of Chicago Press, 1977), 112–113.

49. Michael Harner, *The Way of the Shaman* (San Francisco: Harper & Row, 1980), pp. 4–5.

50. See Mario Califano, "South American Indians: Indians of the Gran Chaco," in *The Encyclopedia of Religion*, vol. 13, p. 484.

51. See Eric Voegelin, *Order and History*, vol. 1 (Baton Rouge: Louisiana State University Press, 1957, passim; also John Carmody and Denise Lardner Carmody, *Interpreting the Religious Experience* (Englewood Cliffs: Prentice-Hall, 1987), pp. 43–54.

BIBLIOGRAPHY

I: Books Suited for Undergraduates

Albanese, Catherine L., *Nature Religion in America: From the Algonkian Indians to the New Age*. Chicago: University of Chicago Press, 1990.

Alexander, Hartley Burr, *The World's Rim: Great Mysteries of the North American Indians*. Lincoln: University of Nebraska Press, 1953.

Bean, Lowell John, *Mukat's People: The Cahuilla Indians of Southern California*. Berkeley: University of California Press, 1974.

Boas, Franz, *The Central Eskimo*. Lincoln: University of Nebraska, 1965.

Brown, Dee, *Bury My Heart at Wounded Knee: An Indian History of the American West*. Toronto: Bantam Books, 1972.

Brown, Joseph Epes (ed.), *The Sacred Pipe: Black Elk's Account of the Seven Rites of the Oglala Sioux*. Penguin Books, 1971.

——, *The Spiritual Legacy of the American Indian*. New York: Crossroad, 1982.

Capps, Walter Holden (ed.), *Seeing with a Native Eye: Essays on Native American Religion*. New York: Harper & Row, 1976.

Chagnon, Napoleon, *Yanomamö: The Fierce People*. New York: Holt, Rinehart and Winston, 1968.

Clark, Ella E., *Indian Legends of the Pacific Northwest*. Berkeley: University of California Press, 1953.

Coles, Robert, *The Old Ones of New Mexico*. Albuquerque: University of New Mexico Press, 1973.

Donner, Florinda, *Shabono: A Visit to a Remote and Magical World in the Heart of the South American Jungle*. New York: Delacorte Press, 1982.

Gill, Sam D., *Native American Traditions: Sources and Interpretations*. Belmont: Wadsworth, 1983.

251

Gregor, Thomas, *Mehinaku: The Drama of Daily Life in a Brazilian Indian Village*. Chicago: The University of Chicago Press, 1977.

Hand, Wayland D. (ed.), *American Folk Medicine*. Los Angeles: University of California Press, 1980.

Harner, Michael, *The Way of the Shaman: A Guide to Power and Healing*. San Francisco: Harper & Row, 1980.

Heizer, R.F. and M. Whipple (eds.), *The California Indians: A Source Book*, 2nd ed. Berkeley: University of California Press, 1971.

Heizer, Robert F. and Theodora Kroeber (eds.), *Ishi the Last Yahi: A Documentary History*. Berkeley: University of California Press, 1979.

Hultkrantz, Ake (tr. Monica Setterwall), *The Religions of the American Indians*. Berkeley: University of California Press, 1967.

Kluckhohn, Clyde, *Navaho Witchcraft*. Boston: Beacon Press, 1967.

Léon-Portilla, Miguel (ed.), *Native Mesoamerican Spirituality: Ancient Myths, Discourses, Stories, Doctrines, Hymns, Poems from the Aztec, Yucatec, Quiche-Maya and Other Sacred Traditions*. New York: Paulist, 1980.

Lopez, Barry, *Arctic Dreams: Imagination and Desire in a Northern Landscape*. New York: Charles Scribner's Sons, 1986.

Macmillan, Cyrus (collected and introduced by), *Canadian Wonder Tales*. London: The Bodley Head, 1974.

Momaday, N. Scott, *House Made of Dawn*. New York: Harper & Row, 1977.

———, *The Way to Rainy Mountain*. New York: Ballantine (Random House), 1978.

———, ed., *American Indian Authors*. Boston: Houghton Mifflin, 1972.

Neihardt, John G., *Black Elk Speaks*. Lincoln: University of Nebraska Press, 1961.

Oakes, Maud, *The Two Crosses of Todos Santos*. Princeton: Princeton University Press, 1969.

Parsons, Elsie Clews (ed.), *American Indian Life*. Lincoln: University of Nebraska Press, 1967.

Pozas, Ricardo, *Juan the Chamula: An Ethnological Re-creation of the Life of a Mexican Indian*. Berkeley: University of California Press, 1962.

Schele, Linda and David Freidel. *A Forest of Kings: The Untold Story of the Ancient Maya*. New York: William Morrow & Co., 1990.

Séjourné, Laurette, *Burning Water: Thought and Religion in Ancient Mexico*. Berkeley: Shambhala Publications, Inc., 1976.

Starkloff, Carl F., *The People of the Center: American Indian Religion and Christianity*. New York: Seabury, 1974.

Sullivan, Lawrence E., *Icanchu's Drum: An Orientation to Meaning in South American Religions*. New York: Macmillan, 1988.

Tooker, Elisabeth (ed.), *Native North American Spirituality of the Eastern Woodlands*. Mahwah: Paulist, 1979.

Underhill, Ruth M., *Red Man's Religion: Beliefs and Practices of the Indians North of Mexico*. Chicago: The University of Chicago Press, 1972.

———, *Singing for Power: The Song Magic of the Papago Indians of Southern Arizona*. Berkeley: University of California Press, 1976.

Warren, Robert Penn, *Chief Joseph of the Nez Perce*. New York: Random House, 1983.

Waters, Frank, *Book of the Hopi: The First Revelation of the Hopi's Historical and Religious World-view of Life*. New York: Penguin, 1985.

Weatherford, Jack, *Indian Givers: How the Indians of the Americas Transformed the World*. New York: Crown Publishers, Inc., 1988.

Welch, James, *Winter in the Blood*. New York: Harper & Row, 1981.

II: Scholarly Books

Amoss, Pamela, *Coast Salish Spirit Dancing*. Seattle, 1978.

Aveni, Anthony, *Skywatchers of Ancient Mexico*. Austin, 1980.

Bancroft-Hunt, Norman, *People of the Totem*. New York, 1979.

Blair, Emma, ed., *The Indian Tribes of the Upper Mississippi Valley and the Region of the Great Lakes* (2 vols.). New York, 1969.

Coe, Michael, *America's First Civilization*. New York, 1968.

Fitzhugh, William W. and Susan A. Kaplan, *Inua: Spirit World of the Bering Sea Eskimo*. Washington, DC, 1982.

Heizer, Robert, ed., *Handbook of the North American Indians*, vol. 8: California. Washington, DC, 1978.

Hudson, Charles, *Elements of Southeastern Indian Religion*. Leiden, 1984.

———, ed., *Four Centuries of Southern Indians*. Athens, 1975.

Kleivan, Inge and Brigette Sonne, *Eskimos: Greenland and Canada*. Leiden, 1985.

Krickenberg, Walter, ed., *Pre-Columbian American Religions*. New York, 1968.

La Barre, Weston, *The Peyote Cult*. Hamden, 1964.

Lantis, Margaret, *Alaskan Eskimo Ceremonialism*. New York, 1947.

Léon-Portilla, Miguel, *Aztec Thought and Culture*. Norman, 1963.

———, *Time and Reality in the Thought of the Maya*. Boston, 1973.

Lumbretas, Luis, *The Peoples and Cultures of Ancient Peru*. Washington, DC, 1974.

Merkur, Daniel, *Becoming Half-Hidden: Shamanism and Initiation among the Inuit.* Stockholm, 1985.

Metraux, Alfred, *Religions et Magies d'Amerique du Sud.* Paris, 1967.

Mooney, James, *The Ghost Dance Religion and the Sioux Outbreak of 1890.* Chicago, 1965.

Opler, Morris Edward, *Apache Odyssey: A Study Between Two Worlds.* New York, 1969.

Ortiz, Alfonso, ed., *The Handbook of North American Indians,* vols. 9 and 10: The Southwest. Washington, DC, 1979.

———, ed., *The Tewa World.* Chicago, 1969.

Parsons, Elsie, *Pueblo Indian Religions,* 2 vols. Chicago, 1939.

Powers, William, *Indians of the Northern Plains.* New York, 1969.

———, *Indians of the Southern Plains.* New York, 1971.

Rasmussen, Knud, *The Netsilik Eskimos: Social Life and Spiritual Culture.* Copenhagen, 1931.

Reichard, Gladys, *Navaho Religion: A Study of Symbolism* (2 vols.). New York, 1950.

Reichel-Dolmatoff, Gerardo, *Amazonian Cosmos* (2 vols.). Chicago, 1971; Philadelphia, 1975.

Roe, Peter, *The Cosmic Zygote.* New Brunswick, 1982.

Stewart, Olmer, *Indians of the Great Basin.* Bloomington, 1982.

Sturtevant, William C. and Bruce Trigger, eds., *Handbook of North American Indians,* rev. ed. Washington, DC, 1981.

Thompson, J. Eric, *Maya History and Religion.* Norman, 1970.

Thwaites, Rueben, Gold, ed., *The Jesuit Relations and Allied Documents* (39 vols.). New York, 1959.

Urton, Gary, *At the Crossroads of the Earth and Sky: The Andean Cosmology.* Austin, 1981.

Walens, Stanley, *Feasting with Cannibals.* Princeton, 1981.

Wauchope, Robert, Gordon Ekholm and Ignacio Bernal, eds., *Handbook of Middle American Indians,* vol. 10. Austin, 1971.

Wood, W. Raymond and Margot Liberty, eds., *Anthropology on the Great Plains.* Lincoln, 1980.

GLOSSARY OF MAJOR GROUPS

Apache: Farmers and raiders recently found in the southwest of North America. Linguistic evidence (similarity to Athabascan) suggests that this people first lived in the far north. Before 1000 A.D. the Apache dwelt in the plains, where many lived until as late as 1700. The introduction of the horse allowed the Comanche and Ute to drive the Apache to the southwest.

Aztec: The Nahuatl-speaking rulers of an impressive empire in central and southern Mexico during the fifteenth and sixteenth centuries A.D. Also known as the Tenochca and Mexica, they probably first arose in northern Mexico as hunters and gatherers. After the collapse of the Toltecs in the thirteenth century, they settled around Lake Texcoco and gradually developed a full empire based on a strong military power.

Chavin: The first high culture of South America, which flourished in the Andean region of Peru from about 900 to 200 B.C. The name comes from an impressive archeological site, Chavin de Huantar, in the northern highlands. Large stone temples characterize this culture, along with carvings of human beings, cats, snakes, and crocodiles.

Cherokee: A people of the eastern woodlands related to the Iroquois. Around 1650 the Cherokee sparsely inhabited some 40,000 square miles of eastern Tennessee and the western Carolinas. They had migrated to this area after being ousted from the Great Lakes by the Delaware and Iroquois. One estimate places their population at the middle of the seventeenth century at about 22,500.

Chiriguano: A South American people living in the Andean foothills of eastern Bolivia and Argentina. As speakers of Guarani, they are related to the Tupi-Guarani, warlike horticulturalists found throughout the Amazonian rain forests. Historians believe that earlier the

255

Chiriguano had inhabited lands in Paraguay but migrated across the Gran Chaco, enslaving such people as the Chane, who had appropriated much culture from the Inca.

Chulupi: A people of the Gran Chaco of South America interesting for a complex, three-cycle mythology of deities who formed the world in primordial times. The gods of the first cycle no longer function in the world. Those of the second cycle set the patterns for initiation rites of women. Those of the third cycle presided over the destruction of heaven that shaped present creation. Nowadays various spirits share the ultimate power that influences all natural and human events.

Fox: Algonquian speakers living in northern Wisconsin who called themselves Meshkwakihug (red-earth people). In the summer they lived in permanent villages where the women cultivated maize, beans, and squash. In the winter the men hunted the bison on the prairies. Their government was democratic, though a peace chief and council of elders held special powers. Medicine dominated many of their religious pursuits and their most important religious organization.

Ge: a South American people inhabiting eastern and southern Brazil, as well as northern Paraguay. Originally hunters and gatherers, they became semi-settled farmers. Presently the various subgroups total perhaps 10,000 individuals. Anthropologists have been intrigued by the complexity of Ge society, in which clan, age, sex, occupation, and moiety (half of a dualistic division) criss-cross to determine interpersonal relations. Shamans have considerable power and government tends to be decentralized.

Hopi: The westernmost Pueblo people, now living in eastern Arizona (in the midst of Navaho lands) and the Painted Desert. Recently numbering about 6,000, they live in the characteristic stone or adobe cliff-apartments known as pueblos, usually on high mesas. Characteristically they form relatively small towns and live by both sheep-herding and farming (corn, beans, squash, melons). Traditionally men were the builders, ceremonialists, and weavers; women gardened, made baskets, and were potters. The rich Hopi ceremonies featuring *kachinas* have drawn the interest of many anthropologists and scholars of tribal religion.

Huron: A people speaking Iroquois who lived along the St. Lawrence river when first encountered by whites in the sixteenth century. They lived in fairly elaborate villages and concentrated on agriculture, hunting and fishing to supplement what they farmed. Men cleared the fields, which women then planted and harvested. Corn, beans, squash, sunflowers, and tobacco were the most important crops. Clans were led by male chiefs who in turn formed a village council. Clan matrons had the key role in selecting clan chiefs. Hurons competed against other Iroquois in the fur trade, the two groups sometimes forming antagonistic leagues that went to war.

Inca: The Andean people who founded the greatest empire in South America. When whites encountered the Inca in the sixteenth century this empire stretched along the Pacific from the north of Ecuador to central Chile, controlling perhaps twelve million people. The Inca developed a complex, stratified social life headed by an aristocratic elite. They built an impressive system of highways, irrigation canals, temples, and fortifications. Farming and animal husbandry gave them a rich economic basis. A principal highway along the coast ran for 2,250 miles, facilitating trade. The Spanish conquerors quickly appropriated the highway system and established lucrative mines, hauling away huge quantities of silver.

Inuit: The self-designation of the Eskimos who, with the closely related Aluet, have been the main population in the Arctic and subarctic regions of Canada, Greenland, Alaska, and Siberia. ("Eskimo" apparently comes from Cree for "eaters of raw meat.") The Inuit are of Mongoloid racial stock, and so differ from many other native Americans. Both their blood types and their languages suggest a different early origin. Inuit religion has traditionally been highly shamanistic, and the severe cold of the far north has shaped most cultural features. Coastal tribes have fished and hunted for seals, while inland tribes have hunted caribou.

Iroquois: A large group of North American Indians speaking languages of the Iroquois family—for example, Cayuga, Cherokee, Huron, Mohawk, Oneida, Onondaga, Seneca, and Tuscarora. These peoples lived around the lower Great Lakes, sometimes spilling into the Appalachian highlands. They dominated the eastern woodlands culture, which was semi-permanent: based on agriculture and housed in palisaded villages that featured longhouses. Men fished, hunted, tracked fur animals, and frequently went to war. Women worked the fields, cooked, and cared for the children. Longhouses formed the basic social unit and were organized along clan lines. Agricultural festivals were the main religious occasions. The Iroquois stand out for their aggression against enemies and their cruelty to prisoners.

Kwakiutl: A collection of groups who populated the northwest of North America, subsisting largely by fishing and distinguishing themselves by their woodworking. Kwakiutl society was stratified by rights to use particular names, wear certain masks, and sing given songs. The southern tribes developed the potlatch most extensively, making of it a full ceremonial through which they ratified social ranks, invited the spirits to work for them, and expressed a full philosophy of material wealth that urged a democratic sharing.

Lakota: The native name for groups also known as the Western or Teton Sioux. ("Sioux," an Algonquian term meaning "snakes," is considered pejorative.) The Lakota lived in Minnesota before moving west onto the plains early in the eighteenth century. They traveled by horse, lived in teepees, and hunted buffalo in Montana, Wyoming, the Dakotas, and Nebraska. In the nineteenth century their leaders (some of the most famous in recent lore, including Crazy Horse and Sitting Bull) rallied them to oppose white soldiers successfully. Indeed, they destroyed Custer's forces at Little Bighorn. However, this prepared their eventual massacre at Wounded Knee. Recently they have numbered about 100,000 living on reservations. Scholars have considered their system of seven sacramental rites a good summary of quintessential plains religion.

Maidu: California peoples traditionally located from east of the Sacramento River into the Sierra Nevada. This geography divided them into groups dwelling in valleys, foothills, and mountain regions. The higher the altitude, the poorer was their material culture. Generally, they lived by hunting and gathering. Those settling in the valleys built large communal dwellings covered by earth, while the mountaineers tended to live in lean-tos. Their government depended on chiefs, who held authority by dispensing gifts generously. Maidu religion employed secret societies, masks, earthen chambers, and the kuksu cult (a series of dances displaying the traditions about the main culture hero).

Mapuche: An Araucanian-speaking people living in the Central Valley of Chile. Although presently about 250,000 Mapuche live on reservations, before the Spanish invasion small farming villages were the rule. Corn, beans, squash, potatoes, and chile peppers were the major crops. Some hunting and fishing supplemented this diet. Llamas served as pack animals and an index of wealth. To counteract the invaders, and later the Chilean authorities, the Mapuche wove their villages into tight military allegiances. They also consolidated much of their political and economic lives. Mapuche rituals continue longstanding Andean themes and are noteworthy for an interest in the cosmic significance of key colors.

Mataco: A people of the Gran Chaco living in northeastern Argentina. Their traditional economy blended hunting and gathering with limited agriculture. They resisted white invasion but recently have often intermarried with people of European blood. Mataco religion has focused on spiritual beings considered to be repositories of power. The spirits of the dead are powerful forces, usually doing more harm than good. Religious rituals placate malevolent powers. As well, they help human beings, who are a composite of material and spiritual forces, keep their balance and make their way in the perilous cosmos.

Maya: A major people of Mesoamerica, currently found in southern Mexico, Guatemala, and Belize. Before the Spanish conquest the Maya enjoyed an impressive civilization based on extensive agriculture, great stone pyramids, and hieroglyphic writing. From about 300 to 900 A.D. the Maya developed a high culture based on earlier Olmec notions and the achievements of Teotihuacan. Maya religion venerated numerous gods of nature and sponsored a great interest in astronomy and mathematics. The Maya calendar, based on close observation of astronomical phenomena, became complex and suffused with religious significance (a way to control time).

Menomini: An Algonquian-speaking people who lived along the current border between Wisconsin and Michigan. Agriculture allowed a sedentary life in villages of dome-shaped houses. Corn, maize, squash, and beans were the staple crops. The Menomini also gathered wild rice, fished, and hunted. In the winter, men also pursued animals for fur. In recent times the Menomini have shown mixed feelings about living on reservations, first wanting to end the reservation system and then petitioning to have it restored (for fear of losing such services as health care).

Nahuatl: A people, sometimes also called the Nahua, who have been the dominant group in Mesoamerica, represented most forcefully by the Aztec empire ruling at the time of white invasion. Nahuatl is the language derived from the Aztecs. Today the Nahua are farmers whose main crops are maize, beans, chili peppers, tomatoes, and squash. Some also raise sugar cane, rice, and coffee. Chickens, turkeys, goats, pigs, and donkeys are the major domestic animals. Each village is divided into sectors (barrios) that hold some cultivated lands in common. The Nahua are skilled weavers of cotton. Nowadays Catholicism has superseded Aztec traditions, but longstanding views of nature as full of spirits often continue.

Navajo: A relatively populous people (perhaps 100,000) of the southwestern United States (New Mexico, Arizona, and Utah). The Navajo are related to the Apache by language, and both groups apparently migrated from the Canadian north between 900 and 1200 A.D. Upon arrival in the southwest, the Navajo were influenced considerably by the Pueblo peoples, who probably introduced them to farming. Navajo mythology stresses the emergence of the first people from under the earth and curing, often through the use of shamanic songs and sand-paintings. Pottery, rug-weaving, and working silver are famous Navajo skills.

Ojibwa: An Algonquian people, also known as the Chippewa, who traditionally lived in the region of the Great Lakes (Huron and Superior). The Ojibwa were migratory, dispersing in family bands during the autumn for hunting. In the summer, bands would gather by rivers for fishing. Some Ojibwa also cultivated maize and gathered wild rice. Birch bark served for constructing canoes (a primary mode of travel) and wigwams. Religious life focused on medicine and sponsored secret societies. Presently about 30,000 Ojibwa live on reservations in the United States and perhaps another 50,000 in Canada.

Olmecs: The first dominant people of Mesoamerica, located in southern Veracruz and the Gulf Coast (Tabasco). Centers excavated by archeologists, such as La Venta, suggest that a remarkable art flourished between 1100 and 800 B.C. Some scholars speculate that the wide distribution of the Olmec style was due to the extensive influence of Olmec politics, trade, and religion. The were-jaguar is prominent in this art, which implies a keen interest in the relations between human beings and animals. Some of the Olmec art is large in scale, and some sites feature huge ceremonial mounds. The labor involved in such sites may suggest a stratified society, with an elite able to command many slaves.

Omaha: A North American people of the plains related linguistically to the Sioux. Some evidence suggests that the Omaha originated on the east coast but migrated westward. Original settlements in Virginia and the Carolinas gave way to settlements in the Ozarks and western Missouri. The Omaha and Ponca then moved north, living in what is now Minnesota until the seventeenth century. Migrations of Dakota Sioux pushed them farther west, into the Dakotas and Nebraska. Their traditional life combined agriculture and hunting. During the spring and summer they were sedentary, fashioning villages composed of earthen houses. In the hunting seasons they lived in portable teepees. The bison was the main game, and Omaha sociology stressed the circle of teepees—the hoop of the people. Shamans were revered for visionary powers, while chiefs ruled ordinary affairs and warfare.

Papago: North American natives who traditionally have lived in the desert areas of southern Arizona and northern Sonoma. They are closely related to the Pima and speak Uto-Aztecan. Because their habitat has usually been extremely dry, they have been able to practice only a flash-flood farming (planting after seasonal flood waters arrived). This was so precarious that they lived semi-nomadically, moving in the dry season to areas where they could draw water from wells. The Papago also gathered wild foods. Social organization traditionally has been the simple linking of villages for mutual help and, occasionally, defense. The precariousness of food has shaped Papago rituals toward a special gratitude for nature's occasional bounty.

Pawnee: A plains people of North America who traditionally lived along the Platte River in Nebraska. The basic social unit was the village, and the Pawnee nation consisted of relatively independent sub-groups composed of several villages. While sedentary they lived in dome-shaped earthen lodges, but while migrating after the buffalo they lived in tepees made of buffalo skin. Pawnee women farmed corn, squash, and beans. After the seventeenth century, when Spanish influence made the horse a cultural factor, many groups became more mobile and so decreased their dependence on farming. Similarly, sedentary arts such as making pottery declined. Shamans dominated traditional religion, offering resources for healing. Pawnee religion stressed the divinity of the stars and the maternal power of corn.

Pueblo: A generic name for the peoples of the southwest who have lived in villages composed of stone or adobe apartments, often ones built high on cliffs. The predecessors of the recent Pueblo were the Anasazi, some of whose sites have been well-excavated by archeologists. The western Pueblo peoples, living in eastern Arizona and western New Mexico, include the more famous groups: Hopi, Zuni, Acoma, and Laguna, for example. Both eastern and western Pueblo have been farmers. Individual towns have functioned as the basic socio-political units, while ritual societies have provided for an elaborate religious life based on seasonal festivals. Kachina dances are a highlight of many of these festivals, bringing into the people's presence the spirits shaping both their crops and their personal lives. Some hunting supplemented the traditional agricultural diet, so hunting also figures from time to time in Pueblo rituals.

Sioux: The popular name (derived from Ojibwa for "snakes" or "enemies") for plains people of three main sub-groups who referred to themselves as the Lakota, Nakota, and Dakota. They have also been known as the Santee, Yankton, and Teton, which suggests their geographical location in the Dakotas and Wyoming. Prior to the seventeenth century, most Sioux lived around Lake Superior, where they gathered wild rice and beans, hunted deer and buffalo, and fished from canoes. Warfare with the Ojibwa drove them westward, where they adopted the plains life that pivoted on hunting the buffalo. The

Sioux have become famous for their elaborate rituals, which included the sun dance, the use of the sweat lodge, and the pervasive use of the calumet or peace pipe. Shamans sought healing powers in visions, while males generally relied on animal helpers and laid great store by personal bravery.

Teotihuacanos: The people residing in Teotihuacan, a city of central Mexico whose excavation has revealed much about classical Mesoamerican culture. Some estimates place the beginnings of Teotihuacan as early as 400 B.C. and it flourished until destroyed by the invading Toltecs between 650 and 900 A.D. Teotihuacan encompassed more than eight square miles, containing many apartments, broad avenues, large plazas, temples, and palaces. Temples to the moon and the plumed serpent Quetzalcoatl indicate major themes of Teotihuacano religion, as does a concern for the dead. The largest pyramid, to the sun, contained more than a million cubic yards of building material, rising to a height of more than two hundred feet. Many features of later Aztec religion, including worship of the Sun and perhaps human sacrifice, seem to have been present at Teotihuacan, as does much of the stratification of Aztec society.

Toltecs: A Nahuatl people who gained rule in central Mexico during the tenth century A.D. and prevailed for more than two hundred years. Their center, near the modern town of Tula (about fifty miles north of Mexico City), arose after they had sacked Teotihuacan. Quetzalcoatl figures prominently in their symbolism, including the names of their great leaders, and they apparently established a modest empire of small states. The Toltecs depended on a military organization, which along with their cults of Quetzalcoatl, the jaguar, and the coyote influenced later Maya religion. The Aztecs were among the people who overthrew the Toltecs, but they drew from Toltec inspiration much of their militarism and religious cult.

Warao: A nomadic South American people (sometimes also known as the Warru or Guarauno) living recently in the Orinoco River delta of Venezuela and Guyana. Their traditional economy has been hunting, fishing, and gathering wild plants, although those living in dry regions have also cultivated plantains, sugar cane, cassava, chili peppers, and watermelons. The Mauritia palm has provided fiber for clothing and hammocks, bread, and liquor. Traditional Warao villages were composed of lean-tos and thatch huts, except in swampy areas, where platforms of logs covered with clay have been the rule. Warao culture is stamped by intricate ties of kinship and shamanic religious rituals, many concerned with healing. Their general ceremonial heritage suggests ties with peoples of the Caribbean, and it is more elaborate than what most hunting tribes enjoy. Striking is the inclination of the Warao toward both a creator god and a temple cult.

Yanomama: A South American people living in the isolated forest of the Orinoco River basin in southern Venezuela and northern Brazil. Their recent tradition has been to live in semi-permanent villages and practice swidden (slash-and-burn) agriculture. To supplement the plantains, cassava, maize, and tubers that they farm, they tend to gather nuts, fruits, seeds, grubs, and honey, and also to hunt monkeys, deer, armadillo, and other forest animals. A favorite crop is tobacco, which many smoke in heavy doses (sometimes as part of shamanic rituals). Cotton is used for trade, clothing, and fashioning containers. Yanomama culture is notoriously aggressive, warfare between neighboring villages being the rule rather than the exception. In this warfare shamans function as primary fighters, sending harmful spirits against the enemy.

Zapotecs: A Mesoamerican people recently residing in Oaxaca in southern Mexico. Now the Zapotecs are Catholics, but their roots lie in a significant Mesoamerican cultural past. Depending on locale, their economy can be that of an urban center or the subsistence farming, even hunting and gathering of rural areas. Subgroups sometimes speak mutually unintelligible languages. The prevailing pattern is organization around villages at the center of agricultural activity (corn, beans, and squash are the major crops). Coffee, wheat, and sugar may also be raised, usually as cash crops. In some places swidden agriculture still occurs. Godparents are an important part of an intricate social order based on kinship patterns, while traditional religion venerated numerous natural forces.

Zuni: A Pueblo people located in western New Mexico near the Arizona border. Spanish explorers credited them with a golden age dominated by a league of seven tribes that had amassed great wealth. Zuni themselves spoke of ancestors coming out of the earth and migrating to their present location. Farming corn and smithing silver are important occupations for men, while women excel at making baskets and pottery. The Zuni generally are peaceful and much involved in elaborate religious rituals featuring secret societies, kachinas, and colorful dances. In modern times the population has declined to perhaps 5,000.

INDEX